MARKETING FINANCIAL PRODUCTS & SERVICES

A handbook of consumer and institutional marketing strategies and critical issues

STEPHEN KERNS, editor

Probus Publishing
Chicago, Illinois

Library of Congress Cataloging in Publication Data Available

ISBN 0-917253-85-X

Printed in the United States of America

1 2 3 4 5 6 7 8 9 0

To my wife Karen for her help and support.

PREFACE

Few industries have undergone the changes that have impacted financial services over the past decade. These changes in competition, product development and pricing have made financial service a more market-driven industry, regardless of whether that market comprises individual consumers or multi-national corporations. A new mind-set has been brought to the field, and "financial services marketers" have become a new breed in both financial services and marketing.

Marketing Financial Products & Services is designed to serve as a handbook of financial marketing techniques and a source book of ideas. The book is intended for marketing personnel at financial services organizations, as well as financial services executives who find that their organizations need to be better attuned to today's marketing realities.

Within this context, several important features have been incorporated into the book's design. First and foremost, we have sought to provide marketing techniques that recognize recent product developments and regulatory changes that impact how specific products and services are brought to market and sold.

In addition, we have sought to recognize the fact that a relatively few people have had long careers in financial marketing. Many in the field have strong business and financial services backgrounds and moved into marketing from operations, administration or relationship management functions. Others have strong marketing backgrounds from retail or industry-to-industry marketing departments in non-financial fields, but limited experience in the special considerations that are part of financial services.

Finally, there are many inherent differences in marketing home equity loans and investment banking services, or retail stock brokerage and institutional asset management. Consequently, the book is structured to draw upon the experiences of a wide range of experts in particular product/service areas.

Their individual and collective expertise provides a well-rounded view of financial marketing today, as well as techniques for marketing specific financial products and services.

The charts and tables in the Appendices are provided as general information to help financial services marketers assess consumer and industrial markets and product and industry competition.

I would like to thank each of the author/experts who contributed to this book. I also would like to thank Karen Ernst, Christopher Krall, Nancy Nemitz, Janie Sergent, Lucia Pellegrini, Ann Kerns and Thomas Walek, who each gave generously of their knowledge and time in helping prepare and review the manuscript. Finally, I would like to express appreciation to the library staff of the U.S. League of Savings Institutions for their help in researching information contained in this book.

CONTENTS

Chapter One

Stephen A. Kerns

Stephen A. Kerns is Vice President of the Weiser Group, a consulting firm that provides marketing advice to a wide range of banks, brokerage houses, insurance companies and other financial service organizations. Mr. Kerns has had extensive experience in developing and implementing financial marketing strategies in his present position with the Weiser Group, as well as in his earlier position with the Chicago Board of Options Exchange.

MARKETING FINANCIAL SERVICES IN A DEREGULATED ENVIRONMENT

Stephen A. Kerns
Vice President
Weiser Group

In the not too distant past, there were a relatively small number of people marketing financial products and services. The marketing emphasis for most financial services providers did not sufficiently exist to create a separate financial services discipline within the marketing field.

That has certainly changed. Some of the most sophisticated marketers in America today work for or on behalf of financial services companies. Many marketing consulting firms and advertising and public relations agencies specialize in financial services marketing. Nearly all the major, national advertising and public relations shops have financial services departments, or at least a stable of financial specialists on staff.

This is all part of the growth of financial services generally. It is an industry growing in the number of products and services brought to market, the number of competitors within individual product areas, and the number of competitors within geographic markets.

These, in turn, are the fruits of deregulation.

There has been so much talk about "The Age of Deregulation" and debate whether it is good or bad, that some key facts occasionally get lost: Deregulation is here, it's continuing and it shows no sign of stopping.

It is an evolutionary process. And, like any form of evolution, it is difficult to determine at what stage in the process we currently find ourselves. How much longer will Glass-Steagall stay in effect? Will savings and loans begin selling insurance? What new derivative markets will the futures and options industries create? How close are we to trading stocks through that long-anticipated "black box" computer system?

For financial services marketers, these questions take on a strategic focus: Who is my competition, and who will my competition be next year? What image does my organization need to project, and to whom? Which market segments are interested in our products and services? How do we determine market interest in each of the growing number of products we offer? How do we assess the value our customers will place on these products?

And what changes need to be made now so we can continue to compete in a changing marketing environment?

It is unwise to look at other industries for strategic answers, because marketing programs supporting financial services—whether provided by a major investment banking firm or a neighborhood S&L—are inherently unlike any other marketing efforts for any other goods or services.

It is not just that there are no tires to kick or doors to slam. The relationship of a financial services customer to his or her financial services provider is different from any other business relationship. After all, the underlying marketing claim of all financial services is that they will directly help a customer's financial health.

MARKETING TO KEEP UP WITH DEREGULATION

For a financial services marketer, deregulation has caused basic changes in strategic thinking. However, these tend to fall under three basic marketing concerns: competition, product attributes and customer service.

A New Competitive Outlook

Financial institutions face new and more complex types of competition. It is not enough merely to recognize that the big boys are coming into your turf, for example, and that they are likely to outspend your advertising budget. Marketers need to assess, on a product-by-product basis, what the *real* impact of this new competition is. Can your new competitor get by with a lower margin, and thereby undercut your existing pricing structure? How does its delivery system compare with yours? Who composes its salesforce? And how many of your customers already have some relationship with this new competitor?

Conversely, when your organization enters a new market, how aggressively can your products and services be priced, and for how long? What will get you established? Price? Convenience factors? Superior product design? What type of salespeople are needed to service customer relationships? Is it necessary, or even advisable, to get high-priced sales talent with an existing customer following, or can you meet your objectives with less experienced people? What sort of natural market exists there for you? And what opportunities exist to cross-sell?

Meeting new competition also requires considerable planning and execution of programs to enhance and, where necessary, change corporate positioning. If your organization is a middle market bank or regional retail brokerage firm, you can continue to thrive even with the influx of money center banks or financial planners. The key is to differentiate yourself by playing on your strengths. Assess what they are and how they relate to your customers' needs, and develop programs that consistently get the message out.

Financial firms often fail at market positioning because the do not give themselves enough time to alter old images or reinforce new one. For example, many bankers throughout the country have resigned themselves to that fact that interstate banking on a nationwide basis is going to be a reality. State laws continue to change. But even where laws have not changed, money center banks continue to open lending offices in key markets that one day could be converted to branches or serve as toeholds for establishing local identities while waiting for out-of-state acquisitions to be allowed (see Table 1).

For institutions in many states—not just banks, but S&Ls and commercial finance companies—the time to examine their long-term competitive outlook is now. New marketing directions, gaining public acceptance of a new image and building new customer relationships can take years.

Similar considerations should be part of the marketing plans of large banks who want to do business in new geographic areas where customer recognition could be very low, or perhaps vaguely negative.

A Changing Product Mix

Perhaps the greatest difficulty caused by deregulation is the competitive disadvantage many firms face by not offering a product line as broad as the

Table 1: States with Interstate Banking Laws

State	*Banks Only*	*Banks and Thrifts*	*Thrifts Only*	*Neither*
Alabama	X			
Alaska		X		
Arizona		X		
Arkansas			X	
California		X		
Colorado				X
Connecticut		X		
Delaware		X		
District of Columbia		X		
Florida		X		
Georgia		X		
Hawaii				X
Idaho	X			
Illinois	X			
Indiana		X		
Iowa		X		
Kansas				X
Kentucky	X			
Louisiana		X		
Maine		X		
Maryland		X		
Massachusetts		X		
Michigan	X			
Minnesota		X		

Table 1 (continued)

State	*Banks Only*	*Banks and Thrifts*	*Thrifts Only*	*Neither*
Mississippi		X		
Missouri		X		
Montana				X
Nebraska	X			
Nevada		X		
New Mexico	X			
New York	X			
New Jersey	X			
New Hampshire		X		
North Dakota	X			
North Carolina		X		
Ohio		X		
Oklahoma		X		
Oregon		X		
Pennsylvania		X		
Rhode Island		X		
South Dakota	X			
South Carolina		X		
Tennessee		X		
Texas		X		
Utah		X		
Vermont		X		
Virginia		X		
Washington		X		
West Virginia		X		
Wisconsin		X		
Wyoming		X		

competition's. This is equally true for consumer- and corporate/institutional-oriented markets.

It is increasingly difficult to market in a *niche*. There still is a respect for *niche* players, but the competitive picture has changed. The idea of excelling at a small set of key services is fine, but customers want a pay-off of some kind. The pay-off used to be that you did it better than larger institutions. But what if another *niche* player, your strongest competition, is acquired by a major, national financial corporation? It is still a *niche* player. Perhaps the management and staff remain unchanged. However, it can now offer not only its special services, but do it with lower fees. Perhaps it now can offer the convenience of bundling its services with related services offered by its parent.

A related problem is maintaining market share in profitable product areas. For example, a savings and loan association may find that the areas of heaviest competition with a bank are those products with the greatest margins and lowest handling costs. The S&L may need to begin offering more sophisticated personal financial services or "business and professional" accounts to maintain its relationships with its most profitable customers. The alternative may be losing profitable business and being left with the low-margin/high-cost services the bank does not want to touch.

Of course, no institution is going to offer every conceivable product. But, many have strategically added to their product lines to enter new business areas. It is safe to say that many also have added to their product lines to help maintain their existing customer base.

The need to develop new products, however, should not be viewed in a negative light. In fact, the need to expand products and services has enabled many firms to redefine themselves to meet new competitive or market-driven needs. A major insurance company may now be reaping more profits from mutual funds than annuities. Similarly, a bank that formerly marketed itself as "full-service" may now be far more involved in interest-rate swaps and financing leveraged buyouts than in "plain vanilla" commercial loans. Perhaps the only consumer services it provides are to the owners of the corporations it services.

The marketing department plays a key role in changing a business plan. As the institution redefines itself, it must change its image, reassess and adjust the communications channels used to reach customers and prospects, and package its marketing messages on a product-by-product basis to speak the language of new audiences. Hand-in-hand with each step in the institution's redirection, marketing functions assist the definition and refinement of overall corporate goals. (See Figure 1.)

Figure 1: Product/Institutional Repositiong

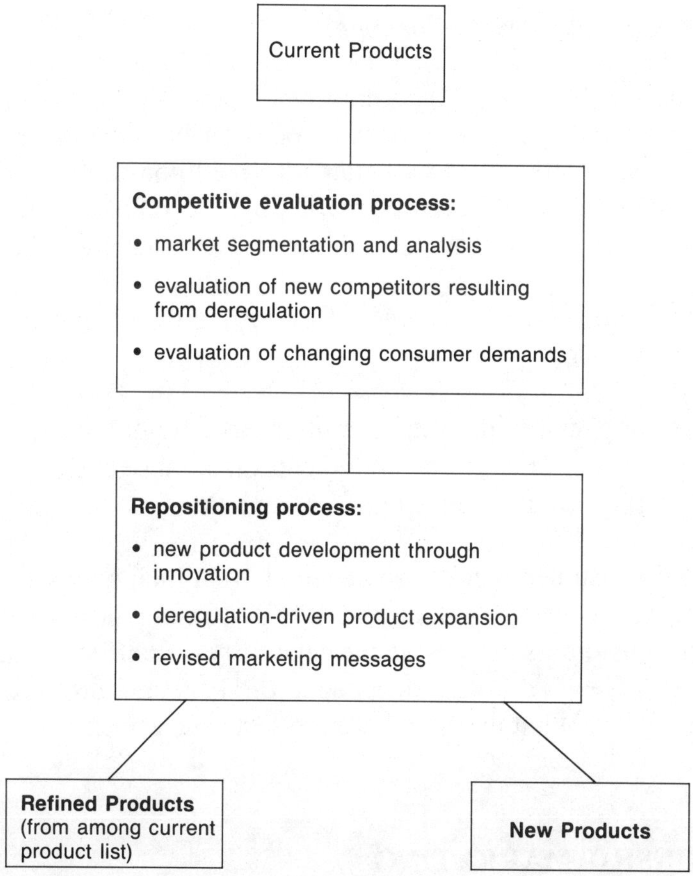

During the first phase of assessing new product areas, market research—too often ignored in the financial services industry—tells management what strengths the institution has that will help it successfully move into new product areas, and what "value added" features will be necessary to effect new market penetration. Research also can help determine how approaches should be made to new customers and how existing customers will react as changes unfold.

In the second phase of the process, marketing communications programs help reach new audiences. Market research helps refine both product specifications and the marketing message.

In the third phase, marketing solidifies the institution's new image and maintains programs supporting it and the new product line.

The New Financial Services Customer

Whether you are marketing home improvement loans or foreign exchange services, or whether your customer is a pension fund manager or options investor, you are marketing to a better informed consumer than did your predecessors in financial services marketing. Throughout the following chapters, you will often hear discussions and see statistics that illustrate that fact.

Today, financial services customers fit a very different profile than they did even ten years ago:

- They are shoppers, willing to take their business down the street for a better rate or better terms. Research indicates that these customers are very cognizant of rates and product features, and these often determine who gets the business.
- Individual consumers tend to be aware of what their needs are and have a reasonably firm idea of what they want to do to meet those needs
- Corporate customers often have the capability on staff to evaluate financial services. They feel less dependent on bankers, brokers and deal makers for advice. What they want are products and services.

RELATIONSHIP MARKETING

There is perhaps no stronger reaction from financial services marketers to the deregulation environment than the advent of "relationship marketing."

Stated in simple terms, relationship marketing is a strategy to attract more business from an institution's best customers. In retail financial services, there is the "20 Percent Rule." Twenty percent of your customers will account for 80 percent of your deposits, commissions, cross-sales or whatever. Relationship marketing seeks to establish closer relationships with this customer segment to create a channel through which more products can be sold.

At many financial institutions with large corporate/institutional customer bases, the position "relationship manager" has existed for several years, but was very much "customer service" oriented. He or she was the person the customer could call to ask account questions or inquire about services. In the case of the latter, someone else would probably work with the relationship manager to make any eventual sale.

This is still true to some degree. But many institutions use relationship managers to spearhead their institutional sales efforts, and their duties and even reporting relationships are based on their role as salespeople. Many organizations have spent considerable time and money training relationship managers to provide highly sophisticated financial advice tailored to meet the specific business needs of their customers.

In the case of banking or corporate finance, for example, relationship managers are selling complex products that often are part of multi-transaction strategies. The relationship manager must take on the role of a business advisor to his or her customer, understanding the customer's business and its operations.

But the general finding of research on customer buying habits of financial services indicates that they are shoppers. The idea of relationship banking or investing is more appealing to financial services providers than to their customers. Hence, there has developed a number of strategies to attract customers to such relationships. Though there will be an overlap in such strategies, they fall within three general categories:

Price incentives: Special offers are made to a targeted set of customers who are most likely to buy a number of different services. The incentive often is on one or a small set of commonly used products with the hope that this will attract the customer to view his or her primary relationship with that institution, and a path will be opened for sale of additional products.

Packaging of services: The most commonly used products and services, or products that often are used in tandem with one another, are "bundled." This packaging of services usually is marketed under a banner of time-saving or convenience for the customer. It also is often combined with a price incentive connected to using products in tandem or "buying the bundle."

Special services: These are methods of telling your most preferred customers that they are your most preferred customers. Special services can range from monthly newsletters, to seminars, to a chance to win a free vacation.

Customer Information File

The final element of a relationship marketing program is a customer information file (CIF) containing a financial profile of each customer. These files have become an integral part of most financial marketing plans targeting individuals and families, and they also are fast becoming popular with marketers seeking corporate business.

CIFs obviously vary from institution to institution, and there are a number of software packages within a broad price range that offer services ranging from the very basic to the very complex. However, the purpose of CIFs remains the same. They are tools that allow banks, S&Ls, insurance companies, brokerages, finance companies, or any organization that wants to cross-sell, a means to identify specific market segments based on income, location, liquid assets, age, family considerations and past product purchases and investments.

The forms filled out by retail sales personnel range from single entries that only track product and account information to those that have space for children's names and ages and personal observations, such as willingness to take risk or specific savings/investment goals. (See Figure 2.)

Corporate/institutional profiles can be pages long, generating a stack of cross-reference printouts. Some firms require their commercial relationship managers or institutional brokers to update their CIFs quarterly or even monthly. (See Figure 3.)

CONCLUSION

It can certainly be argued that, even with the proliferation of financial products over the past 10 years, there is still room for such things as trust, personal service and a long-term customer-advisor relationship.

Figure 2

DEMOGRAPHIC INQUIRY

PERSONAL	OCCUPATIONAL
Name Soc Sec Birthdate Sex Marital Status Customer Type	Title Company Phone Years With
RESIDENTIAL	**BUSINESS**
Phone No. of Adults No. of Minors No. Employed Names/Birth Dates Street Address City, State Zip Years at Current Address	Personal Banker Code Date Last Update Account Opened (Closed) Current Balance Account Opened (Closed) Current Balance Account Opened (Closed) Current Balance
CREDIT	Account Opened (Closed) Current Balance
Credit Rating Date Last Updated	Account Opened (Closed) Current Balance Account Opened (Closed) Current Balance
COMMENTS	Account Opened (Closed) Current Balance

Figure 3

COMMERCIAL LOANS
New Account Set-Up

Batch	Date
Prepared by	
Entered by	

Division _____ Account Number ___________________

Customer Name

MAILING INFORMATION — CODE

Name ______________________________ ________

Address ______________________________ ________

City, State ______________________________ ________

Zip ______________________________ ________

Customer Short Name ______________________________ Social Security No. ________

In Business Since MO.__YR.__ Social Security Code ___ A-Personal B-Tax ID
C-Window using Husband No.
D-Other

CREDIT

Customer Since ________________ Type ___ 1-Prepared by Borrower
Net Worth (in M) ________________ 2-CPA Unqualified
Last Audit Conf. ________________ 3-CPA Qualified
Last Credit Anal. ________________ 4-CPA Unaudited
Last Final Statment ________________ 5-P.A. Statement
6-IRS Tax Return
7-Oth

Figure 3 (continued)

CFT	A/C Type	Standard Industrial Classification Code	Census Tract	Geographic Loc. Code	Credit
____	________	____________________	____________	__________	_____

Primary Officer	Secondary Officer	Address Const.	Zip Code	A/C Review Date	Group Related	Area Code	Telephone Number
______	_________	________	____	__________	Y or N	____	_________

Member 1			Member 2			Member 3		
Division	Account	*	Division	Account	*	Division	Account	*
________	_______	__	________	_______	__	________	_______	__

Member 4			Member 5		
Division	Account	*	Division	Account	*
________	_______	__	________	_______	__

* Status

1 - Primary Owner
2 - Equal Partner
3 - Contact Rep.
4 - Other Member

Meth.	% Fnd in use	% Fnd Comm	Date Com. Bal.	Compensating Balance
____	____________	__________	_____________	____________________

A/C Type ____________

D - Demand
S - Savings
T - Time

Compensating Account #

____

However, such a relationship is harder to find. There are too many hands stretched out to today's financial services consumer, so most of them do not hold onto any one hand very long.

This has caused a fundamental change in the way financial products and services get sold. Marketing and sales used to mean pretty much the same thing to most brokerages, banks and even insurance companies. Sales were made over a desk or a dining room table.

Marketing today is much more complex. Financial organizations wish to develop close working relationships with their customers. Their customers on one hand want personal service, yet do not seem to exhibit the kind of "brand loyalty" that the provider institutions are seeking.

Consequently, a lot of effort is going into three functions:

- Financial institutions deciding what they want to be and whom they wish to service;
- Positioning themselves and their products to withstand the onslaught of new, well-capitalized competitors; and
- Looking for new ways to talk to their customers, in person or through an ever-increasing spectrum of media.

The regulatory outlook, estimates of consumer demand for products, and the willingness of financial organizations to invest time and capital into meeting those demands, will all help open new channels of competition. As they do, the importance of marketing to the financial services industry will continue to grow.

Chapter Two

Bart Zehren

Bart Zehren is Vice President of Marketing Research, Information and Planning Services of Citicorp/Diners Club Inc.

He has a B.S. in Economics from the University of Illinois at Chicago (1971) and an M.B.A. from the University of Chicago (1978).

Formerly, he was head of Marketing Research for Northern Trust Bank, Chicago; Project Manager for Sorkin-Enenstein Research Services; and Marketing Research Manager for Allied Van Lines.

He is a member of the American Marketing Association and of the National Association of Public Opinion Research. Mr. Zehren has taught graduate Marketing Research at Roosevelt University and undergraduate Marketing at St. Xavier University.

MARKETING RESEARCH IN THE FINANCIAL SERVICES SECTOR

Bart D. Zehren
Vice President, Marketing Research
Information and Planning Services
Citicorp/Diners Club

THE VALUE DILEMMA

Research and Marketing in financial services are two topics about which much already has been written, and presumably read, during the past several years. But precious little, it seems, has been written about successfully integrating research with marketing, let alone about using research to integrate marketing with operations, credit, finance, data processing, customer service, sales and sales training, *et cetera*, into a coordinated corporate effort.

However, the attainment of this plateau of influence for research must wait on a solution to the "value dilemma" affecting many of today's corporate (that is, in-house) market researchers. Etiquette, if not sheer political reality, often demands a certain servitude of the market researcher to marketing managers in the development and design, if not the conduct, of projects.

This becomes especially critical in presenting findings, conclusions and recommendations. The success of research within the corporate organization is enhanced by, if not dependent upon, a close working relationship with other areas of marketing, such as advertising and new product development. But unless review procedures are in place that take account of the direct value of marketing research to the firm, this work may go undervalued. Marketing programs that succeed are credited to the marketing manager, usually long after the supportive work of the researcher who recommended a course of action is finished.

The importance of marketing research will be fully recognized only when researchers bring to the corporate table their own plans for action that materially advance progress toward bottom-line organizational objectives.

THE FUNCTION OF MARKETING RESEARCH WITHIN FINANCIAL SERVICES FIRMS

In general, marketing research has four major functions within a firm:

1. Measuring marketing productivity through specialized studies that look at the past (information systems, market or advertising tracking), present (customer satisfaction, brand image and product introduction measurement) and future (new product, new market or new business opportunities studies).
2. Facilitating the management cycle of: controlling performance against plans already in place, solving problems that arise, and planning again.
3. Reducing risk in decisions by measuring the probabilities and potential value of alternative actions.
4. Making marketing managers (and others) better informed.

To enable researchers within a financial services firm to productively perform these functions, their leader must assess the cultural environment of that organization *vis-á-vis* the role and value of marketing research.

Some of these firms, it is found, require dedicated missionary work to establish a budding measure of faith in market research. Others keep their researchers busy with constant projects, tight schedules and firm deadlines. But rare are the financial services firms that recognize the full potential of marketing research within their organizations and demand progress toward that goal.

This chapter presents a few examples of ways that marketing research can reach out and fulfill that potential. The first two of them work on the specific, tactical level: the "moving parts theory" of customer satisfaction and measuring price sensitivity. The others lie close to the strategic domain of the commercial banker and general manager: commercial banking and research, fully integrated strategic information and organizational form.

MOVING PARTS THEORY OF CUSTOMER SATISFACTION

Try to remember back to the first time you rode in a car with modern features like power steering, brakes, antenna and windows, a stereo tape deck, air conditioning and a sun-roof. With all those new and complicated moving parts, didn't it occur to you that, sooner or later, something was bound to go wrong? And it usually did.

This is the principle behind the Moving Parts Theory of Customer Service, which originated from a series of research studies on customer satisfaction for the personal services side of a full-service bank. When the findings showed areas like personal banking services, credit cards and checking services getting relatively lower satisfaction scores while regular savings accounts, and especially safe deposit box services, received the highest scores, the Moving Parts Theory was born.

According to this theory, service areas or accounts having greater transaction volume and/or more personal interactions (thus, more "moving parts") are presumed naturally to produce relatively lower satisfaction levels. After all, what can go wrong with delivery of a safe deposit box service? Originally called the Moving Parts Hypothesis of Customer Service, the concept was elevated to a theory when, upon subsequent studies by the same bank, the effect persisted.

IMPLICATIONS OF THE MOVING PARTS THEORY

One lesson learned from this experience was that the appropriate frame of reference for analyzing such satisfaction scores is to compare the bank's overall scores and those of each department *not* against each other, but each against itself over time. Otherwise ridiculous conclusions such as this can be drawn: "The safe deposit box area is providing a higher quality of service than the personal bankers."

Management must decide how high is up for satisfaction scores for the firm as a whole and for each service area. Only then can judgments begin to be made about the quality of service provided and progress toward goals. Of course, those management decisions need to observe the strategic imperatives of the firm. The bank that is committed to growing its "upscale" business with more sophisticated services and accounts may be well advised to expect increased volume of customer contacts, inquiries, complaints and perhaps even lower satisfaction scores as it embarks on that program.

MEASURING PRICE SENSITIVITY

Perhaps the most difficult and least credible, yet one of the most crucial, measurement issues in marketing research is price sensitivity. The issue arises whether to ask one group of respondents about several prices or to ask each of several cells of respondents about one price each.

A more enlightened view recognizes that perceptions of price are inextricably tied to perceptions of value. Calculation of the optimal balance of these two perceptions has often been derived by assigning theoretical values (i.e., utilities) to prices within attribute bundles that represent products or concepts under study. In less rigorous settings, the price question has sometimes even been left open.

When strong prior knowledge and consumer familiarity are present, or if certain business issues constrain the alternatives in a test situation, these approaches seem to serve well enough to facilitate effective decisions. However, in broader situations of little or no prior learning, where wide bands of price inelasticity exist, or when in the early stages of concept development, these methods do not apply well. In addition, when continuous measurement of a range of prices is needed, no method has seemed very satisfactory . . . until now.

The solution is an outgrowth of the time-honored process of sharing original research through publication, followed by peer review, criticism, adaptation and experimentation.

THE "ASKABLE" METHOD OF MEASURING PRICE SENSITIVITY

In a paper appearing in *Marketing News* (May 14, 1982, Section 1, Page 6) Kenneth Travis presented a fascinating treatment of price sensitivity. It used intersecting lines and points of tangency to represent such concepts as marginal cheapness, marginal expensiveness and zones of indifference.

But the real innovation for survey researchers was the set of four very clever questions Travis used to obtain price/value perceptions from consumers. Listed below in their adapted form, these questions work because 1) they are nearly open-ended as to prices and 2) they beat around the bush rather than ask the key "bottom-line" question directly (leaving that for mathematical derivation). As a result, consumers have no reason to be evasive or to otherwise hedge their answers.

Once the respondent understands the product concept under study, he is given a wide, evenly calibrated number line to use for his responses to these questions:

At what price would this product be so cheap that you would have serious doubts about its quality so that you probably would not buy it?

At what price would this product be inexpensive so that you would begin to have doubts about the quality but you would still consider buying it?

At what price would this product be expensive but you would still consider buying it?

At what price would this product be so expensive that it would be beyond your consideration?

This ingenious innovation was enough to tickle the brain of James C. Adamek, PhD., whose thinking has been in the forefront applied statistics in market research. He added the crowning touch of inserting, after each price question, a ten-point purchase intent question. The result is four pairs of data points for each respondent. When averaged over all respondents, they produce four sets of coordinates on a plot of price versus purchase intent. A curve is then fit to these coordinates and the optimal price is found by using calculus to locate the maximum point of the curve (that is, where purchase intent is at its highest). (See Figure 1.)

The key to this method lies in having a price structure that can be represented by a single point on a number line. However, even a complex price structure, such as a credit card involving both an annual fee and an interest rate, could probably be managed by going through the price questions twice—once to obtain the fee and then to obtain the rate that "is so low that you have serious doubts about the legitimacy of this offer." The resulting eight specialized price estimates, along with answers to four purchase intent questions, permit optimization of the *combination* of annual fee and interest rate that maximize purchase intent.

Figure 1: Price/Value Curve

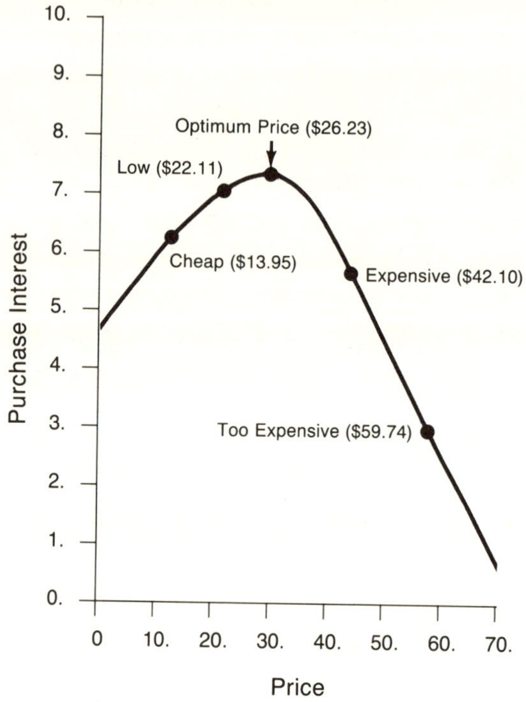

COMMERCIAL BANKING AND RESEARCH

"Follow the Elephants"

Traditionally, what commercial bankers have understood about research has been limited to the annual Greenwich research studies, or Dunn & Bradstreet's reports on prospect companies.

One old-line banker spoke for many when he said his strategy had always been: "Follow the Elephants." Freely translated this means: Follow the biggest banks as they go after the biggest corporations, even their droppings are plenty big enough! And, he didn't need any marketing research to tell him that!

Some of the more up-to-date banks have developed calling report procedures, often using their own in-house researchers to do the analytical (and all too often the woefully manual) dirty work. But the greatest contribution research can make to commercial financial services remains neglected. Wide chasms separate old-line bankers (concerned with evaluating risk and managing spreads) from sales-driven relationship managers (a.k.a. "new line" bankers) from analytical MBA's and market researchers. But, again, the astute researcher can bridge these gaps, while extending the frontier of his chosen field, if the practical use of his work is related to the bottom line.

Integrating Marketing Research Into Sales

The key factor that makes marketing research work in a sales organization is its relevance to individual sales personnel, as well as the overall sales effort. Sales people work on a one-to-one basis, selling themselves and leveraging their relationship with the customer as much as they sell "products." Research to them is the homework they do to prepare for the call.

By making the calling officers' homework the business of marketing research, the innovative financial firm brings together two effective partners. The ultimate result is a recipe designed through market research and followed by the sales team that dramatically improves sales efficiency—while upgrading it to a truly integrated marketing effort.

Nothing comes cheap, of course, especially a major innovation such as this. The price is nothing less than a full scale primary research study of the commercial marketplace. The goal of the study is to learn how to divide the account base and prospect files (i.e., the market) into new and strategically distinct market segments, each having a dominant set of needs and cultural values which can be modeled statistically.

Development of such a major study involves task-force participation by marketing, sales, research and, ideally, senior management to ensure attention to crucial and open business issues. Current use of services, market share, unmet needs, buying motivations and the customer's decision-making processes are obvious "must" topics. Once the study is completed, analysis of response patterns based on "clusters of response" will reveal new market segments that will form the foundation for developing marketing and sales strategies. These will not be groupings by standardized industrial classification (SIC) codes or sales-size, but "needs-based" segments reflecting distinctive and strongly held schools of thought on key issues.

A vital implementation step is the assignment of priorities and strategies across the segments. Marketing programs are then created to apply the communications strategy, develop new services, build sales campaigns, and so on for each high-priority segment. Meanwhile, line management explains to relationship managers which segments are of highest priority.

The next step is the most exciting. The mathematics of the clustering algorithm is used (via discriminant analysis) to produce a proprietary "short-form" questionnaire which will help salespeople evaluate each business account or prospect and place it in the appropriate segment. This short form is the vital bridge that brings the research "down to earth." This research tool can now become part of each salesperson's preparation work for sales calls. With it the sales manager and the field staff can supplement their own skills in diagnosing a prospect's needs, buying patterns and "hot buttons."

The short-form questions should be non-threatening agree/disagree questions or relevant items which can be asked in whatever medium of communication (telephone, mail or personal) the sales staff addresses the customer or prospect.

With adequate experience and effective early results, the best Calling Officers will become adept at working the "short-form" questions into the conversations they have with prospects and customers. (Remember that Sales was represented on the task-force for the project from the very beginning.) Illustrative case studies and success stories can, over time, be developed and incorporated into sales training seminars. Even junior Calling Officers coming right out of training courses can be more productive immediately by sticking close to the literal "short-form" questionnaire in their prospecting work.

FULLY INTEGRATED STRATEGIC INFORMATION

Many service businesses, not just financial, attempt to maximize the value of their internal customer information files. Cross-selling strategies and tactics are developed, 20/80 rules are invoked and promotions are executed on the assumption that historical behavior can be a powerful indicator of similar future behavior. Naturally, the amount of repeat or related purchase behavior that is normal for the product category must be considered. For example, many families tend to have only one Bible in the house, but they may have several cookbooks.

This may sound like common sense but what it really involves is understanding the needs being satisfied by a product and the motivations that underlie purchase behavior. In situations that are not so obvious, such as financial investment services for consumers or businesses, the value of this motivational piece becomes much greater. With the motivations-based market segments and the short-form classification tool in hand, the vision of the truly integrated management database that is actually predictive can now be developed.

It is not necessary to require classification of the entire customer base before applying this principle. However, as prospect and customer classification proceeds, a panel can be built of a representative sample of all customers subdivided by segment. This panel is the integration vehicle. It can link results from ongoing management reports about profitability, cash flow, customer service records, costs of operation, purchase behavior and volume indicators to the specific segments to accomplish the following:

- Validation checks on the analytical and predictive power of the segments in terms of key financial indicators.
- Assessment of the current profitability of serving each segment.
- Tracking purchasing behavior by segment.
- Targeted development of new services or features.
- Deliberate experimentation with programs and actions designed for specific segments.

With this common foundation of strategic marketplace segments backed up by a management commitment to action, the various disciplines of the firm can now, finally, be brought together under a greater discipline. Ongoing market segment research can now be conducted on a business-wide level as the researcher truly becomes a vital member of the management team. His language has, with this integration, become part of the vernacular used by line decision makers. His work becomes part of the sales, marketing and business planning process.

THE ULTIMATE ORGANIZATIONAL FORM

Carrying the twin concepts of sales/research partnership and integrated strategic information one step farther and a level or two higher in the organization may even lead to the firm re-structuring itself to conform to the market's structure. The purpose is to enforce direct accountability for implementation of the strategies that were born of the segments. This applies especially well to multi-brand firms or conglomerates, regardless of whether they are sales-focussed, involved in financial services, or even packaged goods. Of course, no reorganization ought to be contemplated without a compelling reason. But the organization often needs an objective, direct path that runs, if necessary, right through brand and product management all the way to and from targeted consumers and their genuine needs and wants. By definition, brand and product managers have an interest, and indeed a duty, to maintain customer allegiance to their brand or product. So, to lead the organization down this path, a new kind of manager may be needed—the market segment manager. His primary function is to understand the segment: its nature and needs, its wants, whims and wishes. His mission is to achieve numerical goals for his segment (e.g., volume, penetration, market share, profitability, loyalty, etc.). This is a line, not a staff position.

The market segment manager is given authority to transcend established procedures, turfs and old schools of thought in order to re-direct the focus from internal matters toward external market forces. This, of course, is where the focus always belongs, but with product and brand management structures it is only partially realized.

If and when the basic nature or even the ongoing needs of a brand or product comes into question, given changing market forces, the absence of a market segment manager only encourages postponement, rejection or suppression of the inevitable adjustments until, often, a crisis situation is created. By the same token, opportunities are missed for developing truly new brands or products that do not fit neatly under existing organizational categories.

The presence of a market segment manager, however, would acknowledge and address these market forces as a non-threatening, proactive responsibility to be faced, planned for and managed. The market segment manager need not replace today's brand or product manager but must clearly be his/her superior, probably immediate supervisor, so that people resources are assigned and developed most appropriately *vis-á-vis* overall business strategy.

In summary, the fact that market segmentation studies are usually done for, and within, the brand or product structure, ought not obscure the value of applying them at the firm level, where truly strategic issues are addressed. At this level the issues for research supercede any particular brand or product, embracing instead strategic questions such as:

How to allocate investment and operating resources for best market results?

How to organize most efficiently *vis-á-vis* marketplace accountability?

How to stimulate effective leadership and coordinated teamwork toward attainable market goals of the business?

When it operates at this level, marketing research has reached out to fulfill its potential.

Chapter Three

James E. Schneider

Jim Schneider is President of The Jim Schneider Group, a sales training firm headquartered in Oak Brook, Illinois. The firm is unique in custom designing sales training and salesperson selection programs based on the strategies of peak performance sellers.

Since 1968, Mr. Schneider has been one of the country's leading advocates of sales culture in his speeches, articles and consulting throughout the United States and Canada. Thousands of executives have learned to sell in his Feel of Success Seminars.

Prior to forming The Jim Schneider Group, Mr. Schneider was president of two national sales management consulting firms, including Palm Beach Consulting Group.

Before entering the consulting business, Mr. Schneider was Manager of New Products and Planning for First National Bank of Chicago; Trust Marketing Manager for Continental Illinois Bank; and Director of Sales and Marketing for Security Savings of Wisconsin, one of the nation's most profitable S & L's.

Mr. Schneider's sales experience also includes positions as Director of Sales and Marketing for a financial services group that included real estate, insurance, travel and banking, and as a salesman for United Airlines an Inland Steel.

Mr. Schneider is author of a new book on selling, The Feel of Success® in Selling, *and a video series by the same name was recognized as the top sales training film of 1984 by the International Television Association. His firm also operates The Jim Schneider Sales Institute in Oak Brook, Illinois, which provides high-performance sales training to salespeople from all industries and conducts research of peak performance sellers.*

EFFECTIVE SALES MANAGEMENT FOR FINANCIAL INSTITUTIONS (Moving from Sales Basics to Sales Results)

James E. Schneider
President
The Jim Schneider Group
Oak Brook, Illinois

Despite all the industry hype about "sales culture," few financial service organizations have become effective sales organizations.

As an industry, we haven't moved from sales basics to sales results. Increasingly, CEOs are asking their marketing directors such questions as, "I know we've increased our cross-sales ratio substantially, so why aren't we making more money? or, "Why can't our experienced lending officers sell more fee income products?"

Even the most sophisticated sales organizations in the industry are asking, "What's next?" Many have implemented sales tracking, sales training and sales compensation systems, and they're looking for what's needed to move them to the next plateau of excellence and profits in sales.

Sales organizations don't manage themselves. Someone has to drive these marvelous chariots. As the Figure 1 illustrates, effective sales organizations are driven by changing corporate financial objectives. Someone has to communicate the company's objectives, expectations, values, progress and rewards.

Sales management is actually management of a complex web of marketing and human resource issues that provide purpose and reinforcement for the selling effort. Most financial institutions manage sales as a series of continuing "events," not as an integrated climate of sales supports. As a result, sales and quality service never become institutionalized as priorities.

Figure 1: Managing the Sales Climate

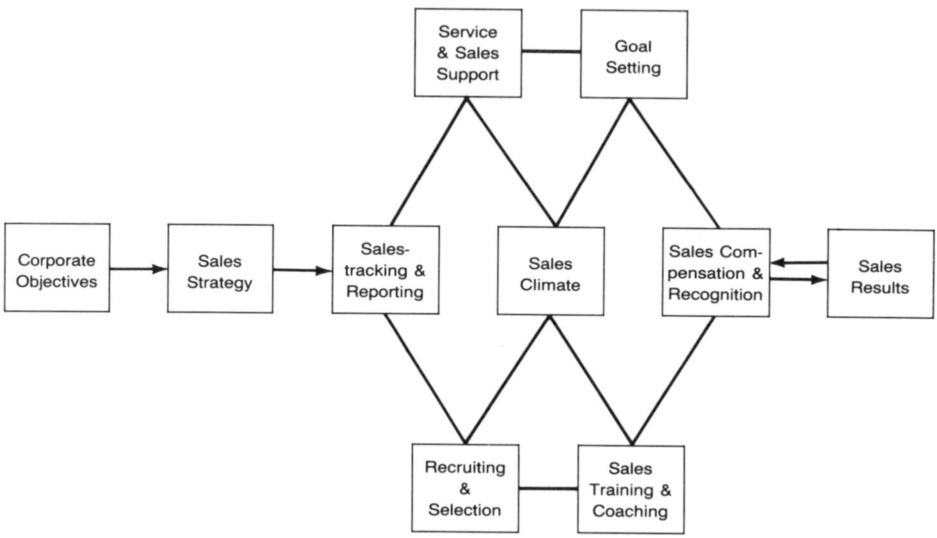

The next wave of sales management is the integration of a company's financial strategies and market research with its sales and service strategies. Most institutions lose potential profits simply because they don't communicate.

At the center of this storm are the industry's new sales managers. By now, most financial institutions have assigned *accountability* for managing sales. Sales managers may be branch managers, business development managers or managers of specific markets, product lines or non-traditional banking products such as annuities or real estate. Many institutions also have company or divisional sales managers.

Whatever their accountability, the primary role of sales managers is sales communication. Companies communicate their values and expectations in everything they do, and in everything they *don't* do. It is the sales manager's job to see that the salesforce gets the right signals and stays on course to meet the organization's financial objectives.

THE SALES MANAGER'S ROLE IN SALES COMMUNICATION

Managing sales results requires managing people, gaining the willing cooperation of the many people who have an impact on sales effectiveness. People are the basic unit of sales excellence.

Sales managers have to sell their ideas in the same way they sell their products. They "sell" selling and peak performance to the salesforce.

New sales managers often struggle with the transition from player to coach. As sales manager, they're no longer judged exclusively on what they sell. Instead, they're judged on their ability to get sales results from other people.

New sales managers soon discover that their role is to solve other people's problems. As sales managers, their time is not their own. Their new role requires them to communicate with dozens of target audiences which have widely different objectives and to communicate the organization's expectations and performance consequences to the salesforce.

Successful sales managers are the most effective when they:

- Sell the mission of solving problems for customers and meeting specific corporate goals so their salespeople sustain their commitment.
- Focus priorities by setting motivating goals and helping their salespeople develop plans to achieve those goals.
- Increase competence and confidence with performance feedback.
- Reward success, even partial success, so it's repeated.
- Select the right people for the right jobs and support them with the training, coaching and resources they need.

THE AUDIENCES FOR SALES COMMUNICATIONS

How sales manager's communicate is shaped by the audience for their communication. The salesforce has a different agenda than executive management, customers, other departments, or suppliers.

Since many of the sales manager's audiences overlap across the functions of sales management, this chapter centers on how sales managers communicate, with the hope that each sales manager will use those communications with the viewpoint of the target audience in mind.

For example, sustaining the commitment and involvement of executive management in the sales climate is essential to getting long-term results. Communication to this audience has to be concise and directed either to financial or long-term strategic implications. Savvy sales managers quickly learn how to interpret and communicate the numbers of sales management to executive management.

In general, other departments want to know that their viewpoints have been considered in sales planning. Operations is usually most interested in cost savings, productivity and hassle-free operations, whereas human resources and training are typically more interested in the impact of sales activities on people and on the way employees are appraised and compensated.

To customers and referral sources, particularly key account customers, sales managers have to communicate their commitment to the relationship, the results they've achieved, and their responsiveness to the customer's needs.

Even suppliers have to be sold. The more your consultants know about your objectives and your problems, the more specific you are about the outcome you want, the more they can help you. By your selling the potential of your relationship, they may be persuaded to give you something extra or to deliver a "miracle" when you need it most.

Communications to the sales force itself requires a segmented approach. The people attracted to different sales roles within the same organization respond differently to various types of communication, based on differences in personality, experience and other factors. The way your sales managers communicate to your branch sales staff should be substantially different than the way they communicate to a commissioned salesforce—an idea reviewed in more depth later in this chapter.

In preparing sales communications, sales managers should first take a few minutes to analyze the objectives, problems and viewpoints of their target audience. Think of your audience as your customer. The Feel of Success® Sales Planner format (Figure 2) is the best way I've found to plan communications with these various audiences.

Figure 2

FEEL OF SUCCESS® SALES PLANNER

Customer's Objectives	What the Customer is Doing Now (Which means)→	What the Customer is Losing	Your Objective (Which means)→	Benefits to Customer (Which means)→	Stretch Benefits	Expected Objections ←
1.	(one sentence)	Loss:	(one sentence)	Feature:		Objection:
		Stretch Loss:		Benefit:		Response:
2.						
		Loss:		Feature:		Objection:
3.						
		Stretch Loss:		Benefit:		Reponse:
4.	Key questions to ask:	Loss:	Reasons for the customer to act now:	Feature:		Objection:
		Stretch Loss:		Benefit:		Response:
5.						

To use the Sales Planner, start by completing column one, the person's business and personal objectives, and then complete the other columns. Always think of the results of your ideas from your audience's viewpoint. In completing column one, think only of the person, not your idea, so your entire communication strategy will be driven by your audience's viewpoint.

Throughout all of your sales communication, stay focused on your audience's viewpoint and on the mission you've set out to achieve.

SELLING THE MISSION

Many sales organizations fail from lack of leadership. Sales management controls the sales climate, but leadership adds the common vision that unleashes energy and motivation.

People do what you want done because they want to do it. They want to be led in pursuit of worthwhile goals. The desire to excel is the most important factor in sales success.

One of the sales manager's most important communication roles is relating the company's mission to each employee's goals. To inspire passion and extra effort, effective sales managers focus attention on a common cause that employees care about, such as dedication to service and solving problems for customers, or becoming the market leader. Having a mission helps employees adapt to change. It gives employees an overall plan with which they're familiar and to which they're committed.

The process of defining a mission for the salesforce begins with management's agreement on a statement of corporate goals for the sales effort which prioritizes what the salesforce is setting out to achieve. In simple terms, this sales mission statement defines "success" for the sales effort.

These discussions often result in a written sales philosophy statement which helps the sales manager exercise leadership in communicating the company's values and sales mission.

In executing the company's sales plan, every sales manager runs up against the company's culture. Savvy sales managers learn to use the culture to communicate their mission.

Since most financial institutions have a strong service culture, and since many of their employees have fears about being viewed as "pushy salespeople" by their customers, we've found it effective for sales managers to position selling in their sales communications as a step up in excellence in service. IBM, the most successful sales organization in history, still positions selling as service with its salesforce.

To solidify sales as a regular way of doing business rather than as a "program" that will eventually go away, sales should also be positioned in communications as a permanent, step-by-step process of serving customers better. The goal is to foster a pervasive attitude that customers come first and that selling is important, expected and the way to get rewarded.

Here are a few other tips for selling the sales mission:

- Constantly use the word "sales" in communications.
- Integrate the company's marketing research data and strategic objectives with your sales training.
- Sell the salesforce on rallying behind a competitive lead product that they really believe in.
- Name the sales process so employees won't label it as a "program."
- Emphasize sales and service expectations and values to new hires during their orientation.
- Assign senior executives a small portfolio of key accounts to contact periodically along with the assigned sales representative.
- Constantly remind everyone of what the organization believes in by pinpointing and magnifying select sales and service incidents in speeches and memos.
- Constantly stress quality rather than price.
- Arrange for the CEO to spend time in highly visible sales activities such as making sales calls, attending sales meetings, reviewing sales reports, and meeting personally with top sales performers.

Once the sales mission is well defined and accepted, the sales manager's most important sales communications revolve around finding salespeople who can sell.

HOW TO IDENTIFY PEOPLE WHO CAN SELL

Sales communications pays off best when sales managers are leading people who can sell. The "200 watt" salespeople shine a lot brighter than "60 watt" salespeople once they're turned on, and communication is much easier.

Not everyone can be a high performing seller. A person's personality and experience may not fit the type of selling he or she is asked to do. As a result, sales managers in most industries set as their first priority the recruitment of salespeople who can sell.

In most financial institutions, sales managers don't communicate their sales personnel needs effectively. They don't recognize the differences that exist among the various types of selling done in a financial institution.

Psychological research of thousands of salespeople has demonstrated that the one factor that consistently correlates with high sales productivity is the person's personality "fit" with what the person is expected to do in selling. Age, gender, sales or banking experience and other factors commonly emphasized in financial industry recruiting have little to do with success in selling.

The research Dr. Arlene Magnus and I have done in salesperson selection in the financial services industry has identified five types of selling roles that take place in financial institutions. In addition, salespeople may also need to be assessed for their potential for sales leadership as managers.

Success in each of the five types of financial industry selling requires different personal attributes, and the people who perform well in each of these selling roles have different motivations and require different communication strategies in training, coaching, reward and motivation. For example, a service seller may be strongly motivated by helping customers or belonging to a successful team, whereas a competitive seller may be more motivated by immediate dollar rewards and personal recognition as a "superseller."

Surprisingly, part-time employees frequently rank among the leaders in bank sales. This is further evidence of the importance of sales personality relative to experience.

Sales managers should first define what sales behavior they expect from people in each sales position. For example, commercial bankers are often selected on the basis of their "number crunching" abilities and then thrown to the wolves to develop business! Next, they should identify the people who are currently peak performers in those sales roles and develop their selection criteria based on the profile of those peak performers, particulary their personality, experience, and "fit" with the culture of the organization and with the audience they'll be selling to.

Sales managers also have to communicate their salesforce needs to the human resources staff. The more precise sales managers are about what they want, the more effective human resources personnel can be in supporting them. Managers can help develop job descriptions, recruiting ads and sales aids that will help draw the right applicants and pre-sell them on your company.

Many of your best potential salespeople can be found inside your organization in positions that don't fit their strengths. By posting new sales positions and profiling employees by personality, you can identify people with sales potential and an interest in selling and "refit" them to the sales positions they're best suited for. Offering cash incentives to employees who recommend people who prove to be effective in sales helps to communicate the priority you're placing on sales recruiting.

Sales managers also need to communicate a career path that will attract and keep good salespeople. Financial institutions tend to hire personnel for entry sales positions, such as teller, and promote these people through a one-dimensional career track to higher levels of selling such as sales counselor or branch manager. Since each of these types of selling requires a different sales personality and different competencies, the best sellers in these categories eventually move to other companies so they can make more money doing what they do best, or they leave branch sales for other job categories.

A two-track career path for salespeople makes it possible for an employee in any selling role to move laterally to other positions or to increase his compensation in his current position by meeting specific performance standards that justify higher compensation.

Sales managers have to continually communicate through their network of employees and outside sales contacts that they seek to recruit people who can sell. By recruiting when they don't need someone, they're never under pressure to hire the wrong person. And when a new hire doesn't work out, the sales supervisor should be urged to replace that employee quickly.

Some institutions communicate their expectations to applicants clearly at the interview stage by asking them to sign a statement which outlines the sales performance expectations for the position for which they're applying.

The personality attributes common to success in all types of selling include a strong drive to persuade for the sake of seeing one's ideas accepted; assertiveness; empathy for other people's viewpoints; and responsiveness to the objectives, style and concerns of other people. To assess these attributes, sales managers should schedule multiple interviews with different people so various members of the sales team can provide feedback on the applicant's versatility in adapting to different people.

Once the right people are in place in the right selling positions, sales managers can concentrate on leadership.

CLEAR ACCOUNTABILITY INCREASES SALES PRODUCTIVITY

Clear accountability is crucial to sales motivation. When sellers are confused about priorities, they don't commit themselves to achieving anything, and when conditions and expectations change fast, as they do during a merger or during the transition to a strong sales climate, employees look for even more clarity.

Sales managers first communicate this accountability in the way they organize their staff or selling.

When a sales manager so organizes selling that branch managers who don't have a strong second tier of management in their branches are expected to do substantial outside calling *plus* manage in-branch sales and operations, neither job gets done well. When branches are organized so first-line supervisors don't function visibly as supervisors with employees and customers, service quality drops dramatically. When institutions operate without a separate, dedicated salesforce for new business development, or for the sale of complicated or non-traditional products, sellers are frequently nonproductive.

The fastest payoff on defining sales accountability results from assigning accountability for retention and development of the 10 to 15 percent of customers and referral sources who produce 80 to 90 percent of the organization's profits.

Relationship management is the rising star of financial sales management. However, its ultimate effectiveness as a concept requires success in personal selling to key accounts. Smart financial sales managers are following the lead of such non-financial companies as IBM and Hewlett-Packard by identifying these key account relationships and assigning customer portfolios to individual sellers so these customers receive extra sales attention.

The sales manager's first impression in communicating sales accountability is made by way of the position description used in hiring and explaining responsibilities to employees. For most financial institutions, these position descriptions communicate few, if any, accountabilities for selling. For many positions the word "sales" isn't even used in the position description, and position descriptions frequently treat all selling positions as if they have the same sales accountabilities. They don't.

For example, if bank tellers interpret their accountability as completing sales, they won't even try to sell because they know they don't have time to sort out the customer's objectives, describe the product and close the sale. Their sales role should be clearly defined as sales referral and what I refer to as "specials selling"—creating opportunities by treating new information such as rate changes as reasons to engage customers in brief dialogues leading to referrals.

The position description spells out what you expect from an employee in this position at this moment in time. When salespeople take on new selling roles or new territories, their accountabilities are almost always different than they were in their previous positions. The position description clearly delineates these differences.

COMMUNICATING YOUR SUPPORT

Leadership is earned, not conferred. Success as a sales manager requires *making time* for communicating with the salesforce.

For the sales manager, resolving even a small problem or distraction for a salesperson is a higher priority than responding to most customers. If just one salesperson is distracted, the resulting drop in performance will affect dozens of customers.

Most sales managers spend too much time supervising their employees and too little time supporting them. The only time most salespeople hear from their sales managers is when they foul up.

The best thing a sales manager can do to increase sales is to spend quality time with each salesperson, looking for ways to support his or her selling. Anything a sales manager can do to support the salesforce is important—listening to them, encouraging them.

The sales manager is the voice of the salesforce. Sellers hold them accountable for meeting their needs. When sales managers free sellers from distractions, they free people for selling.

From a seller's viewpoint, support might be as simple as getting a problem with an expense report ironed out, or as challenging as changing a product or a policy, lobbying for a raise or for a promotion, or selling executive management on the need for important resources.

In-branch sellers typically might want more staff, or on-line relationship summaries and financial counseling software for key account households, sales aids that help them get information from customers. The better sellers might want to be relocated where there's more traffic.

Outside sellers typically might want telemarketing support, sales aids for group presentations, closing call support by executives or product specialists, or better word processing support for proposal preparation and sales letters.

Sales managers can't ignore these requests. They have to convince the salesforce that they're communicating effectively in their behalf. Planning is one of the ways sales managers can demonstrate their support.

SETTING GOALS

Of all the dimensions of sales communication, none has more impact on salesforce motivation than goal setting.

Salespeople who have goals consistently out-perform those who don't. Goals increase motivation by making it possible to succeed more often, and by encouraging self-management. The focus of attention provided by goal setting increases commitment to achieve the goals. A seller is more likely to believe he or she can succeed.

Goals should be set high enough to motivate people to extra effort, yet low enough to provide frequent opportunities for success. People can't do what they can't do, and trying too hard can actually hurt performance. At least 50 percent of the salesforce should meet their goals with reasonable effort.

The difference in behavior between peak performance and average performance is small. Generally, the higher the goals, the better the performance. When goals are set too low, sales managers actually reinforce poor performance.

Improvement is the objective of goal setting. Expect progress, not perfection. It's more motivating for sellers to compete against themselves than to compete against others.

Sales goals should be both measurable and "sales-specific," which means they must be within the seller's control to achieve by a specific date on the basis of his or her effort (rather than being accomplished because of changes in interest rates or marketing support).

Sales managers should set three to five goals per salesperson per quarter. Break these major goals into smaller, step-by-step improvement goals to give sellers more opportunities to succeed. Nothing increases confidence and motivation like success.

Once goals have been set, a sales manager's communication role in goal setting is just beginning. Sales managers need to constantly remind sellers of their successes and their goals. When sales managers frequently check salesforce progress against a goal prior to the goal deadline, sellers are more likely to believe they can achieve that goal.

Once sales managers begin communicating regularly with the salesforce about their progress toward meeting specific goals, sales managers need to know how to give effective feedback on performance.

FEEDBACK: SALES COMMUNICATION AT ITS BEST

For salespeople, performance feedback is clearly "the breakfast of champions." Sellers have a strong need for recognition of their successes so they can sustain their motivation in the face of rejection, resistance and dips and plateaus in performance. Some successful sales organizations such as Mary Kay Cosmetics, were built on the strength of their recognition programs.

Feedback is also a powerful tool for sales managers to use in sustaining effective servicing and referral activity for non-credit staff and third-party referral sources. A quick thank you note can even increase their support. One study found that peak performance salespeople were particularly adept at getting the cooperation of support staff for their customers.

Sales performance is largely the result of the consequences of selling behavior. Behavior that is positively reinforced tends to continue or to increase as sellers work hard to repeat the rewards. Sales behavior that is ignored or punished tends to decrease as sellers work hard to avoid the negative feedback.

Sales managers whose sellers hit a plateau in sales results often can get substantial increases in sales simply by increasing their feedback to sellers on "normal expected" behavior in a 4:1 ratio of rewards to reprimands. *People will work harder and longer for praise than for anything else.*

To program themselves to give more feedback, sales managers should first break sales performance into small steps or behaviors that can be easily rewarded. Salespeople won't repeat or change their behavior unless sales managers are specific. Sales managers should give feedback at a time when the employee can immediately apply it, or immediately after the behavior occurs.

Rewards and recognition have to fit the person. What one salesperson accepts as a reward—such as extra responsibility—another salesperson may accept as punishment.

Every sales manager has a wide selection of inexpensive rewards to call upon ranging from spending extra time with the employee to providing extra chances to learn. One of the best forms of recognition is *customer recognition*, and many firms have developed ways to use direct feedback from customers to reinforce effective sales and service behavior.

Most institutions with advanced sales climates prepare sales progress charts for their sales units and post the scores publicly, quickly and frequently. The impact of this performance tracking is even more powerful when those results are broken into smaller goals for behavior improvement and interim results that lead to goal achievement, and when salespeople record their own progress toward short-term improvement goals, as shown in Figure 3.

Figure 3: Performance Tracking

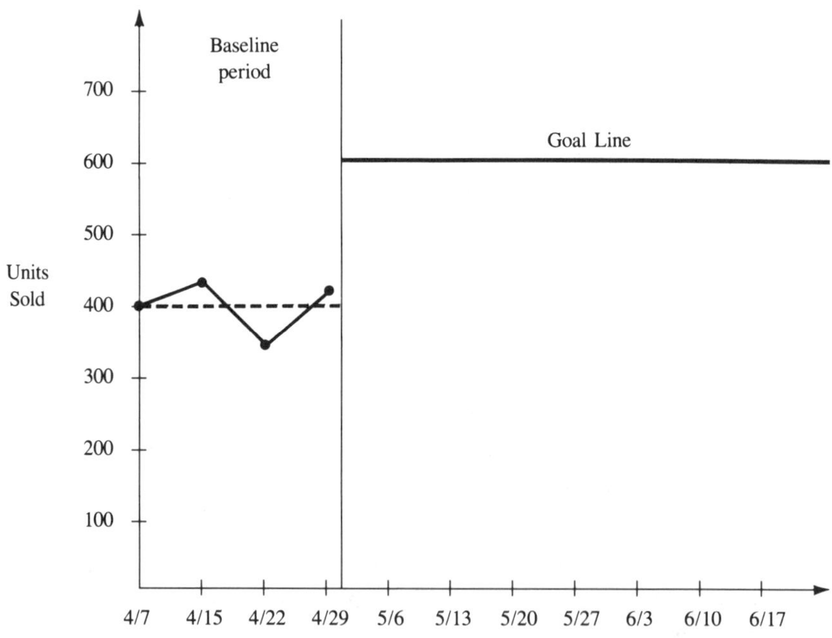

This simple graphing of progress from a baseline record of performance toward a goal encourages self-management and provides immediate feedback to sellers when the sales manager can't be there.

SELLING "PAY FOR PERFORMANCE"

Sales managers can provide effective motivational "hype" and sales communications all year long, but when employees have their performance appraisals and salary reviews and hear little or nothing about sales and goal achievement, the organization communicates clearly that sales is *not* a priority.

Service will continue to be a major responsibility of most financial institution sellers, so base salary will continue to account for the major segment of the branch employee's compensation. As a result, one of the sales manager's key sales communication tasks is to sell the perception that pay and performance are linked. When sales managers fail at this, they quickly lose their best sellers.

The primary communication vehicle for performance review is the appraisal, an event that occurs only once a year at most institutions. The appraisal forms used by many financial institutions don't even refer to sales or to goal achievement. Branch employees throughout the country almost universally report they want more frequent appraisals of their performance than they currently receive.

The perfect appraisal is the one that never has to be held because the sales manager and the salesforce communicate openly about performance throughout the year. Since sales managers don't operate in a perfect world, brief quarterly appraisals for salespeople, separate from the salary review, are recommended.

Effective appraisals are actually performance previews, focusing on what can be learned from the past to improve future performance. They include discussion of sales results, goal achievement, product knowledge, time management, service skills and behavior. To assure that a seller's full performance is appraised, each quarterly appraisal should focus on different issues to supplement the necessary discussion of goals and results. These issues should be included in the written appraisal form.

To assure good communication during appraisals, sales managers should encourage self-evaluation by sellers by talking as little as possible and asking sellers to evaluate their performance independently prior to the appraisal conference.

Since effective appraisals focus on the seller's needs and future performance, the need for training is a frequent outcome of the appraisal process.

SALES TRAINING FOR PEAK PERFORMANCE

The best way for sales managers to communicate sales skills and attitudes is by giving trainees models of good performance which they can imitate. The most effective sales training is based on the successful selling actions of peak performers in your sales climate, and that requires custom design of basic selling concepts around your unique situation.

Who should conduct sales training? Our clients have had their best results with branch managers and other sales managers teaching the fundamentals of selling after receiving training in group leadership skills. There seems to be "magic" in the sales leader taking accountability for the results of his or her salesforce. For advanced sales training and for new-hire sales training, top-performing sales organizations such as IBM often rotate their best sales managers and salespeople as sales training instructors so their strategies, attitudes and values can be modeled for new hires.

10 Key Skills That Sales Managers Need To Communicate in Sales Training

- Selling with purpose: thinking of selling as solving problems and helping customers reach their objectives.
- Setting goals.
- Relaxing by focusing on the customer and involving him, rather than focusing on the product and the presentation.
- Versatility in developing rapport, so that when the salesperson's approach isn't working he or she tries something else.
- Positioning the company and the product as being clearly different from competition.
- Gathering information.
- Recognizing customer objectives and problems and "the feel of the sale."
- Establishing value beyond price by increasing product benefits.

• Spending time with the right prospects.

• Adding to sales by positioning add-on sales as ways of improving the initial purchase.

You'll notice that closing sales and handling objections aren't on the list. Selling is largely mental toughness; the other skills will come naturally.

Repetition is critical to learning. There's a large "aftermarket" for reinforcement of existing sales training since sellers are always at a different "place" in their selling as they gain experience. That's why insurance companies put new salespeople through four or five different sales training courses in their first two years of employment.

By now most financial institutions conduct sales training for the salesforce. To move to the next level of sophistication, sales managers need to develop advanced sales training around what their best performers are doing right.

A major California S&L, for example, prepared videotapes of its best sellers talking about their sales strategies and demonstrating their attitudes. A large southeastern bank has built a sales course for senior calling officers around the strategies used by the 20 best calling officers. These same calling officers appear on videotaped introductions to the program, so their sales trainers have maximum credibility with the calling officers who attend the course. In developing these tapes, it has been found that modelling the attitudes of the peak performers is even more effective than modelling their strategies.

HOW TO LEVERAGE YOUR SALES TRACKING DATA

Most financial institutions operate with some form of sales tracking system. Tracking sales results is one of the basics of sales management, but it won't lead to peak performance selling unless sales managers use that information.

Here are a few communication tips for using the sales tracking system to move your salesforce to the next plateau of sales results:

Communication Tips for Sales Tracking

• Sell "sales tracking" as the basis for reward, even naming the report a "Sales Achievement Report."

• When you train managers and sellers in how to record sales data, train them how to interpret and use the reports.
• Ask managers and sellers to exchange reports and coach each other on how to act on the information in their reports.
• Provide each seller with his or her own monthly report of sales performance and incentive earnings to increase motivational impact.
• Stress effectiveness, not activity.
• Report progress toward goals as well as current sales.
• From the date of your first report, ask sellers to use their reports to set and graph weekly step-by-step improvement goals; for instance, "Sell five CDs with checking accounts in the next week."
• Include everyone in the company in the referral tracking system.
• Review the reports to identify which products sell best with which other products, and train the salesforce to key on those add-on sales opportunities.
• Require sales managers to schedule a brief meeting with each salesperson to review their sales reports the day the reports are received.

Sales tracking provides the basis for establishing standards for sales positions and for setting goals for individuals.

CONCLUSION

Sales management is more than pep rallies, sales contest and memos. Sales managers communicate with every aspect of the sales climate by what they do and by what they don't do.

The sales manager's role in sales communication is to orchestrate these various messages so they work together to support the financial goals that drive the organization.

Chapter Four

Kevin Tynan

Kevin Tynan is President of Kevin B. Tynan and Associates, Inc., a Chicago-based marketing consulting firm specializing in financial and healthcare markets. In addition to developing and executing marketing programs, Tynan and Associates publishes over two million newsletters yearly.

Previously, Tynan was Vice President of Marketing for a billion-dollar financial institution, served two terms on the Federal Savings and Loan Advisory Council, was President of the North Shore Public Relations Club, Chairman of the Illinois Savings and Loan League Marketing Committee and is a frequent media commentator on financial marketing matters.

Tynan graduated with an M.B.A. from Loyola University, Chicago, and a B.S. from the University of Illinois.

MARKETING THROUGH CUSTOMER PUBLICATIONS*

Kevin Tynan
President
Kevin B. Tynan & Associates, Inc.

Customer publications—primarily newsletters and magazines—have been a part of financial services marketing for years. In the past five or so years, however, there has been a growing use and interest in these communication vehicles as an integral part of the marketing plan. There are many ways that customer publications can fill the information gap caused by both the proliferation of new financial products and services and increased competition in the marketplace. And there are several advantages in offering customer publications.

First, using well-designed mailing distribution lists, financial institutions can achieve low waste by sending promotional/informational publications to segments most likely to generate future business and profits.

In addition, unlike mass media, a proprietary vehicle can control the editorial environment and message. If regularly published, this vehicle gives continuity and consistency not found in other communications programs.

Finally, a publication designed for a specific target market achieves considerably higher readership than mass media. Research indicates that

---

* This chapter contains excepts from a monograph published by the Financial Institutions Marketing Association entitled, "Marketing Through Customer Publications," written by Kevin Tynan and William Winter. Used by permission.

a publication designed around an editorial format achieves four times the readership and believability experienced in an advertising format. A controlled vehicle allows a financial institution to enhance its cross-selling power and to strengthen account relationships.

Clearly, a major consideration in developing a customer publication is budget. What you have to spend will determine circulation, number of pages, frequency, use of color, quality of paper stock and other factors. In most cases, your budget will be the key in producing a magazine or a newsletter. A specific objective should be to develop rationale so that management will support an adequate budget to produce the publication you need.

The success of any publication is also shaped by how it is perceived by management. Not only must it meet marketing goals, but it also must convey management philosophy and its goals.

Publications can be divided into two general classifications:

- *Customer Publications.* As the name indicates, this type is directed to existing customers only. These magazines or newsletters can be targeted either to a broad customer base—such as account relationships over a certain deposit amount—or to specific demographic or product groups. The characteristic of such a publication is that its language clearly indicates to the reader that it is being sent to him or her as a customer—not as a prospect.
- *Customer/Prospect Publications.* These publications are designed for prospects and customers. It introduces the reader to the financial institution and is not primarily a cross-selling vehicle. Thus, externally oriented techniques are used.

There are three formats commonly used by financial institutions for their customer and customer/prospect publications.

- *Newsletter.* Normally 8-1/2 x 11 inches in size, this publication expresses urgency, late-breaking news and action to the reader. Articles should be brief and explanatory. It is designed to be a fast read. To be effective, it should come out quarterly or more frequently. It can be used as self-mailer or a stuffer. Most often, one or two colors are used, but four-color can be effective if budget allows.
- *Newspaper.* Similar in scope to a newsletter, a newspaper normally is tabloid in size, thus including more information for the reader. Most often,

this publication is printed on high-grade newsprint with one or two colors. To live up to its "newsy" format, it should come out quarterly or more frequently. (A magapaper—a hybrid using both newspaper and magazine layouts—also has been used effectively.)

• *Magazine*. Through the years, this continues to be a popular type of publication. It has more staying power than a newsletter or newspaper: it is often passed on to others. Normally printed on higher grade paper stock, it uses four-color effectively—although some use two-color to advantage. This is the best vehicle for advertising and stitch-ins are commonly used. Quarterly frequency is best. This is a longer read—with financial institution materials surrounded by general interest or personal money management articles to create a pleasant and informative experience for the reader. More depth in most articles is possible.

MARKETING GOALS AS PART OF PUBLICATION DESIGN

Four broad objectives should underly the basic editorial content of customer publications.

Position Your Institution and Its Products

First, a customer publication clearly should position the financial institution, separating it from its competition and generally supporting the marketing campaign. A customer publication can effectively convey the image of a financial institution, including repositioning following a name change or change in business direction.

In most marketing plans, positioning is a highly important element for both the institution and the publication. For example, does the organization want an innovative or conservative image? Does it want to appeal to a certain type of customer? Should the publication be directed to the middle market or the upscale market? Should it be educational, general interest, or a combination of both?

Your objectives also will be affected by the competition. What type of competitive publication is available? Can your publication fill a niche not covered by competitors? Can a more effective publication be developed than that currently used by your competitors?

Convey Product Information

A custom publication can act as a forum to effectively *inform* customers about products, services and the institution's objectives. It also can be an extremely effective public affairs vehicle in terms of issues management. Furthermore, it can *educate* customers effectively using new and existing products and services.

Support Sales Efforts

Finally, such a publication can cross-sell new and existing services to readers. It can sell the institution as the customers "prime account" relationship.

More specifically, a publication should clearly reflect the objectives of the marketing plan. This may mean meeting a measurable sales goal for a particular product. Or, it may mean penetrating a particular demographic or customer group.

PRODUCING YOUR OWN PUBLICATION

Some financial institutions find it advantageous to produce a publication within their own shop, but this requires certain skills in writing, editing, art direction and production.

There are two basic advantages of an in-house magazine, newsletter or newspaper. One, there is the potential for lower costs if you have appropriate resources. Two, a qualified staff will know your product line and institution better than an outside source. This knowledge—plus a superior understanding of the industry and money management issues—is an important asset in producing a publication internally.

However, there are drawbacks in publishing your own publication. Availability of staff time always is a factor and staff experience and capabilities need to be considered. Further, objectivity can be lost when pressure is brought to bear by department heads, branch managers or management to create a strictly self-directed publication, consequently reducing the effectiveness of the publication.

A marketing director's responsibilities extend beyond the customer publication. Therefore, there is always danger the publication depends greatly on uncontrollable factors such as printers, production houses and other suppliers. Time constraints may preclude full-time attention to the publication.

If you produce your own publication, several considerations need to be dealt with. One major consideration is the distribution channels for which the publication is designed. For example, a statement stuffer requires certain size and weight limitations. Therefore, design must take into consideration how the publication is folded to achieve greatest impact. Self-mailers will require attention to such items as weight, postal requirements, labeling, impact, and so on. Four primary means of distribution are: (1) conventional outgoing mail, (2) self-mailer, (3) door-to-door distribution or distribution through branch offices and (4) newspaper insert. Or a combination of the four may be used.

For budgetary reasons, estimating costs when doing your own publication is crucial. Items to be taken into consideration are:

• Writing, rewriting, editing and coordination of the internal staff and freelancers. Editorial charges will vary greatly based on these individuals' experience.

• Artwork expense will depend on whether it is original artwork, clip art, stock photography, studio photography or on-site photography.

• Printing prices will vary widely based on equipment, paper quality and number of colors. Competitive bids are essential.

• Distribution costs will range from minimal (if included in outgoing mail) to more expensive first-class postage. The most commonly used postage is third-class bulk.

• In comparing in-house costs to outside expenses, be sure you allocate salaries, benefits and overhead.

SYNDICATED AND CUSTOM PUBLISHING

While there are advantages to producing your publication inside the organization, there also are excellent reasons to have it done by professional outsiders. Most often, marketing and public relations staffs of financial institutions are small, and the use of a custom publisher becomes a cost-effective alternative.

Although an outside supplier can frequently be of great assistance in publishing a custom periodical, there can be disappointments along the printed path. Some agencies that specialize in newsletters may have little familiarity with particular industries such as financial services. It can be expensive in terms of time, to educate someone about the business. It's best to ask to meet with the editor or writer who will be your editorial contact so that you can assess his or her competency and compatibility. You cannot judge the supplier strictly on the basis of the presentation delivered by the company's principal or salesperson.

To avoid problems, require firm, written, comparable estimates for all publishing assignments. Specify the type of paper you expect, whether the delivery will be in convenient cartons and whether you'll own the rights to the name you select. Some suppliers might provide quotes based on use of a low-priced paper. Others might register a new newsletter title in their firm's name, thus making it impossible for the financial institution to continue using this title if they cancel the firm's publishing contract.

Selecting a Supplier

Here are several other specific factors to examine when selecting a supplier:

• *Experience.* What is the publisher's client base? How many years have they been in business? What are their samples like? Are they financially stable?

• *Quality of Execution.* This is easily determined by reviewing past work of the publisher, talking to current and past clients and examining results generated by their publications. Is the publisher experienced with the financial services industry? Is the staff knowledgeable and capable of writing the type of materials necessary for your publication. Can they get the publication out on time? Can they deliver on their promises? A simple check of past performance will verify this.

• *Flexibility.* Can the publisher respond to your needs? Do they offer a full variety of formats, schedules, design and writing styles? Can they react to sudden changes in marketing direction or schedule? Are they willing to work with you on a "can-do" basis or do they have printing and scheduling inflexibilities that will encourage crises?

• *Depth of Service.* Are they a full-service publisher? Can they provide all services needed to publish your vehicle? Can they create a turnkey operation for you?

• *Value*. Interestingly enough, price often is not as important as value. A seemingly inexpensive publication can be costly when measured against execution and cross-selling ability. A poorly designed publication that misses the target market is costly in terms of effectiveness.

• *Personal Chemistry*. This is the ability to mesh with the publisher during all phases of production. Are they encouraged to be members of your team? Do they exhibit creativity? Do they bring new ideas? Do they spark projects? Do they understand your needs and marketing objectives? Do they have a feel for your institution and where it's going?

Once a custom publisher has been selected, it is important that several considerations be kept in mind:

• *Relationship*. A supplier relationship should be viewed as a client-agency partnership. The mark of a good publisher is how well they deal with your problems. The publisher should be as closely informed as possible about marketing goals and directions.

• *Objectives*. Clearly defined objectives of the publication are critical to the financial institution and the publisher. Start with the marketing objectives and discuss what is expected of the publication and the publisher.

• *Editorial Meetings*. Regular editorial meetings are essential to the success of a publication. Generally, meetings should be directed at planning for the immediate issue and subsequent issues.

• *Client Prime Contact*. It is essential that *one* person from the marketing department be assigned as a prime contact with the publisher. This person should act as a funnel for all details of the publication and interaction with the institution's staff.

• *Publication Importance*. For a publication to be successful, it must be treated as an important part of the marketing plan; as such, schedules and the staff's dedication to the publication are a necessity.

• *Assistance*. If you have a problem that needs attention, do not let it become a crisis. Ask your publisher for help.

DEVELOPING YOUR PUBLICATION

The contents of the magazine will reflect your marketing objectives.

Basically, there are two types of publications: (1) a total custom publication where all copy and artwork are developed specifically for a single financial institution, and (2) a syndicated publication where portions of the publication may be shared among non-competitive financial institutions. In some cases, a syndicated publication will consist of nothing more than a logo identification of a publication. Between these two basic types is the semi-custom publication—a hybrid between syndicated and custom.

Most publications used by financial institutions today fall into two categories: (1) general interest, with a wide variety of subject matter including travel, personalities, money management, and so on, and (2) money management, with content dedicated solely to personal financial matters including better buying, taxes and financial planning. To determine which format is appropriate, you must analyze your objectives and markets.

It is important to remember that a publication's appearance is evolutionary—it will change over time to fit market conditions. A general guideline is that every issue is unique unto itself. Evaluate each issue and use that evaluation to fine-tune subsequent issues. As market conditions or management objectives change, the publication can also change.

Balance is critical to a publication's success. Editorial materials must be appropriate for the target market. If your market is diversified, your editorial can be diversified. For example, you may have editorial divided 40 percent to seniors, 30 percent for retirees, 20 percent to new families and 10 percent to young professionals. Other publications may be directed to just one of these groups. As you refine your publication, it is important to draw a response from all representative groups—customers, management and employees.

• *The 50-Percent Rule*. For readability, one standard in developing editorial balance for the publication is that hard-sell topics should not exceed 50 percent of total editorial content. This can vary from issue to issue and still be effective, but when it hits the 70-to-90-percent hard-sell range regularly, it moves the piece from a publication to an advertising vehicle. There must be a payoff for the recipient of the publication. The reader should find the publication informative, entertaining and useful in his or her daily activities.

• *Developing Subject Matter*. The list of appropriate subjects for a financial institution publication is almost endless. The best method of developing editorial is to examine all pertinent events that will take place in the next six months at the financial institution, be they product, event or public relations related.

• *Artwork Options.* When designing a publication, there are a number of artwork options available. The design of the publication should dictate narrow artwork options. A few of those artwork options are: (1) custom photo versus stock photo, (2) illustration versus photography, (3) colors/black and white versus four-color, and (4) paper quality.

TARGETING YOUR PUBLICATION

Targeting your publication to certain segments often pays dividends.

The size of the market will dictate the practicality of segmenting. For example, it may not be advantageous to create a publication for an extremely small market due to prohibitive costs. When examining this possibility, determine how much business this target market can produce, and whether it would justify the time and cost involved in creating the specialized publication.

In some cases, particularly in large institutions, the use of two publications may be an option to reach marketing goals. For example, a financial institution may want to send a newsletter to its general customer base and then use a more sophisticated publication for its affluent customers. As another example, a financial institution breaks out target markets and creates separate newsletters for each one—seniors, small business owners, professionals, and others.

DIRECT MARKETING DEVICES

Direct response mechanisms are effective marketing devices that should be considered seriously in a publication. These mechanisms elicit inquiries, create traffic and provide the opportunity to cross-sell additional services. You are actually giving the customer as many ways as possible to respond. However, a word of caution. Any direct response mechanism must be followed up by your staff or a marketing reversal will occur. If a timely response is not forthcoming, the customer may become disillusioned and seek a similar product or service from a competitor. Direct response mechanisms include:

• *Response Card.* It is important the card be properly designed and placed in the publication to generate maximum response. A poorly designed response card can cut response by as much as 80 percent. Graphics are extremely important to gain attention.

• *Applications.* These can be included in a publication to be completed by a customer and then brought in or mailed to a nearby branch office or processing center. The type of product offered will dramatically affect the number of applications returned. For example, experience shows that a pre-approved credit card will outdraw a complicated insurance product by a considerable margin.

• *Catalogs and Brochures.* Existing or specially designed catalogs and booklets can be included in magazines, or an article may direct customers to a branch location to pick up these materials.

• *Cut-out Coupons.* While not as effective as tear-out return cards, well-designed cut-out return cards within the editorial (usually as part of an article) can elicit good leads.

• *Toll-free Numbers.* Properly highlighted, these convenient numbers are a strong complement to direct mail offers.

EXECUTION

There is no substitute for good execution in producing a publication.

Publication research has been conducted extensively to measure readership and other market factors. This research varies little among geographic locations and target groups. The findings suggest there are two key points that determine whether your publication will be read. They are:

1. *Sort Time.* This occurs when an individual sorts through incoming mail—discarding those items that look uninteresting or are viewed as junk mail. At this point, your publication either will be put aside for future reading or it will be discarded.

2. *Reading Time.* The second stage—as important as the sort—takes place when the individual prepares to read the materials he or she has saved. At this point, your publication is in competition with several others. To survive this second stage, your publication's graphics and editorial section must be appealing and provocative. A sharp cover will lead recipients to turn the page. Interesting headlines and graphics will get the reader into

a story. An interesting and well-written lead will challenge the person to finish the piece and move on to next article.

In many respects, a bad publication is like a bad advertisement: it doesn't get read. Here are four sets of questions you may want to review in determining the quality of your publication:

1. Is there a payoff for your reader? In other words, is the publication appealing enough so that you would read it yourself?
2. Is the publication easily read? Is there a nice blend of quick-read material and in-depth articles?
3. Is the publication too self-serving? Is it simply an advertising piece? Have you created a publication too myopic in scope?
4. Does your publication have a personality? Is it distinct enough to stand out when compared to other publications—both newsstand and controlled publications?

A publication should not be undertaken as a short-term venture. It should be viewed as a two-year proposition at least, and should appear at least quarterly to be effective. Any less than this normally indicates to customers and management confusion and a lack of direction.

As in all advertising, *consistency* is a critical factor in the success of a publication. It must be published on a regular basis to create awareness and sales. Research has shown that the longer the life of a publication, the higher the accumulative cross-sell.

EVALUATING YOUR PUBLICATION

As is the case with any part of the marketing plan, a publication should be evaluated periodically and scientifically.

Normally, it is not prudent to evaluate before the fourth issue since it will take at least three issues for a customer to realize a publication is being sent from a financial institution on a regular basis. Furthermore, it will take up to the fourth issue for a customer to become familiar with the publication and the institution. After the initial evaluation, a general rule is to evaluate once every two years. This gives adequate data for the institution to refine the publication and reflect changes in the marketplace.

The two most common means of measuring a publication are:

1. *"Stitch-in" Questionnaire*. It is critical that this type of questionnaire be properly designed. A variable—such as whether the questionnaire is postage-paid or not—can seriously affect the response. It is recommended that a qualified market research individual or marketing consultant be employed to conduct the research.
2. *Random Phone Survey*. This is the other popular measurement method. Again, a professional market research individual or consultant should conduct the study.

When measuring publication readership, some of the most common questions are:

• Do recipients read the publication? What do they like about the publication? (Here, the publication should be divided into common editorial topics such as money management, travel, product and services, health, and so on.) What other topics are important? (Normally, an open-ended question is preferable to suggested subjects.)
• Questions on publication quality also are important: How do readers rate the quality of the publication? Do they have a better image of the institution because of the publication?
• Then, there are cross-selling questions—an indicator of extreme interest to top management. Here are two: Has the reader signed up for or inquired about other products or services specifically because of the publication? If so, what products and services?

MERCHANDISING FAVORABLE RESULTS

As previously indicated, top management's response can be as critical to a publication's success as that of the customers. If the publication is to continue, management must be informed about its effectiveness, especially its ability to cross-sell products and services.

With this data, management is clearly able to measure advertising dollars against publication dollars in bottom-line terms. (It also is a good idea to include this readership data in your employee publications.) If your publication receives recognition from trade associations and other sources, it's important to communicate this to top management.

As mentioned earlier, a publication is an ongoing process. Therefore, research should be used to improve the publication from issue to issue. If research shows an inadequacy, adjustments should be made quickly.

If your budget does not allow research, periodic critiques are valuable using staff or non-marketing insiders. Some key issues to examine are:

- Does the publication meet specific marketing objectives?
- Is the publication integrated within the marketing plan?
- Is the content balanced to attract major target markets?
- Should outside help be brought in to evaluate the redesign of the publication?

CONCLUSION

Since customer publications have proven to be an effective way to sell financial services and to better inform the customer, it is important to view them as an integral part of the marketing plan.

Industry observers predict that customer publications will continue to grow more sophisticated and target-oriented in the financial services businesses. Also, it's been noted that customer publications are one component of direct mail—the fastest growing segment of the financial services marketing dollar.

Regardless of whether a financial institution decides to produce its customer publication entirely on its own, turns the project over completely to an outside vendor, or does some of both, the project should be undertaken with the intent of using the publication as a professional and potentially very profitable marketing technique.

Chapter Five

Robert A. Raucci

Robert A. Raucci is a Financial Marketing Consultant practicing in Chicago. In a career that includes client and ad-agency experience, he was a Vice President and Account Supervisor with agencies handling marketing communications for a major money-center bank and a $2.2 billion thrift in Illinois. As Director of Advertising with a multi-unit bank holding company, he handled the marketing of four banks. His experience as a Vice President of a major thrift and financial sales company round out his extensive financial service background.

His education includes Northwestern University, the University of Oklahoma and the University of Southern California.

MARKETING TO TODAY'S ONE-STOP FINANCIAL SERVICES CONSUMER

Robert A. Raucci
Independent Marketing Consultant and Financial Writer

THE ONE-STOP FINANCIAL SERVICE CENTER

The One-Stop Financial Service Center has been the dream and goal of financial institutions for many years. Banks and thrifts have longed to be all things to all people. And perhaps for a while they were. But that was when they shared what amounted to a monopoly on financial services, which were simply mortgages, checking accounts, savings accounts and loans—hardly "all things" by today's standards. "We had a monopoly and it was lovely; now there's a market and we're losing market share," opined Walter Wriston, retired Chairman of Citicorp.

Deregulation and advances in technology have changed all that. When we think about one-stop financial service centers today, a seemingly unlikely candidate for the title pops up: Sears! Sears, the nation's largest merchandiser of consumer goods, has now extended its marketing philosophy to include financial services—"To deliver the greatest number of financial services to the largest number of consumers in the most efficient manner possible."

Other retailers such as J. C. Penney, Montgomery Ward, and K-Mart are also expanding into the financial services. K-Mart has stated it intends to open financial centers in at least 1,000 stores. These retail giants, with consumers walking into their stores from coast to coast, will inevitably capture a substantial share of clients.

Nonbank competitors have joined with consumer conglomerates such as General Motors, Metropolitan Life, and Chrysler Corporation to create a revolution in the financial services industry. By expanding their product lines and taking advantage of their distribution capabilities, they hope to bring the widest possible array of financial services to their huge customer bases.

These new entrants into the field of financial services are staffed with people who have been raised and nurtured with a market-driven philosophy. Market forces are creating both the demand and opportunity for financial service providers to meet the challenges of today's consumer. Those who meet these challenges will ultimately succeed.

WHAT DRIVES THE MARKET?

In the bygone era of financial services, banks and thrifts were much like gas stations. With a station on every street corner and no discernable difference in a gallon of gas from one station to another, petroleum companies had two options to increase sales: reduce price or offer incentives, such as glassware and dishes.

Banks and thrifts, the only "full financial service" providers at the time, occupied a similar position. They offered higher rates and premiums to promote deposit generation. They opened branches in outlying areas, primarily to protect pockets of existing customers and, in some cases, to increase market share. Eventually, automatic teller machines were installed to add 24-hour service convenience and to reduce pressure on lobby facilities. And, generally, the banks and thrifts succeeded unimpeded by any signigicant competition and with casual regard for consumer needs.

But this was before deregulation and the swift advance of technology that has since wiped out traditional thinking about the marketplace, product development, pricing and service delivery.

Retailers began to enter the financial services arena, and with their market-driven organization and in-place distribution systems began to diligently cultivate financial relationships. With extensive research capabilities and a market-driven orientation, their impact on the marketplace became readily apparent. Traditional financial service marketers finally began to recognize the necessity of adopting a market-driven culture.

Unlike the package goods industry, in which the product is king and consumers can feel it and see it, in financial services the consumer is paramount and the successful provider is the one who meets all their financial needs. Satisfying these needs dictates a strategy that cultivates relationships—a combination of products and services in a relationship package that satisfies both present and future consumer needs.

Cultivating relationships involves the communication of concepts, rather than just the promotion of products and services. The "human" factor is the element that confers value in the consumer's mind. Relationships should have a permanence analogous to that of families; consumers must be made to feel comfortable. An environment that builds trust, credibility, and the acceptance of customers' needs leads to sustained relationships and long-term customer satisfaction.

TECHNOLOGY AND CHANGE

Advances in technology have been influential in the creation of new approaches to financial service marketing.

Institutions adopted automation, an early technological advance, as a means of supporting their back-room accounting systems and to reduce the voluminous warehouse of paperwork. The microfiche presented another opportunity to reduce the unwieldy growth of customer files.

Today's advances in technology have greatly exceeded those humble beginnings and have expanded into the marketing of financial services. Technology improves both the sales and delivery of financial services today.

To be an effective marketer of financial services, it is almost a given that an organization have a Central Information File (CIF). In the past ten years, the development of CIF computer programs has brought this technology within the grasp of most financial service institutions.

A CIF system, for marketing purposes, typically furnishes information as to what a customer base looks like. Marketers need this information to develop programs dealing with research, direct mail, telemarketing, and various forms of customer segmentation, as well as strategic planning and results analysis.

One of the most important questions a CIF can answer is, "Which of the households or customers I presently do business with is most likely to buy the product or service I want to sell?" The answer, of course, to this and other questions is essential to an efficient and effective cross-selling effort and the building of multiple account relationships.

While this form of information technology has been a vital force in the marketing of financial services, technology advances in the area of service delivery have been equally influential. Distribution plays an important role in differentiating financial service providers.

Electronic banking networks, automatic teller machines (ATMs), point-of-sale (POS), and home banking represent the three primary areas of evolution.

Successful marketers must ask themselves: How will this technology affect our ability to deliver business at a profit? Ten years ago, ATMs were an experimental technology; today they are a matter of survival for financial institutions that intend to retain their customer base.

Relatively speaking, POS and home banking are still in the early stages of development.

POS generally is described as the actual transfer of funds from a customer's bank account to a merchant's account. For example, a POS card (a debit card, not a credit card) may be used at the check-out counter of a supermarket to pay for groceries—dollars to make the purchase are instantly transferred from customer to merchant.

Home banking services are made available through special equipment displaying sophisticated graphics generated by videotext systems.

Bank of America presently boasts of some 16,000 subscribers and is a close competitor of Chemical Bank as the leader in home banking. Home banking is approached from a market-driven orientation. However, questions about what services consumers want and how much they are willing to pay will determine how widespread this technology will become, and how quickly.

The list of new players in the home banking market leaves no doubt that the potential for market share expansion is promising. Trintex, a new corporation formed by Sears, IBM and CBS, will provide computer and telecommunications systems (IBM), entertainment and information services (CBS), and electronic catalog shopping and financial services (Sears).

FINANCIAL SUPERMARKETS

Today's "financial supermarkets" are nationwide as well as regional and local. The trend of non-banks entering the financial service market continues, while mega-financials such as Citicorp, American Express and Merrill Lynch seek new ways to attract more and more customers.

Relationship marketing of financial services is evident in successful institutions, whether they target narrow or broad markets. Tailored investment portfolios with a number of savings and investment products, plus secured and unsecured credit lines, encourage consumers to establish long-term relationships. The institutions provide for their consumers' current needs, and assure them that their changing needs over time will be met.

IDS Financial Services

IDS, owned by financial giant American Express since 1983, has been offering financial products to consumers for over 90 years. Its salesforce of almost 6,000 includes people from all walks of life, some of whom have worked with customers whose children and grandchildren are now clients.

This form of multi-level marketing produced an average sale of $5,000 in 1985. Their financial planners boosted new product sales by 44 percent in September of 1986, bringing sales for the first three quarters of the year up 3.5 percent, to $1.7 billion.

With plans to make substantial inroads into consumer lending with under-secured credit lines, IDS moves closer to its ultimate goal of satisfying 90% of its customers' financial needs.

Merrill Lynch

Merrill Lynch introduced its Cash Management Account several years ago, targeting upscale, sophisticated investors. Offering a wide choice of investments, instant borrowing power, bank checks, an automatic sweep feature and comprehensive statements, Merrill Lynch has succeeded in attracting and holding a dominant market share in this category.

Similar "cash management" types of accounts are offered by many other prominent securities firms, including Smith Barney's "Vantage," Fidelity's "Asset Management," and Kemper's "Money-Plus." The establishment of long-term relationship is common to all accounts.

Sears, Roebuck And Company

Sears credit cards are held by almost 44 million households. The nation's largest source of retail credit has nearly $14 million in receivables, representing a formidable distribution network already in place.

The "Discover Card" was introduced by the Sears Financial Network in January of 1986. It offered up to 1 percent cash dividends on purchases, money market interest rates on savings, nationwide charge accounts, cash at ATMs and Sears stores and checking privileges. Additional services have been added since its introduction, but more importantly, cardmembers are exposed to the benefits of the Sears Financial Network, which includes:

- Dean Witter—Investments, stock brokerage and portfolio management.
- Coldwell Banker—Residential and commercial real estate services for buying, selling and investing.
- Allstate Insurance Company—Life, casualty, and property insurance products.

By tying all of these elements together with their retail operations and nationwide distribution network, and promoting through an aggressive television, newsprint and direct mail campaign, Sears has produced some impressive results. According to a 1986 survey by *American Banker*, Sears ranks first in the minds of consumers as the brightest star in the financial services industry, above such giants as American Express, Citicorp, Fidelity and Merrill Lynch. The survey further points out that the number of consumers who say they buy financial services from Sears has increased to 30 percent from 11 percent. (See Figure 1.)

Banks such as Citicorp (nationally) and First National Bank of Chicago also offer one-stop financial service menus.

Citicorp, serving 23 million households and operating 1,190 offices in 42 states, is the largest banking company in the country. Citicorp owns thrifts in major markets such as Chicago, San Francisco, and southern Florida. In addition to its proprietary network of ATMs, Citicorp is considering an alliance with Tokyo's Dai-Ichi Kyango Bank to extend electronic teller cash withdrawal to each other's customers. Dai-Ichi is the world's largest banking company.

Figure 1: Which Financial Giants Lead the Pack?

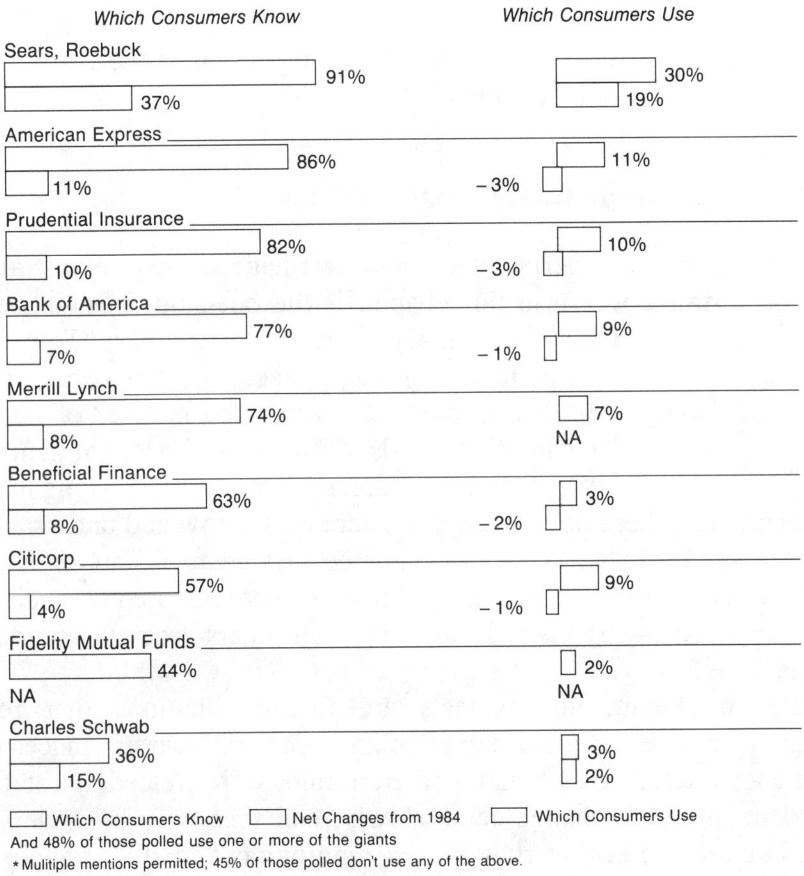

Source: *American Banker,* Sept. 23, 1986.

Like Citicorp and First National Bank of Chicago, banks and thrifts all over the country are beginning to offer a full complement of financial services to augment their goal of becoming a *home* to the nation's one-stop financial service consumers. This has been accomplished through subsidiaries and through special agreements with national brokerage firms and private firms such as Invest and Dreyfus.

The securities industry, too, has been swept up in the financial supermarket craze. A number of independents have sold to national full-line firms and large regionals, while some giants have sold out to insurance companies, diversified financial firms or retailers.

Interstate banking, "reciprocal" state banking laws and the emergence of credit unions have further intensified the competition in the battle for the financial service consumer's attention.

ESTABLISHING MARKET OBJECTIVES

Marketing objectives define the goals of financial service institutions. Since our prime concern in this chapter is the one-stop financial service consumer, we will define our primary objectives as follows: "To generate new customers and engage them in multiple account relationships, and to maintain existing customers through increasing the number of accounts they presently hold." Or in other words, customer and account generation through efficient and effective satisfaction of current and on-going needs.

To accomplish these objectives, marketers must know and understand the environment. Financial services cannot be viewed in isolation. The elements of the environment—Competition, technology trends, social and economic trends—influence the way the consumers "see" the product or service.

Clearly, marketing professionals are facing situations that require development of new strategies to effectively deal with circumstances never before encountered. Traditional marketing rules were created in a static environment in which change came slowly, and then only by government edict. Marketers must work with the environment to differentiate their companies' positions within the financial services industry generally. Understanding how the various forces in the environment interact, and being alert to changes in those forces, enables marketers to see their products and services as consumers see them.

Knowing the consumer and identifying the consumer's needs is absolutely vital to the positioning of financial services. As pointed out earlier, the most effective strategy stresses the building of relationships, rather than just the promotion of products; and the communication of concepts as opposed to the mere dispersal of information.

Pumping out more TV ads and print ads—mountains of direct mail dumped on consumer doorsteps—does not solve marketing problems. It leads to a monumental clutter. At a time when few people can remember yesterday's newspaper headlines, it becomes obvious that information today has become disposable.

Relationship marketing of financial services is the key to extending current customer activity, and to adding new customers. Its essential elements include:

- A core service around which the relationship can be built.
- Structured pricing that provides an incentive for consolidation or packaging of accounts.
- Establishment of a sales culture.

The core accounts being offered, such as checking accounts, money market accounts or brokerage accounts, depend on primarily two factors:

- The financial service provider (thrift, securities firm, bank, *et cetera*).
- Demographics/Consumers.

Pricing practices that create incentives for account packaging must also be considered. Pricing will be influenced by activity, balance parameters and volume discounts. Customers must understand the advantage of consolidating their financial relationship and the resulting impact on fees and rates.

Establishing a sales culture may be easy or difficult, again depending on the identity of the financial service provider.

As we have seen, in organizations committed to a market-driven philosophy, such as Sears, Merrill Lynch, American Express and other major retailing and financial giants, selling is a natural extension of that philosophy. However, in some financial institutions, most notably banks and thrifts who have historically relied on interest spreads to pay the bills, this has not been the case.

Successful financial service providers realize that knowledgeable, motivated and experienced people with selling skills are best suited to helping customers solve problems by guiding them through the wide array of services and products. And in the process, utilizing cross-selling to provide better service and consolidation of accounts, will lead to long and profitable relationships.

Cultivating relationships is not just a marketing objective; it is a matter of survival. The tools are there for marketers to use. Consumers can no longer be taken for granted. They must believe you have the best way to satisfy the needs that drew them to the market to begin with. Consumers must be made to feel special. Technology itself does not interest consumers, but its benefits to them does.

Not all consumers are willing to consolidate their financial needs with just one provider. But establishing account relationships built on trust, credibility and superior satisfaction of needs will separate the winners from the losers in financial services.

CUSTOMER SATISFACTION AND CROSS-SELLING

As competitive pressures and the demands of consumers challenge financial service providers, retaining current customers and adding new ones become critical to survival. A true understanding of today's consumer will enable institutions to meet that challenge, and cross-selling plays an important role in this respect.

Marketers must learn that it is easier and much less expensive to sell two or three additional services and/or products to existing customers than it is to sell one service to one or two more additional customers. Cross-selling from expanded product lines is one of the benefits of the relationship marketing approach to selling financial services. The customer who has been satisfied and has developed a sense of trust is most likely to utilize three or four or more financial services from the same institution.

This strategy means that financial service institutions must adopt a sales culture and make optimum use of employee skills and technology. Institutions cannot be simply order takers. Elaborate menus of financial services do not sell mutual funds, CDs, or cash management accounts. Marketers must recognize that customers not only have more funds to be tapped, but also more needs for different services that change over time. An aggressive, sales-oriented approach is the key to an efficient and effective response.

Studies show that the more accounts a customer has with a financial institution, the more stable the relationship. More product/service usage by a customer goes hand-in-hand with longer relationships, and this, in turn, makes it less likely that the customer will look to a competitor for financial advice.

Using cross-selling to provide more efficient service and to promote multiple account usage by customers is crucial to building long-term, profitable relationships.

The vital elements in establishing a proper sales orientation include:

- Commitment to a sales culture.
- Effective sales training.
- Efficient sales-support (e.g., CIF and advertising).
- Measurement of sales performance.
- Rewarding outstanding sales performance.

While a strong sales culture is essential to generating business, remember that good service, or "delivering the goods," is equally critical to keeping business.

COMMUNICATIONS PLANNING

Once marketing objectives have been established, the time is right to develop the marketing communications plan. Whether or not this is to be done internally or through an advertising agency is of little importance here. Market-driven approaches are based on understanding consumers and their needs, on developing "want-satisfying" products and services and on building relationship.

Advertising and promotion are only a part of the marketing strategy. They can communicate, they can reinforce positions, but they do not solve problems.

Providing the marketing communications planners with marketing objectives and with summaries of background data and research gives them all the information they need to develop creative media strategies and tactics designed to achieve those objectives.

Creative strategies provide a foundation for positioning in the marketplace. Choosing the positioning goal which best serves the organization's marketing and communication objectives establishes the basic creative strategy statement.

The communications plan will, of course, detail media tactics and budgets required to attain the objectives. Given sufficient time to digest all objectives and research, planners will be better able to prepare an effective, efficient plan covering all forms of communications and to evaluate which methods best suit both products and services.

It is impossible, within the limited scope of this chapter, to suggest to financial service marketers which marketing communications methods would best suit their particular needs. There are many factors peculiar to each provider that will influence such decisions.

Generally, when discussing the effective communications of financial services, one might say that 1) television is best suited for reaching mass markets, but lacks the ability to explain the complexities of financial services; 2) direct mail is better suited to targeting and explanation of complex investment offerings; and 3) newspapers can reach a broader market while still retaining the ability to clarify financial offerings. In any event, this is strictly conjectural, and the tools for reaching consumers are best chosen by the experts with a demonstrated ability to produce results.

TOMORROW'S CONSUMERS

Finally, a commitment to satisfying the present and ongoing needs of consumers requires marketers to analyze trends in demographics over the next five years, ten years, and through the end of the century.

These trends are part of our continuing effort to know and understand the environment. According to the U.S. Census Report, the next 13 years will bring:

- Lower birthrates.
- An aging population.
- High immigration.
- A rising percentage of racial minorities.

These trends will seriously influence the way financial service marketers look at the consumers of tomorrow. Lower birth rates attributed to later marriages, a higher divorce rate and greater female employment will mean an increase in the cost of child care.

The United States will have 110 million households by the year 2000, about 27 percent more than in 1986. Table 1 shows the number of households headed by people of various ages. Heads of households under age 30 will decline substantially, while there will be a surge in middle-age and very elderly households.

Table 1: Our Population Mix Grows Older

Head of Household	*1986*	*2000*	*Change*
Under 25	5.2*	4.9	-6%
25-29	10.0	8.0	-20
30-34	10.6	10.9	+3
35-44	18.6	26.8	+44
45-54	12.8	22.7	+77
55-64	12.9	13.9	+8
65-74	11.1	11.6	+5
75 & Over	7.7	11.3	+47

*In millions

Source: U. S. Census Bureau.

THE FERTILITY RATE IS LOW

The median age of the American population is being pushed up by a low fertility rate, which in 1972 dropped below the population replacement level (an average of two children per woman) and has stayed there since (see Figures 2). Most of America's meager population growth between now and 2000 (barely 12 percent in 13 years) will come from immigration.

Low birthrates mean a steadily aging population. By 1990 baby boomers will be between 35 and 50 years of age. This will probably create a decline in the need for "starter" homes, as there will be fewer young adults in the 1990s. Baby Boomers will increasingly seek the advice of financial planners. More and more, consumers will arrive at retirement age with lump-sum retirement monies and the desire for optimum income generation from their investments.

Financial service marketers must be alert and responsive to these trends in a continuing process of self-education. The ability to satisfy consumer needs today does not guarantee the ability to satisfy those needs tomorrow.

Figure 2: The Fertility Rate Is Low (Average Number of Children per Woman)

Source: U. S. Census Bureau.

Chapter Six

Ronald B. Millman

Currently a senior associate and account management executive with the Chicago-based Financial Relations Board, Mr. Millman has more than 25 years of experience in investor relations.

He formerly was head of his own consulting firm and held management positions with three national public relations agencies, including five years as general manager of Doremus/Chicago, specialists in marketing financial services.

Mr. Millman is an accredited member of the Public Relations Society of America and serves on the association's local Board of Directors.

Through the years he has written and lectured extensively on financial relations. He has won numerous professional awards.

MARKETING EQUITIES THROUGH AN EFFECTIVE INVESTOR RELATIONS PROGRAM

Ronald B. Millman
Senior Associate
The Financial Relations Board
Chicago, Illinois

Each year Corporate America spends upwards of $4 billion on investor relations. Companies employ a variety of strategies in attempts to convince the Wall Street professionals and the average investor on Main Street that their equity and debt offerings are much more rewarding investments than others in the marketplace. By doing so, they are not trying to manipulate their stock price, but rather to build a solid base of appreciation for their achievements, their management and their prospects for future growth.

Being primarily an information process, investor relations' budgets include a great deal of printed materials: these take up approximately one quarter of annual corporate IR expenditures. The costs of internal staff and the services of outside professional consultants to develop and disseminate the information are estimated at about half the total. Top management involvement is valued at about 10 percent; and the balance is devoted to out-of-pocket expenses.

Is it worth the time and money? Can a company really influence the decision to buy, sell or hold a particular security? Most assuredly the Blue Chip corporation will always have its loyalists. So will the company developing a singularly unique product with great earnings potential.

For the rest of us, however, gaining attention in a highly competitive marketplace requires a full-scale continuing sales effort, just as would be employed in selling any product or service. When you think about investor relations in these terms, the effort takes on the proportions of a standard Marketing 101 textbook case history. You have readily identifiable and well-established marketing channels, made up of a network of national and local brokerage firms. You know who your customers are: individual investors and institutional money managers. You even know who you are competing against for the investment dollar. The primary competition consists of the 5,000 or so other public companies. Also competing for the investment dollar are various alternatives including bonds and mutual funds to options, index futures, thoroughbred horses, Broadway plays, stamps, collectibles, limited partnerships and so on.

The first step in preparing to market your equities is to identify the messages that will influence potential investors. You then target the particular audiences for those messages. Knowing what you want to say and the audience to whom you want to address your messages, it follows that you can then select the programming vehicles that will best serve as a bridge between the two.

WHAT MAKES YOU AN ATTRACTIVE INVESTMENT?

Positioning your company for a marketing effort begins by determining the type of investment vehicle you represent. Are you a junior-Blue Chipper, an established veteran, a growth stock, an emerging industries company or a turnaround situation? Each group has its own followers within the investment community.

That established, you can assemble the facts that will convince investors of the long- and short-term growth potential you can offer them.

What will turn an investor on to your stock? Every company has something that makes it an appealing investment. Could it be your continuing earnings growth trend, new products or a history of rising dividends? Perhaps it is an ability to outperform the industry, regardless of economic circumstances.

In determining what sets you apart from all the others, you should not only look for the obvious, but also delve into some of the seemingly inconsequential aspects of your operation. For instance, your industry ranking certainly is important, but don't overlook a particularly unique marketing strategy, or long-standing customer relationships that have been built upon a highly successful service program. These less obvious points just may be the investment appeal that distinguishes you in the eyes of investors.

The anticipated growth within your industry and the markets you serve are also good indicators of the potential for your company as an above-average investment opportunity, especially when juxtaposed with your status within the industry. If possible, add some pizzazz to the presentation of your market position. Assuming you are the dominant supplier in your industry with a 20 percent share, look outward and talk in terms of the estimated 80 percent potential that lies ahead of you, rather than focusing on your present competitive position.

Financial performance provides still another means of demonstrating your investment qualities. Be sure to look beyond your balance sheet and income statement. Evaluate such ratios as sales per employee or per assets, inventory patterns and retention rate. Cashflow, the basic measurement of the money coming in and going out of the company, is becoming increasingly more important to security analysts.

Whenever possible, compare your financial statistics with the rest of your industry. Media General and other commercial databanks can supply you with these competitive rankings. In many cases your trade association may also maintain such performance records.

THE MANY FACES OF WALL STREET

The investment community is fragmented, consisting of a number of formidable forces. There are active players, influentials and intermediaries. All of these groups represent opportunities that must be addressed as part of your Investor Relations marketing efforts.

The Big Players: Professional Money Managers

At one time the stock market was dominated almost exclusively by individual investors. Then came the explosion of mutual funds, pension funds, insurance companies, investment trusts and others, consolidating the cash from many sources into a single, much larger investment force. Now these institutional investors overwhelmingly control the mood and direction of the market. They are aided in their pursuit of performance by teams of sharp-eyed security analysts whose job is to discover potential investments, and by sophisticated computer programs that will tell them when to buy and when to sell.

The popularity of funds grew out of a faster-paced, more complex investment environment. Individuals with a limited amount of money to invest became bewildered by the various alternatives. Still wishing to participate in the stock market, they turned to mutual funds. These institutions had the research capabilities. They were able to purchase stocks at advantageous prices. Of late they have also adopted such esoteric trading strategies as a stock purchase and corresponding futures or options hedge for protection, along with computer-driven signals of when to sell.

Mutual funds attract upwards of 200 billion in investor dollars annually. There are more funds than public companies listed on the New York Stock Exchange; others are being introduced each day. Specialties have developed among mutual funds. There are funds that will only invest in emerging companies, and others that look for contrarian situations. Many concentrate within a particular industry or industry sector. Such specialization enables you to directly target your investor relations activities at the funds that invest in your type of company.

The money managers and security analysts who make the buying and selling decisions for these institutions are part of a much larger group. With their counterparts at insurance companies, banks and pension funds, funds control portfolios with an estimated value in excess of $3 trillion.

You can readily identify those analysts who may be interested in your company. They are listed by their industry specialty in the directories of the Financial Analysts Federation, located in New York, with various local chapters across the country. Magazines such as *Institutional Investor* and the *Financial Analyst Journal* will also help you determine the top managers and analysts tracking stocks within a particular industry group. Other magazines and newspapers, including trade publications, frequently quote these people in articles about the industry.

Once identified, the institutional investor can be reached through many of the established tools of investor relations, including printed material such as your annual report and 10K, as well as some of the more detailed information pieces prepared specifically for this audience.

Face-to-face meetings with management are important to financial analysts. These sessions can be a simple one-on-one meeting in your office or a formal multi-media presentation, either before an investment analyst society group or at a private meeting that you or your investment banker organized.

Analysts do not only want to learn about your company and its plans for future growth; they also want to know about you as a manager. In one survey of institutional investment professionals, management's competence was second only to the corporation's price/earnings ratio among the factors used in selecting stocks for investment. Return on investment was third, followed by earnings growth record, market share, long-term record, price per share, balance sheet strength, industry group, U.S. economic conditions and the quality of company products.

Mr. And Mrs. Investor: Still A Force

While institutions dominate the market, individual investors remain an important factor, and they, too, must be addressed in your investor relations program.

According to the New York Stock Exchange, approximately 47 million Americans are invested directly in listed public corporations, or in mutual funds. The median portfolio is $6,200.

Shareholders are almost divided equally between men and women. Most are between 21 and 44 years old, college graduates in white collar professions with incomes between $25,000 and $49,000. Following the general population of the United States, New York has the largest number of individual investors, with Los Angeles and Chicago in second and third place respectively. Only about 15 percent live in non-metropolitan areas.

One out of every four shareholders made their first investment through an employee stock purchase plan. Only 14 percent said they use discount brokers and approximately 30 percent invest through mutual funds.

While most investors are followers of whatever trend is currently popular, there are also many individualists. Some of them employ research techniques that, though unconventional, are no less probing than those of professional security analysts. For instance, one New York school teacher actually spent several days on the construction site of an Atlantic City hotel/casino before deciding to invest in the operator's company. She wanted to see for herself that the facility was on schedule toward the promised opening date.

A California lawyer regularly scans the help-wanted ads for investment tips. If he sees a company hiring an inordinate number of engineers and production workers, it is a signal to him that something big may be in the offing. He then checks around to see if the company recently received a major new contract or is gearing up to introduce a new product. One time he went so far as to apply for a job, just to see what all the hiring was about.

In the case of companies with well-known consumer franchises, many investors base their buying decision on favorable experiences with the product or service. Even some professionals admit to being swayed in this manner.

Reaching those individuals who might be interested in your corporation as an investment is not as easy as getting to professional asset managers. There is no directory that can tell you who they are, where they live and their specific investment strategies. Some commercial mailing lists purport to have the names of active or aggressive traders, but they are not very accurate.

There are, however, several organizations for individuals who invest regularly. One is the National Association of Investment Clubs. Located in Royal Oaks, Michigan, it represents some 6,700 clubs, with 101,000 members. The estimated average portfolio of a member group is about $90,000. The NAIC has a number of local, regional and national events through which a corporation can promote its stocks and bonds.

The Chicago-based American Association of Individual Investors, with 100,000 members, reaches a more sophisticated market segment—people who wish to direct their own investing strategies.

Shareholders: A Pre-Sold Market

Communicating with your stockholders to convince them to buy more shares in your company—or hold on to the ones they already own—is much easier than reaching any of the other audiences within your investor relations plan.

The Securities and Exchange Commission mandates that companies provide their investors with financial reports and certain other information on a timely basis. The marketing-astute corporate executive recognizes that this audience deserves much greater attention. For just as it is easer to generate repeat business among existing customers, so are satisfied shareholders a primary target for additional stock purchases.

So beyond the annual and interim reports, many corporations also use regional meetings to communicate with their investors in other parts of the country. Others maintain special toll-free 800 numbers so that shareholders can secure up-to-the-minute investor information.

Knowing that their shareholders could represent a powerful consumer force as well, there are companies that offer their investors coupons or discounts on the products. Others will rally shareholder support behind political issues that could hamper the corporation's operations.

Direct communications to shareholders who have their stock held by brokers was once next to impossible without the broker serving as an intermediary—a slow and costly method. Since January 1986, however, companies have been able to mail annual reports, interim reports and other corporate information, or call requesting proxies, by obtaining a list of all street-name shareholders who do not object to receiving such material. Lists are available from the Independent Election Corporation of America, Lake Success, New York.

BROKERS: THE MIDDLEMEN

As the officer of a public company, your contact with brokerage firms probably centers on their investment bankers or merger specialists. But since it is so difficult to reach potential individual investors directly, the 40,000 or so registered brokers in the United States become an important audience in any investor marketing program. In effect, they are your retail salesmen.

Before marketing your company to the broker, you must work through the firm's research department. Brokerage firms establish all sorts of criteria for the stocks to be recommended by their brokers. For some it is a matter of per-share price or shares outstanding; for others, it is a long history of earnings.

Brokerage firm security analysts are no less diligent than the institutional analysts in their study of the factors on which to make an investment recommendation. In your investor relations marketing plan, therefore, you should treat these sell-side research analysts just as you would their buy-side associates. They can be identified through the same sources, reached through the same media and are supplied the same information.

While many firms will only permit their brokers to sell stocks that were approved by their research departments (they can always take orders to buy stocks selected by the customers), others give their brokers the latitude to make their own recommendations. In those instances where there is such an opportunity for independent initiative, brokers should become another audience in your Investor Relations program.

Brokers can be identified through a number of sources. Various commercial mailing list vendors offer regional breakdowns. Some can even provide you with the names of the top producing brokers in each firm and each office within that firm. There are also broker publications such as *Registered Representative.*

Brokers want the same information as analysts and other investment professionals. In addition, they need selling material, just as you would provide product catalogs to your salesmen. In this case, it should be something that effectively describes your company and its investment appeals in a few succinct paragraphs. Give them enough facts so that they can tell their clients about you during a brief telephone conversation. If there is interest, then more detailed information and the brokerage firm's research report can be sent to the prospective investor.

THE TOOLS OF INVESTOR RELATIONS

Information—Wall Street demands information. Not the sort that scandals are made of; but rather, the facts and figures that help investors make more intelligent investment decisions. The primary function of investor relations, therefore, is to employ various proven methods to communicate corporate data to the publics involved in the investing process.

The techniques that deliver those messages are as diverse as the audiences they are meant to reach.

Communicating Through Investment Community Contacts

With due respect to those in direct-mail advertising, nothing sells a product better than a personal contact. The axiom is just as true in investor relations as it is any other sales situation.

Analysts and brokers want to meet corporate management before making an investment decision. It's not that they are a gregarious group; rather, they believe they are able to gain a better insight into the company's corporate culture through a direct interface with the CEO.

Some company officers seem to rebel against the idea of meeting with these professionals. They cite the fear of having to give away too much competitive data or making projections that will come back to haunt them. Others say: "Why should we make their job any easier for them?" For the recalcitrant, perhaps the New York Stock Exchange's position on the relationship with company officials and security analysts will put the matter in proper prospective. This excerpt is from the NYSE Company Manual:

> Security analysts play an increasingly important role in the evaluation and interpretation of the financial affairs of listed companies. Annual reports, quarterly reports, and interim releases cannot by their nature provide all of the financial and statistical data that should be available to the investing public. The Exchange recommends that corporations observe an "open door" policy in their relations with security analysts, financial writers, shareholders, and others who have a legitimate investment interest in the company's affairs.

Other exchanges have similar regulations and the SEC has consistently encouraged corporations to maintain "continuing and meaningful" relationships with the financial community.

Personal Contacts

Ideally, a company wishing to establish itself within the investment community would send its CEO or CFO on the road as the company's primary salesman of its securities, calling an analysts and brokers in an effort to win their support.

However, these executives have a more immediate responsibility to the shareholders, and that is to effectively operate their company. Therefore, when corporations do make missionary sales calls on investment professionals, the role falls to surrogates. In the case of larger, more established organizations, it may be someone from the treasurer's office or a member of the internal investor relations staff. Smaller companies may employ outside agencies to undertake this effort on their behalf.

Whoever makes the calls, the purpose of these visits includes distributing the latest corporate financial material and answering questions concerning company operations. In the process, these "missionaries" should be able to identify those professionals who show sufficient interest in the company to receive a personal call or visit from the CEO, those who should be invited to meetings that will later be held in that city and those who should be added to the company's mailing list.

Meetings

Outside of personal visits, the next best approach for telling professionals about your company is through organized meetings. Some are sponsored by investment bankers, others by local investment analyst societies. Undoubtedly the most effective type of meeting is the one sponsored by the company itself. Because you are in control, you are able to invite only those individuals who, by past experience or predilection, would have an interest in your stock.

Regardless of who makes the arrangements, the format of a typical meeting begins with remarks from the CEO. Slides or a short film help set the stage for a discussion of the company's investment appeal and the marketing considerations that will produce future growth in sales and earnings.

Since professionals want to see management depth, other members of the corporation's executive team should participate. Vice presidents could discuss marketing, R&D and manufacturing; the CFO could review the financial statements.

The entire meeting should be planned to take between 30 and 45 minutes, with time left for questions immediately following the executive presentation.

Product demonstrations are acceptable, especially if it is a new or extremely exciting product.

Those in attendance should be given an information packet, including the company's latest annual report and interims, a financial fact book, publicity reprints and product literature. If a great many financial statistics are being used in the presentation, printed copies of the information should also be included in the kit. It saves your audience the necessity of taking notes during your presentation.

When planning a meeting in an unfamiliar city, you should determine local custom: in some, breakfast meetings are acceptable; in others, an early dinner. Normally, however, luncheons are the standard.

It is advisable to contact several of those who attended the meeting for their evaluation of the presentation and management's handling of the question-and-answer session. This information would be helpful in making changes that would improve the next meeting.

Meetings can be videotaped and copies offered to other professionals. Video is not new to the investment community (Merrill Lynch has had TV capabilities since the late 1960s). Today it is estimated that 88 percent of all brokerage firms have VCRs in some, if not all, of their branch operations.

Other Tools

There are a few other types of meetings that would be worthwhile in an Investor Relations program. Chief among them are the smaller, less formal get-togethers with no more than a handful of participants. Many executives plan these sessions as breakfasts or dinners when in a city on other business.

Also effective are the sales meetings that many regional brokerage firms regularly conduct for their registered reps. Held either before or after the market, they give you an opportunity to talk to some of the people who are actually selling your stock. You should take that opportunity to learn what their customers are saying about you.

A new method of communicating to investment professionals is the Telescan Corporate Forum, an on-line computer service operated from Houston. The participating company enters an opening statement into the system. More than 5,000 subscribing money managers, security analysts, stockbrokers and individual investors then use their personal computers to ask questions about the company. The entire interchange is available for others to view at a later time, and the company can update its presentation by putting its press releases into the system.

Among the meetings of marginal value are the so-called stock brokers clubs. In most instances companies must pay to make a presentation, and then attendance is encouraged through raffles and other enticements. No one comes to learn about the company, but rather to network or see if they won a prize.

Annual Meetings

Many companies give perfunctory attention to the annual meeting, but these events can be used quite effectively in reaching shareholders, members of the professional community and the media. Attendance should be encouraged through direct invitations from the chairman, president or CFO. Product demonstrations should be planned and refreshments served. Some companies videotape their annual meeting presentations and offer the tapes to brokers or analysts who could not attend. Others print and distribute complete meeting transcripts.

COMMUNICATING THROUGH PRINTED MATERIALS

Annual Reports

There is a big difference between the simple presentation of material information that the SEC requires in an annual report and what most corporations issue each year. Using slick four-color productions these reports not only present the financial results of the year just ended, they also give management an opportunity to articulate their aspirations for the future. Therefore, annual reports cover new marketing strategies, new products and other corporate developments. They include forecasts for the industries served and the company's competitive position within those industries. Many include features on executives on the rise and employees who have made significant contributions to the company's progress. Some boast original art; others have photos to compete with those of Ansel Adams.

Besides informing shareholders about their investments, annual reports are used in many other ways. They are distributed to financial analysts and brokers who regularly follow the company. They are used to introduce the company to new financial professionals. Many corporations also use them in their recruitment efforts. They are sent to customers and suppliers, bankers, employees and media.

While the annual report has a great many readers, it is read in one of two different ways. Most of us start with the cover and finish at the back. Financial professionals, however, usually start at the back. They look at the auditors' opinion to see if there was a qualification. They pore over the financial statements and footnotes, ending with the shareholder letter and any special statistical presentations, such as a 5- or 10-year table of financial highlights. If time permits, they will then read some of the other sections and flip through the pictures.

Besides the financial statements, footnotes and opinion, analysts usually look to see if the following points are adequately covered when they evaluate an annual report:

Financial Highlights. Is this presentation clear and unambiguous?

Shareholder Letter. Does this present the highlights of the past year in an objective way? Is it relevant to the company's results and candid in appraising problems? Is there a statement regarding short- and long-term corporate goals and how and when management expects to achieve them?

Officers and Directors. Does the annual report include the age, background and responsibilities of officers? Is there a description of company organization? Are the outside affiliations of directors noted? Have principal personnel changes been fully explained?

Management Discussion. Does it have a complete breakdown of sales, materials, costs, overhead and earnings? Are explanations of unusual developments included with management's response? Is there a report regarding taxes and tax status?

There has been a great deal of discussion regarding the value of the current format for annual reports. Whether it continues in its present printed form, or as some advocate, assumes an all new format (perhaps as videotape or computer floppy disk), this document will remain the most important financial presentation any corporation makes in the course of a year.

Quarterly Reports.

Annual reports are supplemented by interim statements, which have become more informative through the years. Some have evolved into shareholder magazines with several pages of feature articles, pictures and graphs showing industrial and corporate growth. Post-annual meeting reports are another effective tool, especially if there was an interesting question-and-answer session.

Financial Backgrounders

A booklet with commentary and financial and industry statistics has proven to be another valuable investor relations tool, particularly when dealing with professional analysts. These fact files provide much of the historical background information and industry forecasts necessary for analysts to formulate their research opinions. Briefer, less detailed versions are better suited for brokers in their retail sales efforts on your behalf.

Reprints

Copies of favorable articles from the business and trade press make excellent mailers to the financial community and shareholders. Copies of brokerage firm research reports should also be considered for shareholder mailings, as a way to reinforce their decision to invest in your company.

Other Mailers

Many corporations maximize the cost of their dividend mailings by including a pamphlet on products, an ad reprint or some other type of sales literature.

Others have added a short attitudinal survey regarding the reasons why shareholders chose to invest in the company, an evaluation of the company's shareholder communications program, or opinions on certain issues that might affect the company.

Welcome letters to new shareholders, special mailings to both investors and investment professionals on important corporate developments occurring between quarterly reports, copies of executive speeches, even applicable issues of employee publications are still more examples of printed materials distributed within a well-rounded investor relations program.

Mailing Lists

All of these materials would be useless without a means of assuring that they get into the hands of the right people. It is critical that your financial mailing list be kept current. In addition to those who write in requesting your financial information, those who are known to follow your industry should be included, along with those who follow your competitors and those who follow stocks in your current situation, be they emerging, growth or turnabout.

As both printing and mailing costs rise, many companies have begun to question the benefit of including certain parties on their financial mailing list to receive expensive corporate information. Some have removed libraries or businesses for which they have no individual's name.

Mailing lists should normally be purged at least once a year by using a reply postcard that must be returned by a specified date if the individual wishes to continue receiving your material.

COMMUNICATING THROUGH MEDIA

The reach of information presented at a meeting of investment analysts is limited to the primary audience. So is the mailing of a financial fact book. For these reasons, publicity and advertising, with their ability to spread your message to a far wider audience, play a crucial role in most all-encompassing investor relations programs. How else can you disseminate important financial news or messages regarding important corporate strategy?

Financial Publicity

The first element in any media relations effort involves the prompt and full disclosure of the information that will influence an investment decision. In this category are announcements of quarterly results, acquisitions and mergers, changes in dividends and dividend policy, important executive appointments, new product developments, strikes or union settlements, major new contracts and pending litigation.

Feature Articles

The second ingredient in financial media relations involves cooperating with editors and writers in the development of profiles on the company, its executives, corporate activities or products. Each major business publication devotes considerable space to such articles.

Financial Advertising

Your corporate messages can also be delivered through paid space in publications and on radio and TV. Many companies—particularly conglomerates' industrial concerns—employ "image" advertising to describe the diversity of their operations. Others report their earnings and dividends through notices in the principal financial newspapers. Many more offer their annual reports through special advertising sections prepared each spring.

Media Outlets for Your Corporate Messages

There is an array of business and financial publications for both publicity and advertising. Included are:

National Daily Financial Newspapers. *The Wall Street Journal* is the largest and best known. With bureaus strategically located in money centers around the world, the *Journal* reports on corporate and investment news. Other daily financial publications include *Investor's Daily* and the *Journal of Commerce*. The national edition of *The New York Times* and *USA Today,* the nation's largest circulation newspaper, also have sizable sections devoted exclusively to business and financial news.

Daily Newspapers. Every metropolitan newspaper has a financial section. Some are quite extensive; others are no more than a few pages. Besides local and national business news, they include tables of stock prices from the New York, American and OTC markets.

Financial News Services. Besides publishing *The Wall Street Journal,* Dow Jones also operates a news service that transmits an endless flow of corporate, business and economic information into brokerage firm offices and other media outlets through the "Broad Tape" (as opposed to the narrower Dow Jones tape that carries stock prices). Its principal competitor in this effort is the Reuters Economic News Service, operating 24 hours a day with worldwide coverage. Both Associated Press and United Press International also provide financial news. Their stories are sent to all major newspapers in the country, plus radio and TV outlets.

Periodicals. *Barron's, Fortune, Dun's, BusinessWeek,* and *Forbes* are among the leading publications covering the business and investment scene. There are also more specialized magazines, such as *Financial World, OTC Review,* and the *Wall Street Transcript,* which prints the full text of corporate presentations to the financial community. The National Association of Investment Clubs publishes *Better Investing* and the American Association of Individual Investors has its own monthly journal for members.

General magazines, such as *Time, Newsweek,* and *U.S. News and World Report* also have sections dealing with business news and economics.

Investment Newsletters. Many newsletters earn their reputations by spotting economic trends and heretofore undiscovered companies. Each one has its own criteria. Some will only evaluate companies selling above certain price levels. Others want a certain market capitalization. Industries are important to the editors of some, and earnings history is the primary consideration for others.

Electronic Media. The amount of business news being carried on radio and TV by the regular networks and local news programs alike is increasing. Public Broadcasting Service produces "The Nightly Business Report" and "Wall Street Week." On cable TV and UHF, there are numerous stations that broadcast financial news, interviews and stock prices all day long. Many of the local all-news radio stations broadcast financial reports several times each hour.

Trade Publications. After reading *The Wall Street Journal*, the astute investment analyst reads the leading magazine within the basic industries he or she follows. These trade publications help spot trends in products and marketing, personnel changes and other such information that may not be covered by the major business publications.

SEEKING OUTSIDE HELP

Depending on the degree and sophistication of activities to be undertaken, managing an investor relations program could be a full-time assignment.

In most major corporations, it calls for an officer-level executive, backed by a staff of perhaps two or three professional specialists.

Smaller companies do not have the luxury of such an organization. The responsibility, therefore, falls to the CEO and CFO: together, they usually write the shareholder communications, issue the press releases and maintain contact with Wall Street.

Rather than doing it themselves or using a large internal staff, many companies secure their investor relations assistance from outside agencies who make the street contacts, initiate the media coverage and prepare the shareholder materials. There are a handful of national firms specializing in this area, and most others usually have one or two professionals on staff with investor relations skills.

When attempting to select a firm to assist you in the implementation of your program, some of your basic considerations should be:

- The agency's long-standing relationships with other companies of your size, along with a documented history of helping clients win market support.
- Size of staff devoted to corporate investor relations.
- Ratio of staff to clients.
- Experience in all of the areas of service you will need to achieve your program goals.

As with the services of lawyers, accountants and management consultants, an investor relations agency is likely to charge for its services on the basis of specified hourly rates for the people assigned to your account.

EVALUATING THE PROGRESS OF YOUR INVESTOR RELATIONS

Marketing Program

Just as you would measure the ability of your Marketing Department to meet predetermined objectives, so should your investor relations program be held accountable for its performance. Among the standards that might be used in that evaluation are the number of new market makers inventorying your stock, the number of new brokers and institutions who are supporting you, the number of research reports written and the number of magazine articles appearing about your company.

Another method of measuring the effectiveness of the program would be to compare the increase in stock price and price/earnings multiple from the outset of the campaign to the time of the evaluation. Study the gain in market value. Ask yourself what you would have received if there was a one-million share offering at the beginning of the program? Next, compute what that total would be if the same amount of stock was to be sold today. The difference in proceeds would be the most meaningful gauge of just how successful your investor relations program has been in marketing your company's equity.

Chapter Seven

Patrice L. Peltier

Patrice L. Peltier is Vice President and Director of Marketing for Xerox Financial Services Life, a recent addition to the Xerox financial services organization. Peltier joined the company in June, 1985, as part of the start-up team and has been learning (the hard way) about establishing new distribution systems ever since. Prior to joining Xerox Financial Services Life, Peltier was Director of Insurance Sales Promotion for Kemper Financial Services. A Phi Beta Kappa graduate of Indiana University, Peltier's industry experience began in 1977 when she went to work in public relations and advertising for Prudential.

MARKETING THROUGH A DISTRIBUTION NETWORK

Patrice Peltier
Vice President and Director of Marketing
Xerox Life

There's nothing terribly mysterious about establishing a new distribution network. Asking the right questions—and knowing where to look for the answers—is what this process is all about. The questions are the same whether your company is selling mutual funds through insurance agents, insurance through stockbrokers, annuities through banks, unit investment trusts through financial planners, or any of the other combinations of financial products and distributors.

ASSESSING THE INDUSTRY'S EXPERIENCE

You should begin by asking some questions about the industry experience of your chosen product within your chosen channel of distribution. For example, if yours is a mutual fund company that wants to sell its funds through financial planners, then you need to acquaint yourself with the experiences of companies already selling their funds through financial planners. What amount of total mutual fund sales in the previous year or years has been sold by financial planners? What is the sales trend—up or down? Who are the other manufacturers selling their funds through planners? Which financial planning groups are they distributing for? How are they reaching their distributors? How effective are their methods? How competitively are their products priced? Is there a niche—an unfilled need—available in the marketplace?

Now that you know some of the questions, where can you get the answers? A good starting place is industry groups like the American Council of Life Insurance, the Life Insurance Marketing and Research Association, the Investment Company Institute, American Bankers Association, Bank Administration Institute, and the U.S. League of Savings Associations.

Often, there are also more informal groups of companies who have agreed to exchange information. The Network, for instance, is a group of insurance companies that shares information on request. Industry journals also often publish lists of the top companies in a particular marketplace, ranking them by sales volume. If you have chosen experienced professionals for your marketing staff, they may well have a network of contacts within competitive organizations. Or they may have come from a competitors' organization, which would certainly make the job of finding out what other companies have experienced much easier. And, if you have contacts within your chosen channel of distribution, they will often be able to tell you who else is manufacturing the product, which distributors are selling the product for them, and how much volume that particular distributor is doing with your competitors, if not how much volume your competitors are doing overall.

You also will want to know as much as possible about your competitors' products and their marketing approach. You can get this information by using your contacts within your competitors' organizations and your contacts within your chosen channel of distribution. You can also often very easily obtain information by simply walking into a distributors' office and picking up sales material or responding to one of your competitors' ads, either in trade or consumer publications.

DETERMINING THE NEEDS OF YOUR DISTRIBUTION CHANNEL

The next area for intelligence gathering is your distribution channel. Identify the salespeople within a distributing organization who will be responsible for your product. Talk with them and ask the following questions:

- How much of your product is the organization selling?
- Whose products are they selling?
- Why are they selling your product? The others?

• How complex is the sales process for your product?
• What is the level of expertise within the organization's salesforce, with respect to your product?
• Will the organization and its salesforce need much training, sales support and/or administrative support to sell your product?

Sales and Marketing

Let's look at the makeup of the salesforce and marketing organizations.

• What are the their backgrounds: college educated, highly technical, sophisticated, beginners or people who have worked in other careers?
• Do they tend to stay in this industry for many years, or move on to other pursuits?
• What motivates them? What are their concerns? Their needs?
• How do they see their role *vis-á-vis* the consumer?
• What kinds of products do they sell now and why?
• What is their sales process like? Do they sell over the phone or in person?
• Do they rely on high volume or large average ticket size. Do they know their clients well?
• How much control do they have over what their clients buy?

Marketing Materials

The way you position your product and the kinds of marketing materials you prepare for your distributor must be tailored from one distribution channel to another.

You will find that stockbrokers are very different from insurance agents who are different from bankers...and financial planners vary greatly one to another. Insurance agents will read ratebooks and product guides; stockbrokers won't. Insurance agents will fill out forms; stockbrokers won't. Stockbrokers talk about basis points and market risk. Insurance agents talk about love, responsibility and whether providing for your family isn't more important than buying a new refrigerator.

The product may be exactly the same, but your materials must reflect your understanding of exactly how your distributors will sell it and why.

Perhaps this sounds obvious. Perhaps it sounds easy. Yet the surprising truth is that few manufacturers have grasped the distinctions between the various channels of distribution—and fewer still have acted on this information.

Compensation

Also of importance (for both the organization and it salesforce) is the compensation received for selling your product:

- What level of compensation is required to be competitive with other issuers of your products?
- How does this compensation compare with the compensation paid by other kinds of products the salesforce can sell?
- What else is going on in the industry, the market, the economy and the government that might have a positive or negative impact on your product?

Regulatory Concerns

You also would want to explore any potential regulatory considerations:

- If you work with a bank, can it sell your product directly or must it have a subsidiary agency which will make the sale and receive the commissions?
- If so, does this subsidiary already exist?
- If not, is the distributor willing to establish a subsidiary?
- What is the time and expense involved?
- Are there licensing considerations?
- Will the stockbrokers need to be licensed as insurance agents?
- Will the insurance agents need a securities license?
- How difficult and expensive is this process?
- What support would the manufacturer be expected to provide?
- What percent of the organization's existing salesforce is already appropriately licensed?

UNCOVERING THE NEEDS OF THE CONSUMER

It's also important to know as much as possible about how consumers perceive your product, and seek distribution networks that have experience addressing these concerns. Look at your potential customers and ask these questions:

- Why will they buy it?
- Do they buy other products that meet those same needs?
- How do they choose?
- Does your product meet additional secondary needs?
- Where do they buy your product? From which channel of distribution and why?
- What features of the product are most appealing to consumers?
- Are there needs consumers have that aren't currently being met by products like yours?
- Are there changes forthcoming in the marketplace (for instance, resulting from the economy or government regulations) which will increase or decrease the need for your product?

To some degree, you can get this information, in a rather unscientific way, by asking these questions of people in the salesforce in your potential channel of distribution. This will give you a gauge of how well they understand your product, as well as some insights in how your product should be sold.

You also can do your own personal survey of people within the market segment you have targeted. Traditionally, issuers of financial products have used these informal approaches and called the results "market research."

In the last few years, industry organizations have been commissioning more sophisticated market surveys. If your company does formal marketing studies, include questions to consumers about where they purchase and use that information in establishing your network.

STRATEGIES FOR DISTRIBUTING YOUR PRODUCT

Existing Systems

Depending upon the extent of your available resources and how the time available to you to get your product to market, you may decide to use an existing distribution system. In almost every area, you will find that brokers (or middlemen by another name) are already distributing products to your chosen channel. These middlemen may be distributing your competitors' products or they may be representing unrelated types of products. Either way, they already have the retailing staff in place and the contacts made with the people you want to reach.

If you have limited time and/or money, this may be an excellent option, although you will give up a certain amount of control over the individuals who represent you and just how they do that. You may even decide that this is an excellent interim approach until you can find—and afford—a retailing staff of your own.

Developing Your Own External Network

If your money and staff are limited, you'll want to be choosy about the distributors with whom you work. Some methods of reaching distributors may elicit a big response and leave you with an impressive number of distributors, most of whom aren't going to do much business for you. If you do not have the luxury of a large wholesaling staff that can afford to spend time following up a million leads to nowhere, you'll be wasting your time.

Unless you are taking the luxury route, you will want to determine how much money is available to hire wholesaling staff and put them on the road. How quickly you want to build your distribution system should depend, in part, upon how quickly you can expand your operating functions to accommodate sales activity.

For example, assume you have found that stock brokerage firms need extensive training and joint sales support to sell your product. If you are staffed to provide this for 4 firms, don't sign up 12. As a newcomer in an expanding, competitive marketplace, you cannot afford to make mistakes. Expect to go overboard initially in providing what you promised—it's an investment in future success. For better or for worse, word of mouth travels fast within a distribution channel. If you look like a winner, that message will likely reach the next firm on your list before you do.

The Process of Prospecting

Once you determine how much you can spend on reaching your distribution channel and how quickly you can reach and service them, you can begin prospecting. If you are planning to be selective, you probably can put together your own call list. You may already know which distributors would be able to give you the kind of volume that would make it worth your while. If you do not you can use your network again to help you. You also can examine directories and industry reference books, such as *Best's Insurance Reports*, *The Discount Brokerage Directory*, *Standard & Poor's Security Dealers of North America*, or the *U.S. League of Savings Associations Directory* to jog your memory and gather more data.

There is a variety of methods to reach your prospects: First, provided your list is small enough, the most effective way to contact your prospects is with a personal letter. Your letter will introduce you and your firm and indicate that you'll call soon for an appointment. Obviously, the next step is to get an appointment.

Second, if you would rather take a "broad-brush" approach, you may choose to prospect through advertising or direct mail or a combination of both. If you do not know where to advertise, your advertising or public relations agency can help you identify the publications which have the audience you want to reach.

Next, if you are a do-it-yourselfer, you should use the *Red Book,* which is available in most public libraries. As for direct mail lists, they can be bought from trade associations or publications or independently compiled lists. Again, if you do not know where or how to buy a list, your advertising or direct mail agency can help you.

Finally, you also can attend industry and association meetings. But because everyone from the individual sales rep and his office manager to the head of an organization may be attending, you could talk to a lot of people without ever meeting those you really need to know.

THE IMPORTANCE OF PERSONAL CONTACT

The "broad-brush" approach will yield a lot of contacts, but it is only the first step. It's very rare that sales agreements are signed without any personal contact. If you are fortunate enough to be offering a product that's easy to understand, easy to sell and in great demand, your advertisements and direct mail programs may well be enough to get people to contact you. In most cases, though, there are so many issuers vying for a distributor's attention that it takes a personal visit to focus the distributor's attention on you.

In fact, in these times of concern over the financial stability of certain institutions, you should be prepared for a lot of personal contact before the sales agreement is reached. Don't be surprised if a distributor wants to see annual reports and financial statements, and wants to meet with members of your senior management. A potential distributor may even want an independent auditor or actuary or some other outside consultant to study your organization.

Once you've made it past the distributor, be prepared to lavish personal attention on the distributor's salesforce, too. Salespeople are bombarded with direct mail programs and product kits; even the more studious among them seldom read this mountain of material. In most cases, it will take a living, breathing wholesaler sitting in the office to get the salesperson interested in selling your product.

Building a Team

At some point in this process you will need to assemble a team of people to develop your product, market it, sell it and then administer it. Many financial organizations are tempted to assign these duties to people already performing similar functions within your organization. They also often hire some entry-level people or let some promising neophytes within their organization try their hand at new responsibilities.

What they really need are people who have had substantial experience marketing what you want sold. Look for the people who have a good track record with your chosen distribution channel. And then look more closely for those who are creative, dynamic and willing to be aggressive. Your team must be capable of reacting to opportunities in the marketplace faster and more competitively than the bigger, more established players—that is always their weakness, and your advantage.

If you cannot find (or afford) all the people you require at this level, you may get the expertise you need by using outside consultants. You may even consider entering into joint ventures with organizations that can provide the services you need. As the financial services marketplace becomes increasingly dynamic and competitive, more and more organizations are turning to arrangements such as these as faster, more cost-effective alternatives to building a staff and developing all these functions internally.

However, as you go about establishing your team, be certain to choose individuals or partners who are already experienced in your distribution channel or who have the ability to cross over. An underwriter who is experienced in issuing group insurance is unlikely to have the mental set required to underwrite interest-sensitive policies distributed through stockbrokers. A job candidate's experience with your product will not necessarily mean the person is a good fit with your chosen distribution channel.

The Sales Staff

If you decide to establish your own distribution staff instead of using an existing network, you once again may be tempted to opt for the cheaper route and hire beginners. This may work well if there is a great demand for your product and the sales process is not complex. Otherwise, resist!

If, instead, you hire sellers who are already successful in your channel of distribution, they will be much more cost-effective in the long run. They know the market and can really produce. They will have established rapport and credibility with people in your prime market. They'll get you in to the big hitters faster and easier than a neophyte can. What's more, as a "newcomer" to the system, your firm needs to establish itself quickly as a professional, knowledgeable company that provides a quality product and backs it up with quality service. You won't make that first impression if your salesforce is obviously new to the business.

Internal Wholesalers

You also may have an opportunity to use "internal wholesalers" in addition to or in place of your own wholesaling staff. An internal wholesaler is an individual on the distributor's staff who is responsible for promoting sales of a product or group of products among the distributors' salesforce. In some cases, you may be able to strike a deal with a distributor that will lower your wholesaling costs, or at least ensure a warm reception in your distributor's camp. For example, some manufacturers pay all or part of the salary of an individual who is selected by the distributor and works for the distributor but whose primary responsibility is to encourage the distributor's salespeople to sell the manufacturer's product.

In other cases, you may help the distributor find an individual to fill this job even if you don't help pay the salary. Unless you are willing to pay part or all of the salary, you may find the distributor has a tendency to hire less experienced, and therefore less expensive, individuals for this position. Naturally, it's to the manufacturer's advantage to have an experienced individual in the job. In fact, some manufacturers estimate that an experienced person will start producing business 12-18 months faster than an inexperienced one.

Management Support

Top-down management support is always important, but when you are establishing a new distribution system, it's critical. First, you need top-down support from your own management, and this support must be visible to your prospective distributors. The best situation, probably, is to have senior management that has a firm understanding of the job ahead and some pretty realistic expectations for how and when it will be accomplished. However, senior management must be prepared to stand by the internal marketing staff through the herky-jerky sales results that are typical during this start-up process and provide the time and resources to get the job done.

Equally important is the need for support from your distributors' top management. That does not mean that senior management must be your *entre* into a new distributor. However, in addition to getting approval to sign the agreement, you will need a commitment from senior management to actively promote your product. And once you've got that, you also need the support of the person within the distribution organization who is ultimately responsible for sales of your kind of product. Making certain you have commitments is an important part of the selection process.

Evaluating Your Success

How and when will you know whether your network is working? To a great extent, how quickly you can expect results depends upon the complexity of your product and the familiarity of your distributors with this kind of product, as well as a host of external factors such as market conditions, the overall economy and the political scene.

In a very general way, you should know early on whether what you are doing is likely to succeed. For instance, once you start calling on prospective distributors, you will know by how they respond to your product, your presentation and your marketing materials whether you're headed in the right direction.

Even if everyone responds favorably, however, you may not be bombarded with business right away. It takes time for sales agreements to be made, for salespeople to feel comfortable with you and your product, for old selling habits to change and new loyalties to be created. Be patient.

As a rule of thumb, you can expect to spend the first three to four months just calling on prospective distributors. Then you will probably spend another three to four months calling on them repeatedly, until people feel comfortable enough with you, your company and your product to begin selling it. Each time you hire a new wholesaler or open a new territory, you should expect to wait at least six months before you see a bottom-line impact. Once you have made an impact, do not try to move on too quickly. You must continue to work within a distribution system building your base and protecting yourself from all the other manufacturers who want to get into that system, as well.

You will no doubt also want more specific measures of your success. You may find it helpful to determine what your competitors' experiences have been. How much business did they do during the first six months or first year? How much of your type of product was sold in the industry in the last six months? In the last year? And, without fail, keep looking at your bottom line. How do your costs compare with projected earnings? You may have a loss the first year, but will that business be profitable next year?

CONCLUSION

Establishing a distribution network is really a process of asking the right questions. Since your product's market position depends so heavily on how it is distributed—and by whom—taking the time to get and evaluate the answers is imperative to successful sales.

Chapter Eight

Joe Marconi

Joe Marconi is an advertising, marketing and public relations professional whose writing has been published internationally in newspapers and magazines. He has edited textbooks and interviewed public figures from sculptors to rock stars. He has written of families in crisis and of stock options trading.

While heading the communications department of a national securities exchange, he also served as executive producer of an award-winning public information film.

More awards followed for his work in public relations and for ad campaigns with which he's been associated.

He is Executive Vice President of Weber Cohn & Riley in Chicago, where he is head of client services and business development.

MARKETING TO RE-ESTABLISH CONSUMER TRUST (*or* OPEN FOR BUSINESS—BEFORE AND AFTER THE FALL)

Joseph Marconi
Marketing Consultant and Executive Vice President
Weber Cohn & Riley

For generations some institutions were, quite simply, held sacred. The bank, for instance, was small-town America's bedrock. The savings and loan, that place that loaned you the money to buy your home, start your business and send your kids to college, was that most solid of entities around which entire cities blossomed. The doctor would pass away one day and the blacksmith would give way to the garage mechanic, but the banks and savings and loans would live forever. They had to—they had all the money. Right?

Wrong

The number of failures of banks and thrifts in the 1980s is staggering and the problem is forecast to worsen.

Bad loans, bad investments and in some cases outright theft or old fashioned embezzlement has rocked the financial community to such an extent that the old jokes about grandpa's money being safer stuffed in a mattress than deposited with a bank aren't quite so funny anymore.

Consider, too, the condition of some of the most revered houses on Wall Street. One of the most elite members of the exclusive circle of investment banking houses was rocked by losses and driven to the brink of financial ruin. The reason for its plummeting from grace was said to be a battle for control by its two egotistical top officers. Tens of millions of dollars in losses and the market goes unblamed. No charges of recession, depression or politics. Instead, the public is told it is the arrogance, selfishness and petty jealousies of the managers who drove the firm from shining star to shambles.

Another case is the national brokerage firm that spent millions of advertising dollars annually to inspire confidence and reinforce its image of a well-established first-line firm. Little wonder then that in 1986 Wall Street and the public alike were shocked and stunned when the United States Government charged this firm with, of all things, kiting checks. It was as if an environmental group had been charged with dumping toxic waste.

A firm like the investment banking house doesn't allow the arrogance of its management to bring down the walls of a great and historic financial empire. A prestigious retail and institutional brokerage giant wouldn't commit something so blatant an act as multi-million dollar check kiting. Yet both happened, inspiring many an investor—indeed, many an investment profession—to wonder if indeed nothing was sacred anymore.

Surely there are many solid financial institutions we can count on to be there with the flag waving and the books balanced by nightfall.

But one of them was not a major midwestern bank where a run of bad loans and a loss of corporate depositors drew the federal government in to bail out and save the once mighty giant.

These examples would make fascinating folklore if they were limited to a handful of tales. Alas, the accounts of scandals and foul-ups facing the financial industry abound. The business pages of the daily newspapers, while once considered by the average reader "the boring part of the paper," with stock tables, closing averages and an investment tip or two, now are rich with columns and articles on takeovers, raids, swindles and high crimes to rival the police blotter.

Corporate moguls Ted Turner, Ross Perot, Rupert Murdock and Carl Ichan have become true celebrities, and subjects of controversy, respected and feared.

What's happening to American business? How can the staid old pinstripe conservatives fall to new low levels of public trust? More importantly, how does the firm, corporation or institution regain the public's respect for its products and its name?

There are a number of ways to re-establish consumer confidence, but they first require an analysis of how a company loses it. This is not a problem that lends itself to easy solutions. Let's establish a framework and see where our problems begin and how to determine our best responses to them.

THE MEDIA'S EYE ON BUSINESS

We live in a time of extreme media domination. Where once television was considered exclusively an entertainment medium, it is now a primary force of information and a pivotal influence. Networks spend millions not only to produce, but to promote their newscasts. Documentaries and magazine shows abound.

While the program "Wall Street Week" may still be considered esoteric or elitist, CBS's "60 Minutes" or ABC's "20/20" can take an obscure entrepreneur or corporate CEO and make him or her a "household word" overnight.

Sometimes a company or firm doesn't even need its own scandal or crisis to have the public's confidence in it shaken.

Guilt by association is still a valid concept. By the end of 1986, the name Ivan Boesky was on page one of every big city paper and on virtually every page of most of the financial magazines.

Mr. Boesky may take credit for helping the masses learn the definition of the term "inside information." His celebrity made the entire securities industry part of a running joke for months. Brokers and traders far removed from Mr. Boesky's dealings were at least temporarily faced with having to re-establish the ethics of their profession. Arbitrageurs were considered by many to be, simply, hopelessly corrupt.

It is unreasonable and unfair, of course, to make television once again the scapegoat by claiming that it continually sensationalizes and blows subjects out of proportion. Television is only one component of a highly influential media.

Only a few years ago, analysts were sounding the death knell for the printed word. Newspapers were folding and magazines that had been major cultural forces, such as the *Saturday Evening Post*, *Harpers* and *Look*, were vanishing from our newsstands and our lives.

But as trends come and go, not only has print journalism, for no apparent reason, enjoyed a resuscitation of sorts, it too has become a major force in shaping opinions and lifestyles. Such periodicals as *People, Cosmopolitan* and *Gentlemen's Quarterly* tell us how to dress, pose and stay in fashion.

Whereas once the *Wall Street Journal* dominated and shaped our opinions of business and business leaders, almost suddenly *Forbes, Fortune, Business Week, Barron's, Dun's* and a score of "vertical trade" publications were becoming for many people every bit as much mainstream reading as *Time* and *Newsweek.* Even *TV Guide*, once considered a fluffy digest of little more than channel listings, has claimed to be the largest circulation weekly magazine in America and carrys articles and editorials on politics, technology, and business ethics.

People were not only reading these magazines—they were believing them.

Today's business leaders, citing their responsibility to stockholders, feel obliged not only to comment but to mount a major campaign of response and retaliation. Media specialists, research teams, advertising and public relations consultants are mobilized, and if the rumor mill, TV or the press hasn't sufficiently blown the issue out of all proportion, the professional communicators may well do so.

It is, after all, professional communicators we can credit for such contributions to our language as "buzzwords," "credibility gap," "crisis of confidence" and an endless stream of named scandals that end with "gate" in tribute, of course, to the Nixon's Watergate.

RESPONDING TO NEGATIVE PUBLICITY

Having provided this general overview of the high level of vulnerability that exists in the marketplace today—where businesses can no longer succeed or fail strictly on the apparently antiquated standards of quality of products, service, convenience, cost or location—let's examine some companies' attempts to re-establish consumer trust.

These corporations, at a retail consumer level (nonfinancial services), had to deal with concerns which reached panic proportions.

Tylenol pain reliever capsules and Contac cold capsules had been reported to be laced with poison. Deaths had been reportedly attributed to the capsules.

Many owners of Ford Pinto compact cars were charging that an improperly placed gas tank would cause the car to explode into flames when struck from the rear by another vehicle.

Jewel Food Stores, one of the largest grocery chains in the midwest, was reported to be selling milk that was contaminated. Numerous illnesses and some deaths were attributed to the product.

What is noteworthy in these instances is that each case had the potential to put the company out of business. Certainly, the challenge of re-establishing consumer trust can be no greater than when the product is claimed to result in a consumer's death.

Remarkably, not only were the companies not driven from the marketplace, but they all remain respected, profitable entities. While it may be years before all lawsuits are resolved, the fact that the companies are solidly prospering at this writing is testimony to, and a direct result of, their stability in the marketplace.

Prior to the crisis, each company had a long history of heavy advertising. Each had nurtured for years a reputation of service to the consumer and high product standards.

In the case of the Tylenol and Contac capsules, the swift response of the companies (removing products from the shelves, urging consumers to return or destroy any product on hand, replacing products with tamper-proof tablets) earned high marks for integrity and support and sympathy for the companies' plights.

The Ford response was somewhat less successful to the extent that the model, its image severely damaged, was ultimately discontinued. The company itself, however, continues to be hugely successful, its image untarnished.

The Jewel company closed down the dairy that was the source of the contaminated product, urged consumers not to risk using any of the product on hand and retained a well-known competitive dairy to replace the store's own brand on its shelves. TV messages of warning and reassurance were delivered personally by the company's chairman, who looked appropriately concerned.

In each instance the companies followed a classic formula for responding to crisis situations:

1. Publicly acknowledge the problem.
2. Investigate the range and scope of the position.
3. Designate a single spokesperson to present the company's position.

4. Present and maintain the positioning of the company in a larger context than the problem.

The response in the area of financial services follows the same formula as nonfinancial consumer marketing. Effective public communications, like good marketing, adheres to some basic principles, which are non-product-specific.

Consider what factors inspire consumer confidence in a product or service, financial or nonfinancial. Indeed, consumer confidence may be the reason why we select one firm over another, whether we are choosing a bank, a broker, a mutual fund or a bottle of aspirin. Our considerations may include:

- The history of the firm, institution, product or service.
- The reputation of the firm as it evolved during that history.
- Our opinion of the founder and/or management.
- Competitive pricing.
- The firm's word-of-mouth reputation.
- Policy regarding customer satisfaction.
- Convenience of doing business.

Certainly we could poll our friends and create a lengthy list, but the essence of consumer confidence can be summed up in the word trust and trust is largely drawn from our experience or understanding of the firm or corporation's reputation as a frame for the product.

The Ford Motor Company had a long history of producing quality products priced competitively. When the Edsel proved to be a misjudgment of public tastes, the company quickly discontinued the model and the public continued buying Fords. When the Pinto, as noted, was reported to be flawed, the company continued selling its other models at a brisk pace. To the consumer, the positioning was clear: the model might be a loser, but the company on balance does a good job. The Ford Foundation had historically been a kindly benefactor, the company a good neighbor in the community.

So it goes in the financial services area. People's "hot buttons," "turn-ons," and "warm fuzzies" are the same: they are largely emotional decisions.

Is the crisis of a bank any worse in the eyes of its customers than a scandal involving McDonald's would be to its shareholders and the public?

Not at all.

Mobil Oil Company reacted to the "gas crisis" of the 1970s with the creation of advertorials, paid advertisements to address charges in the media and public perceptions that the gasoline shortage was a fraud, that oil companies were unnecessarily inflating prices and gouging the public.

The campaign garnered nearly as much attention as the crisis itself. Never before had a major corporation so aggressively taken on its critics and the media, buying space to authoritatively detail its side of the story and how it felt it was misunderstood and maligned. The Mobil public relations crew was dispatched to issue releases highlighting the main points of the advertorials. Copies were circulated to legislators and persons of influence. A Mobil spokesman was a familiar figure on news and talk shows. Many said the purpose was to divert attention from the high price of gas to the unfairness of the media and the lack of facts supporting the charges against big oil companies.

Overall, Mobil was hailed as one gutsy outfit, challenging its critics with nothing less than full page, point-by-point statements of its case in *The Wall Street Journal* and elsewhere.

Mobil stockholders loved it. Media and legislative attention seemed to shift to Exxon and Shell, whose responses to charges of windfall profits in the face of a crisis seemed very timid and defensive in comparison. Mobil, although a giant already, became virtually the spokesman for the oil industry because its management chose to usurp the role.

Continental Bank, on the brink of disaster after a devastating series of bad loans, employed a strategy that was similar to that of Chrysler Corporation when its stock fell through the floor and heavy losses were incurred. Both opted for government support and a changing of the guard. The new regime brought with it its own track record of successfully building, managing and overcoming competitive challenges.

Who wanted to buy a Chrysler product when the company looked like it might fold?

The answer is anyone who believed in America, apple pie and former Ford superstar Lee Iacocca, who challenged consumers in ads stating "If you can find a better car for the money—buy it!"

Ads and public relations projects turned Iacocca into a folk hero of sorts. He was the guy who was going to roll up his sleeves, challenge his people to build a quality car, guarantee it and tell the American public it was now up to them—to save a company, jobs, and be part of a renewed Spirit of America.

It worked: Lee Iacocca is not only credited with selling cars and turning around the direction of the company's stock and profit picture, but his autobiography (part of the image-building) became a national best seller and he was frequently mentioned as a possible presidential contender.

Similarly, Continental Bank, humbled by its plight following the scandal-plagued Penn Square deal, accepted help from the government in the form of loan guarantees, and recruited John Swearingen, former head of Standard Oil of Indiana, to lead the charge back to stability. He was a recognized, first-rate CEO and his reputation alone assured the bank's creditors and the public that a serious reorganization had begun under first-string leadership.

Continental's road back was built largely on assurances by the new management that this was a "new Continental" without the managers or philosophy that got it in trouble before. Only time will tell how effective a long-term solution this will prove. An operation the size of Continental often makes commitments based on analysis and judgment, not collateral. How the judgment of this group compares to that of its predecessors remains to be seen.

But as a short-term solution to regaining the confidence of the marketplace, the appointment of a management team with a good track record, integrity and personal charisma was enough to have the financial community willing to take another chance on Continental.

We must be aware of the double-edged sword carried by the "kings of the mountain." When Continental was one of the great powers of American banking it wielded that power, saying yes to some and no to others. Clearly, when you're on top there are those who wish you ill, who like to see how the mighty have fallen.

In 1986 alone, according to the Federal Reserve Board, some 135 banking institutions failed. Many believed they got what they deserved. It is one of our more curious contradictions that as we seek to get close to wealth, we take a certain pleasure in seeing the wealthy having the tables turned on them.

In few industries is this more true than in insurance. This industry can point to an all-time low level of consumer confidence. While there is a recognition of the clear value of the insurer, the protector, the perception is that large insurance companies have all the money in the world, gather it with hollow promises, and go to any lengths to keep it.

Insurance companies, as a rule, have a lousy image going in and it only seems to worsen with time. Consider some of these more well-known insurance company themes:

"You're in good hands..."
"Like a good neighbor..."
"For all the decisions that you make..."
"Get a piece of the rock..."

Good hands? Good neighbors? No word-of-mouth spreads as quickly as that regarding an insurance company that tries to duck paying a claim. Consumers don't want the insurance company's slogans about neighborliness—they want their claims paid. Promptly.

For years, insurance companies prospered by selling whole life policies with low face-value amounts and inflated premiums. Life insurance agents touted money waiting for the retiree that resulted from years of premiums earning less interest than that of the minimum passbook account. When the pocket calculator came in and people began calculating premiums plus interest times 35 years, the bottom fell out of this market and with it much of the company's credibility.

Furthermore, there is a perception that insurance company money, like "government money," is somehow there for the taking and is "less stolen" through fraud than other money. "Let the insurance company pay for it," or "Just put through an insurance claim for it" are common phrases in our everyday vocabulary.

Liability insurance and malpractice insurance carry premiums so high as to border on the absurd. Yet, those who provide such services are among the most frequent victims of lawsuit settlements and awards going to those simply seeking "easy money."

The insurance industry in the 1970s and 1980s has undergone and continues to undergo a revolution. Many insurance companies that were fat with profits in the Sixties and took a beating in the Seventies are coming back strong in the Eighties. Mostly they are coming back through acquisitions, mergers, diversifications and new products.

Many insurance companies now own or are part of networks of real estate companies, brokerage firms and or lending institutions.

In early 1987, the Comptroller of the Currency approved the petitions of several large New York banks, thus paving the way for the banks' managing mutual funds, underwriting securities and providing investment banking services.

One executive recently noted that this is the era in which every bank wanted to be a brokerage firm and every brokerage firm wanted to be a bank. The particular executive speaking was head of marketing for a mutual fund group, owned by an insurance company, which had recently acquired a brokerage firm.

WHAT TO TELL THE CONSUMERS

What all this means at a consumer level is uncertain—except in how it's marketed.

Can a consumer believe in a brokerage firm if the most famous names in today's brokerage business are accused wrongdoers? The key to building consumer confidence and consumer trust is a fairly elementary proposition: start by telling the truth.

In the brokerage business, begin by positioning the brokerage firm before the crisis. Tell the public some of the things the firm is doing to inspire confidence, to reinforce its integrity.

Following the E.F. Hutton scandal, that firm hired comedian Bill Cosby to help restore its tarnished image. Mr. Cosby was, at that point, television's highest rated performer and the celebrity endorser for about a half-dozen products from autos to snacks to soda pop. (In advertising, the practice of attempting to transfer and capitalize on the appeal of a person from one context to another is called "borrowed interest.") Hutton tried to capitalize on the public's affection for Mr. Cosby as one of TV's best comics and to link that affection to its own name and products.

The resulting campaign was tepid at best. The public had no trouble believing Mr. Cosby sat with children, teasing and eating snack foods. It did, however, have trouble buying Mr. Cosby's professional discussion of how he believed he could "count on Hutton because of their 83 years of uninterrupted performance."

Error number one: it was widely reported in the news media that Mr. Cosby was paid an amount estimated in the seven-figure range for his "remarks." Number two: the public knows Mr. Cosby's endorsement is for sale. Number three: 83 years of uninterrupted performance doesn't speak at all to the honesty, integrity or expertise of the firm.

Hutton might have done better to have someone other than a famous comedian point out in print and TV ads the fact that the firm announced early in 1987 that it would buy back certain revenue bonds that had dropped in value after being downgraded. It seems that, upon review, Hutton felt its brochures implied the bonds would always sell at par. The firm felt there was reason to believe it had unintentionally misled its customers. It so prided itself on its integrity, honesty and service to its customers that it was ready to assume the losses.

That message, transmitted in a news release, a letter to customers and prospects, in ad copy and in seminars, would speak more to the point of reestablishing consumer confidence than would all the slogans, jingles and celebrity endorsers in Hollywood.

Additionally, a risk with celebrity endorsers is that they will often outshine the product. This was certainly the case with Bill Cosby and E.F. Hutton.

There appears to be a reluctance to deal with reality on the insurance side of the aisle. Let's return again to the theme of simple truths.

First, let's acknowledge that insurance agents are *salesmen*. The effort to portray these energetic, hardworking souls as "special agents" is a disservice to them, a dishonest way of relating to their public.

Furthermore, the concept of calling prospects with the request for 20 minutes to discuss something new and of interest to them borders on outright fraud. What they want is an appointment to attempt to sell insurance. Many "agents" have been directed in their training programs to go so far as to say "I'm not going to try to sell you any life insurance." The reason for this is the belief that no one believes he or she wants to buy insurance and unless this point is addressed first, the "agent" will never get the appointment.

On the contrary: Large insurance companies spend millions of dollars a year trying to increase awareness and recognition for their products only to have a salesman for them phone for an appointment with a promise "not to try to sell insurance." It would be wise to put aside the slogans and jingles about friendliness for a moment. Allow the marketing campaign to show your product as having value. Propose a list of questions to ask your current insurance "agent" regarding the value of your insurance program given today's economic climate. Site cost of living and income ratios over the last 3-, 5-, and 10-year periods. Offer a list of features the prospect should know about today's catalog of insurance products (annuities, trusts, IRA's, and the like).

Sell insurance. Offer newsletters explaining what's new in your business and compare your innovations to other competitive enterprises.

Avoid over-promising. Don't be so eager to close a sale that you'll promise anything. Too many people are led to believe the insurance policy they're buying is actually some type of unique, diversified investment program. It is through such deals that all company and salesperson credibility is lost.

Summarize the benefits of what you're selling in bold type on a single page. Most insurance applications are so packed with fine print and disclaimers that they perpetuate, if not generate, the lack of consumer confidence.

Marketing some highly speculative instruments can often pose a challenge. Futures, options and "junk bonds" are among those products which are tough to market even without a scandal to overcome. This is largely due to a lack of understanding among both professionals within the financial community and public investors. "Junk bonds" carry high risk but often afford opportunities for profit that make that risk worth taking. Futures contracts and option contracts can be used as hedging vehicles in even the most conservative of investment strategies.

No sooner had futures and options achieved a degree of acceptance and legitimacy due to their use by some banks, insurance companies and pension funds, than concern arose over "program trading," a strategy which seeks to profit from moves in stock prices relative to moves in the highly volatile new stock index market.

The stock, options and futures exchanges have produced extremely well-written material that helps to explain the markets and their movements. They've also invested tens of thousands of dollars on broker and investor education. Profit opportunities in these markets are so great that there appears to be a determined effort on the part of the investing public to want to overcome their fears of the market and take the proverbial plunge.

But how do you create consumer confidence, much less re-establish it, when rumors continually abound relative to the image of the young traders?

Imagine trying to market futures after a leading financial publication has just accused one of the largest trading firms with attempting to corner the market in a particular commodity. Or imagine trying to market stock options when an exchange has just publicly filed charges against a trader for attempting to use options to manipulate the value of the option's underlying stock.

These scenarios, however, pale by comparison with traders being escorted from the trading floor in handcuffs and charged with dealing cocaine on the exchange floor. Accounts of this event were front page news, and a residue of concern and mistrust will linger for years to come. The guilt or innocence of the accused 10 of nearly 2,000 traders is, for purposes of this work, irrelevant. What is important is the image and opinion the public, the press and the financial community holds as a result of the experience. It was critical that the exchange respond quickly, honestly and establish an impression that it did an adequate job of policing its members.

WHAT STEPS SHOULD YOU TAKE

The way to deal with such occurrences and attempt to re-establish consumer trust—the only way—is through honesty. The process is not complicated:

1. Select a single spokesperson to address the subject. People "close to the source" may be knowledgeable and well-connected, but may be lacking in an understanding of the totality of the matter.
2. Don't exceed credibility. People are willing to accept blemishes as well as beauty marks—don't try to pretend they can't possibly exist. Besides, few corporations or individuals are such great liars as to not get blown over in a lie backfiring.
3. Try to break the news before the media gets wind of it. They might misinterpret the range or scope of the matter. You'll also hold psychological advantage in being the one to initiate the subject.

4. Acknowledge what's going on. Say you're investigating, you're cooperating with other parties involved and a report will be forthcoming. And make sure this all happens.

5. Anticipate the worst-case scenario. Thoughtfully rehearse your responses to the toughest possible questions. It is critical to establish assurances that you are informed, confident and responsive.

6. Advertise your position through both paid ads, press releases and the availability of a speaker. The public and industry respect a leader who tackles a problem head-on. If this seems a big-ticket item (and advertising often is) remember it may be the most important investment your company or firm ever makes.

7. Don't let your spokesperson upstage the product. Certain public relations figures and spokespersons and advertising people (creative and executive) have taken on a celebrity status of their own. That's dangerous as it allows feelings for the individual to distract from re-establishing trust in the product.

8. Always attempt to position yourself well before the crisis. Be visible, be competent, be available and know that building a reservoir of goodwill will allow you to draw from it later if you need to put a "crisis incident" in a larger context of having done the right things properly. The CEO or manager who refuses to talk with the media or respond to inquiries in the good times shouldn't expect understanding and support when times get tough.

9. Accept the counsel of professionals. Having made the point earlier that professional communicators can sometimes overdo it and blow a situation out of proportion, don't overlook the fact that many public relations people have had considerable experience in helping to restore trust after a crisis. Seek their counsel and determine if they can be of value in your situation.

10. Put it in writing. The aftermath of a crisis is a time when rumors abound. Whether in an ad, newsletter, mailing or press release, commit your position to writing and be consistent in your follow-through.

Remember, the vehicles are there to be used—newspapers, television, radio, mail or the speakers' platform. The basic steps to re-establishing consumer trust are the same as those used to establish that trust initially. Be honest, be available, be credible and be confident that there are few things that cannot be overcome by demonstrating the kind of integrity you want your public to see in you at the start.

Chapter Nine

Ronald Friedman

Mr. Friedman is a consultant in marketing, product development and positioning for financial services, communications and travel related organizations. His client list includes firms such as Dreyfus Corporation, Citicorp, Continental Insurance, Response Analysis Corp., William Erty, and Bozell, Jacobs, Kenyon & Eckhardt.

He is also Adjunct Professor of Marketing at the Fordham University Graduate School of Business, New York, with an emphasis on financial services marketing.

Mr. Friedman previously served as Vice President of Marketing and Advertising and Vice President, Marketing Services, for American Express; Vice President of Marketing for Continental Equities, the broker/dealer unit of Continental Insurance; and Vice President of Marketing for Cable Health Network. He also has held senior positions at major national advertising agencies where he specialized in both packaged goods and systems marketing.

He is a Registered General Securities Principal and Registered Security Representative.

RETAIL MARKETING OF MUTUAL FUNDS

Ronald Friedman
Marketing Consultant

INTRODUCTION

The mutual funds industry is experiencing phenomenal growth. Mutual funds assets under management rose from $135 billion in 1980 to $716 billion in 1986. There are now over 1,800 mutual funds available for purchase, up from 550 in 1980.[1] Sales in 1986 alone totalled $216 billion (not including money market funds) compared to only $10 billion in 1980. At year end 1986, a total of 46 million mutual fund accounts existed—a growth of 11 million accounts in only one year. Types of funds run the gamut from growth to growth and income to income to option income to international to sector funds and many more. Mutual funds are conceived, manufactured and marketed by a range of financial service companies including stock brokerage firms, insurance companies, banks and thrifts; the deregulatory environment encourages more entrants.

This dramatic growth suggests that there will be both survivors and dropouts in this market and that consumer confusion exists in the marketplace. It suggests that mutual funds are not just "sold" and the longer term winners will be those entrants who establish an image, identity and franchise for their particular mutual funds or mutual fund families. Mutual funds require a disciplined marketing approach (as opposed to sales-oriented only) approach in their creation, manufacturing, distribution, and selling to enhance chances for success.

---

[1]Investment Company Institute, April, 1987.

It is believed the same disciplines utilized in the marketing of packaged goods and services apply to mutual fund marketing. The needs of both the ultimate consumers and distributors must be considered. But, there are numerous key differences in emphasis when marketing mutual funds as opposed to other product categories. Among the unique considerations in mutual funds marketing which will be addressed here are:

- Multiple and alternative distribution channels.
- The primary importance of the distributor: should marketing through a salesforce be selected? These considerations, however, should not eliminate sensitivity to the ultimate consumer's needs.
- Regulatory and compliance issues involving the Securities and Exchange Commission (SEC) and the National Association of Securities Dealers (NASD) and the impact on communications materials developed—including advertising, direct response, sales promotion and public relations.
- The varying degrees of sophistication and product knowledge of the distributor and the ultimate consumer.
- Pricing and compensation scenarios.
- The high degree of "retail"/"sell-it *today,*" orientation.
- The relatively sparse use of primary marketing research.
- The preponderance of "sales-" as contrasted to "marketing-" oriented fund managements.

The wide variance within the mutual fund industry in addressing these and other marketing related factors suggests opportunities for the marketing professional in the mutual funds industry, provided there is true commitment from top management to the marketing discipline.

THE "MARKETING" VERSUS "SALES" ORIENTATION

In 1985, the American Marketing Association (AMA) revised its definition of Marketing to "the process of planning and executing the conception, pricing, promotion, and distribution of ideas, goods, and services to create exchanges that satisfy individual and organizational objectives."[2]

---

[2]"AMA Board Approves New Definition," Marketing News (March 1, 1985), p. 1.

More concisely, "Marketing is the anticipation, management, and satisfaction of demand through the exchange process."[3] It involves marketing research to develop and introduce products or services desired by consumers (and distributors), stimulating demand, facilitating purchase, regulating peaks and valleys for demand and fulfilling consumer (and distributor) expectations.[4] Marketing involves all the actions in conceiving, defining and getting a product or service from the producer or manufacturer to the target audiences (wholesaler, distributor, retailer, ultimate consumer) and then reinforcing the purchase decision to obtain repeat purchasers. Brand awareness, distributor and consumer trial, and usage or repeat purchase must be generated in a timely and cost-efficient manner, with the understanding that investment spending of marketing dollars will likely be needed up-front. This statement of what Marketing is true for mutual funds marketing, and adoption of these ideas can considerably improve marketing and sales performance.

In fact, the mutual fund industry is flooded with product manufacturers who are not versed in "Marketing," who do not understand its definition and who equate "Selling" with "Marketing."

Selling is *product driven* and implies the logic of "selling" whatever the company makes. *Marketing* is *market driven* in that it makes what consumers and distributors desire. Selling is a critical component of marketing, but not a substitute for it.

In most mutual funds organizations, marketing professionals are not hired; if hired, they are not supported with the tools or granted the commitment from top management to get the job done—that is, to apply a marketing discipline. Why is this so? Perhaps because top management does not understand the marketing approach; perhaps because top management is not willing to invest in marketing programs; and/or perhaps because elements of the mutual fund industry are short-term oriented—after a quick buck.

With over 1,800 mutual funds (and more appearing every month)—many of which are not differentiated from competitors—supply, it could be argued, already has exceeded or will shortly exceed demand. A marketing

---

[3]Joel R. Evans and Barry Berman, *Marketing* (Third Edition) (New York: Macmillan Publishing Company, 1987), p. 9.

[4]Ibid.

approach seeks to identilfy differences in consumer and distributor needs and can help develop the products to satisfy them. It is long-term oriented, yet recognizes the need to establish and attain short-term goals.

MUTUAL FUND MARKETING STRATEGIES: THE PRODUCT DEVELOPMENT PROCESS

In developing and marketing mutual funds, at least a dozen strategies should be addressed (see Figure 1). Note that Marketing Research is included as a strategy because it is applicable to each of the other strategies. Critical to this discipline is the underlying assumption that less time and effort and more effective targeted results will occur if this process is followed. Throughout this discussion, specific considerations for marketing mutual funds as contrasted with marketing classical packaged goods will be highlighted.

Figure 1: Marketing Strategy Diagram

Marketing Research

When creating mutual funds, the role of Marketing Research pervades and should precede every step in the process. Simply stated, Marketing Research is "the systematic gathering, recording, and analyzing of data about problems relating to the marketing of goods and services"[5] to help in the solution of marketing problems. Both secondary research (searching through data previously gathered for purposes other than solving the existing questions) and primary research (data to be freshly collected and analyzed) should be employed to obtain answers to specific questions about product design.

What does this mean for mutual fund creation? It suggests that when analyzing competition, consideration should be given to product offerings and features, pricing, distribution channels, portfolio management, performance track records, analysis of advertising, sales promotion, sales kit efforts and the regulatory and compliance environment. This will help locate a niche, a market segment, an opportunity for the new mutual fund that make it somewhat unique or positively differentiated from the competition (see the section on positioning below). Alternatively, if the new mutual fund is just a clone of existing products, research is likewise required to ensure the relevant duplication features are incorporated. After product introduction, Marketing Research regularly and systematically should be employed to evaluate performance against marketing objectives so that logical modifications can be made.

Critical to the effective use of research in mutual funds marketing is the recognition that research should be performed among proper target audiences—the ultimate consumer and, in the case of "load" funds which are distributed via salesforces, also among distributors. Arguably, the distributor's active role in presenting the product to his customer is more crucial than in packaged goods marketing. Thus, it makes sense to evaluate the distributor's viewpoints, recognizing both the distributor's short-term interest in his commission income as well as his long-term interest in maintaining his customer relationship.

---

[5] Ralph S. Alexander (Chairman), *Marketing Decisions: A Glossary of Marketing Terms* (Chicago, Illinois: American Marketing Association, 1960), pp.16-17.

Marketing Research data can also be creatively employed in development of communications materials to ensure that the mutual fund is appealing to customer needs and wants or is creating the relevant needs.

Mutual fund marketers often shy away from research because it seems like a "theoretical" exercise which costs money and time. There is no question that short cuts can be taken and that research should only be employed when it is practical—when it helps solve problems—and not as an exercise. But it is argued here that the mutual funds marketer cannot afford to entirely omit research. Research does not eliminate judgment; it help to make more informed decisions. The cost of product launch failure will far exceed the cost of any reasonably defined and well-considered Marketing Research program.

Product

New product ideas and creativity are not the exclusive domain of the marketing function. Input from team members should be solicited up-front: this means that Systems, Operations, Compliance, Legal/Regulatory personnel, the salesforce, advertising, sales promotion, public relations agencies and portfolio managers are vital cogs in the mutual fund product development and launch process. Each can contribute to the enhancement of product attributes and features. Here, too, up-front participation and continuous communication with the team create a sense of "ownership" among the team members and enhances the likelihood of timely support in recognition that marketing does not and cannot exist in a vacuum.

A product concept statement defining the mutual fund or family, how it will function, the consumer and distributor benefits, the unique features and how the benefits can be supported, rationalized, and defended, must be written in a few sentences or brief paragraph. This concept statement for the mutual fund sets the tone for further development of marketing strategies. It can be used in concept-testing marketing research among the target audiences to assess the new fund's overall appeal, and specific appeals to be highlighted in communications. Further, with so many fund categories (growth, income, option income, global, sector, and so on.) the product mix of the family must be assessed so as to provide a compatible and sufficiently diversified family membership.

Positioning

The overall marketing strategy which embodies all the individual strategies is positioning. Positioning determines who the mutual fund will appeal to and what it is about the mutual fund the target audiences (consumers, distributors) need or want that this product can provide better than or, at least as well as, other products. Positioning creates the impression of uniqueness or differentiation, determines the stance to set this fund apart from the competition, establishes just who the competition is, defines the target audiences both demographically and psychographically (in terms of attitudes and lifestyles), segments the markets and allows the mutual fund marketer to emphasize or downplay certain product features to select market segments. This too is analogous to the marketing of packaged goods, wherein both trade (such as food, drug mass merchandiser outlets) and consumer market segmentation decisions are made. A clear positioning statement sets the overall direction for the other marketing strategies. These strategies must be consistent with the fund's positioning statement.

Place

An early mutual fund marketing decision centers around distribution, or place. Should the mutual fund be marketed directly to the consumer via direct response marketing techniques while avoiding a third-party distributor? Or should wholesalers be employed to market through stockbrokers, financial planners and/or insurance companies? Can the fund be distributed both through third parties as well as directly to the consumer?

Decisions on each of these choices carry additional ramifications. For example, the consumer and distributor audiences must be further refined/segmented. The issue arises as to whether multi-distribution channels can work. Will distributors be sufficiently upset to remove the product from the shelf if the mutual fund manufacturer also markets directly to the ultimate consumer? How can all parties be satisfied? The present market trend is toward multi-distribution channels, yet this path canceals landmines which must be discovered and dismantled. Further, pricing through each channel and compensation of the various distributors must be resolved. In contrast to the concerns of packaged goods marketers, who have only recently developed direct marketing as a supplementary distribution channel, mutual funds marketers find direct marketing very viable, and the role of distributors in actively "selling" mutual funds is generally far more prevalent than in selling packaged goods.

Pricing and Profitability

Obviously, it is a goal of virtually all products and services to price for profit. The key is to find the price which helps secure relevant volume to optimize profitability. Mutual fund pricing considerations are similar. Furthermore, the price should support positioning goals; for instance premium pricing might be supportive of a more upscale mutual fund offer...but it might not. Packaged goods such as premium priced coffee would reasonably be targeted to up-scale, perhaps more sophisticated consumers with higher discretionary income. But if a mutual fund has high up-front fees, it could be counter productive to attracting the more up-scale consumers who, by dint of their wealth and investment clout, expect fee concessions. So pricing decisions become more complex in the mutual funds arena

When marketing directly to consumers, *no-load,* or no up-front sales charge, is generally the rule. A few mutual fund marketers, relying on the strength of past performance of portfolios, are now charging low front end charges to direct purchasers. *Load* funds or funds sold through third-party distributors have up-front sales commissions, and some have contingent deferred sales charges (back-end loads) when moneys are withdrawn within a certain period of time after investment (usually four to six years). No-load or load funds may also have 12-b (1) charges (named for a Securities and Exchange Commission regulation) which come out of the fund's assets to pay for distribution costs. The competitive analysis should provide relevant data upon which to base pricing decisions—and perhaps to stimulate innovative pricing decisions.

Promotion

The promotion strategy for mutual funds encompasses the activities of advertising, direct response vehicles, sales promotion, including sales promotion kits and sales support materials as well as public (consumer) and industry/trade relations. The promotion process, including development of a clear creative strategy, mirrors the efforts in marketing consumer packaged goods. To provide optimum guidance for the creatives, the creative strategy components are as follows:

Objective. A clear statement of the position the mutual fund seeks to occupy in the target audience's mind. What must the communication accomplish in order to be judged as successful?

Target Audience. Define it, demographically and psychographically.

Competition. Who is the competition? What competitor is the enemy?

Promise. What are the benefits to the target audience?

Support. What features or rationale allow you to make the Promise?

Tone. For mutual funds, the tone is usually serious and/or prestigious and/or reassuring.

Mandatories. What *must* be said or included in design of the creative product—including the company's graphics, slogan and legal requirements?

Net Impression. What should the target audience take away from the advertising or promotion (in one sentence)?

A crisp, clear, creative strategy, on one page, will enhance the likelihood of a better creative output and creative breakthroughs.

In mutual funds marketing, promotion should strive to achieve or enhance a marketing partnership with distributors, if third-party distributors are used. To this end, lead generation efforts utilizing targeted consumer lists and direct response testing can find qualified consumer prospects. These leads can be provided free or at a minimal cost to the distributors. For direct-to-consumer marketers, state of the art multi-media direct response marketing techniques are invaluable. Direct response provides the opportunity to test creative and media alternatives as results are quantitatively measurable.

A major consideration and a constraint to the creative process is that, in addition to the normal internal legal review and clearance which is standard for all communications efforts, the NASD Rules of Fair Practice are applicable to companies registered under the Investment Company Act of

1940. Also, judgment by the NASD regarding whether a communication is misleading considers, but is not limited to the following factors:

1. The overall context of statements.
2. Varying levels of detail or explanation depending on the target audience for a communication.
3. Overall clarity of the communications.
4. Special care taken to ensure that presentation of investment results are not misleading as regards data provided and relevance of time periods illustrated, and to ensure that historical results do not claim to predict the future; as well as clarity of charts; adequacy of summary results; inclusion of relevant charges and expenses.
5. Specific consideration in presenting capital results, total return illustrations, yield data, and comparison to other investment products or services.[6]

The mutual fund's compliance officer should be kept involved continuously in the promotion to reduce unnecessary time delays. Sufficient time must be allowed for NASD to review creative materials prior to release. (Guidelines for companies' activities during the initial year of operation are more stringent in requiring advance comments from the NASD prior to media insertion.) Further restrictions exist as to what can or cannot be said when a prospectus is or is not included with the communications materials. There is no doubt that creativity is constrained in the regulatory environment in which mutual funds must operate.

Compliance, Legal

It is imperative that sufficient time for red herring and prospectus review be allowed in anticipation of a new mutual fund offering. This chapter is not designed to be a compliance manual; however, it is urged that the mutual fund's attorney and its compliance officer be part of the product development process in order to avoid legal, regulatory, and compliance pitfalls and delays in product launch.

---

[6] National Association of Securities Dealers (NASD) Manual, *Investment Company Securities*, Section 5286, Commerce Clearing House, Inc., 1986.

Packaging

In consumer packaged goods marketing, the exterior package design elements are obvious. The fragrance industry provides a classic example of how package design helps create an image for a brand. Packaging works with the other marketing strategies to support the brand's positioning in the minds of consumers and the trade.

Likewise in mutual funds marketing, the package has a comparable role, although not quite so obviously. Elements of the sales promotion kit provided to consumers and distributors should have a distinguishing look that is consistent across each element, ranging from the prospectus and dealer selling guide to consumer brochures, co-operative advertising mats and such. The same considerations evident in developing the creative strategy for advertising development hold for package design. If the mutual fund package is "fighting" for shelf space in a stock brokerage firm's office, it should be made to stand out. And the method and components or delivery also create opportunities for differentiation. If a family of mutual funds is being offered, it is crucial that a consistent look and theme, both visual and written, be applied. Most important, package design must be supportive of the desired positioning.

People and Performance

In marketing mutual funds and, for that matter, financial services overall, it is vital that all relevant internal and outside personnel be involved up-front and continuously in the product development process: sales, marketing research, operations, systems, compliance, legal, finance, customer service, portfolio management, advertising, sales promotion, public relations agencies and financial printer. This will enhance the likelihood that all relevant issues are addressed in a timely fashion and are competently solved. It also gives joint "ownership" of the product to the participants. "No surprises" should be the order of the day. Yet marketing should lead the new product process and should assume responsibility to construct the agreed upon mission, performance and timetable goals.

The support and commitment of top management is required to communicate marketing's leadership role. With this commitment to the Marketing discipline comes the responsibility of marketing to be the diplomatically assertive leader for the team and to ensure ongoing communications.

Customer Service

As in packaged goods marketing, brand awareness, trial, purchase and repurchase must be secured when marketing mutual funds. But on both the consumer and distributor levels, mutual funds deal with considerably higher dollar purchases. This suggests the vital importance of impeccable, reliable, prompt customer service to consumers, institutions, distributors—to all target audiences. To obtain repeat purchase, ideally, the mutual fund's investment performance should be outstanding. But hand-in-hand with performance there must be customer-service orientation throughout the mutual fund organization, to communicate with the customers, to see that administrative details are accurate and consistent with compliance requirements, to ensure that client contact and telephone personnel are courteous, friendly, professional, responsive, and to ensure that adequate telecommunications lines (including sufficient 800-number capability) and personnel are available. Further, customer service has a great opportunity to resell the mutual fund and to cross-sell other investment products offered by the firm. And given that this function has direct contact with customers, it should also encompass marketing research role. Proper training, discipline and motivation must be imparted to customer service personnel. Customer service goes a long way towards fulfilling the image and positioning goals of the mutual funds organization.

SUMMARY AND CONCLUSION

This chapter has lobbied for a disciplined marketing orientation to mutual fund development and enhancement. It acknowledged the vital role of sales as a component of marketing. It identified the key marketing strategies that should be considered and the elements within the strategies to be addressed. The tactics or execution of the strategies will serve to differentiate from among other mutual fund products to consumers, institutions and distributors. Finally, it has emphasized that teamwork throughout the organization is required continuously and that the marketing approach can succeed only with top management's support and endorsement.

Chapter Ten

Anne Brennan

With over 12 years in the direct marketing industry, Anne Brennan has been involved in promoting a wide variety of consumer products through direct mail, telemarketing, broadcast and print. She started her career with a small New York advertising agency and publisher, where she wrote copy for a variety of self-help products.

Ms. Brennan began her career in financial services in March, 1983, when she joined Citibank USA to manage customer acquisitions for a new financial product introducing the concept of remote consumer banking. In 1985 she was promoted to Vice President, National Expansion Marketing.

Since November, 1986, Ms. Brennan has been with Chase Manhattan Bank's Direct Response Banking Group as Director of Acquisitions for their three bankcard brands, revolving credit line product, and National Deposit business.

Ms. Brennan is a frequent speaker at direct marketing and financial services industry conferences and seminars, and contributes to industry periodicals. She also serves as guest professor at the Direct Marketing course sponsored by New York University's School of Continuing Education.

DIRECT MARKETING OF FINANCIAL SERVICES
How, When and Why You Should Consider "Branchless" Marketing

Anne Brennan, Vice President
The Chase Manhattan Bank, N.A.

Branch marketing is driven by the need to get a certain number of people, determined by your goal for market share, to leave their homes or offices to open an account, deposit or transfer money, or apply for a loan.

In order to direct these decisions, you must:

1. Write a detailed marketing plan (including a full product profit and loss projection).
2. Present it for management approval.
3. Convince Systems, Operations and Customer Service that this really *is* a good idea.
4. Hire an advertising agency.
5. Create and run ads in local newspapers.
6. Create branch signage (and convince branch managers to install it).
7. Offer an incentive to get customers in the door ($50 deposited into their new account, or premiums such as toasters, would do).
8. Create training materials and train branch personnel to field questions about the product and promotion.
9. Cross your fingers, and hope that the week your campaign breaks the worst weather in 50 years doesn't hit your area.

10. Last but not least, hope that the branch personnel remember to code and count the returns, so the incremental business will be accurately attributed to your program.

If you were using direct marketing, steps one through three would be the same; but then the process starts to change. Let's assume you were using the mail to sell your product. You would need to:

4. Select your vendors (agency, printer, lettershop, and so on).
5. Buy a mailing list of qualified prospects.
6. Create a direct-mail solicitation package.
7. Produce and mail the piece directly to your potential customers.
8. Receive the responses and book the resulting accounts.
9. Track your returns against the money expended to evaluate the success of your program.

Direct mail is more precise and effective than other sales media for several reasons:

- You are dealing with "qualified" prospects, people who presumably (if you have chosen your list correctly) have the ability and *propensity* to buy your product.
- You have more *control* over the process; nothing "falls through the cracks." You are not dependent on other people who, while very willing, may not be putting your objectives first on any given day.
- Perhaps most important, through *your* direct interaction with the customer you become master of your own destiny because responses (and deposits) come directly to you.
- You also get to build a database of customer names from the reply coupons—perhaps the single most important tool for future direct marketing.

Direct marketing allows a financial organization to finely segment its universe of prospects, target the right offer to the right people, and deliver that offer to their doors. It also allows the institution to track the success of its marketing programs *and* build a base of proven *buyers* for future cross-sells.

There are, however, products which simply cannot be sold through the mail, and those will be discussed later in this chapter.

THE DIRECT MARKETING CUSTOMER

When Messrs. Sears and Roebuck started selling their wares via the mail around 1890, they were pioneering a whole new distribution system for goods and services. They also were creating an entirely new type of *customer*, one who was not afraid to send his money to some remote location to purchase merchandise he had not seen.

Today's direct marketing customers are not all that different. However, today, in addition to being trusting, they are usually harried and stressed, with little time or desire to "shop around." They are discriminating, too, and have money to spend—but *only* on products or services for which they have a real need.

Some of your current customers may also be direct marketing customers. However, a great many may not be now, or will never become, direct-mail[1] responsive. On the whole, a financial institution, and any other type of direct marketer, are much better advised not to try to convert such customers, but rather to better target those people within and outside their customer bases who already *are* mail responsive.

WHY THE MEDIUM DRIVES THE PRODUCT

One of the first things to acknowledge is that there are many products that financial institutions just cannot seem to market successfully through the mail. They include:

- Anything that requires a long application. Response falls in direct proportion to the number of items requested on the account form.
- Any product that requires a lengthy explanation or a significant amount of disclosure copy. Let the branch personnel sell the more complicated products; use the mail for the simpler products.

---

[1]"Mail" is used as a generic term for all direct response media: mail, print ads, radio and TV commercials with a 1-800 phone number.

• Checking accounts are especially difficult to sell through the mail. It seems people will not send the money they need to pay bills and buy groceries away to some remote location. (One funny thing about consumers: they never doubt that the checks they mail to pay their bills will get there, but they're always *sure* their deposits will get lost.)

Financial services products that do lend themselves to direct marketing are:

• **Credit cards.** Response increases in direct proportion to credit line size, and pre-approved offers draw up to 50 percent more responses than those not pre-approved.
• **Money market funds and certificates of deposit.** Consumers seem to understand these products now, and have become somewhat comfortable with buying them long-distance. However, a toll-free phone number to answer questions and help close the sale can be a crucial factor in the success of your campaign.
• **Revolving lines of credit.** Customer response tends to follow the same parameters as credit cards.
• **Mutual funds.** This is largely due to the efforts of major marketers of mutual funds (especially when marketed as IRAs). But keep in mind that mutual funds are a two-step sale—the bulk and weight of the disclosure booklet makes it impractical to include in an initial solicitation mailing.

BUILDING A DIRECT MARKETING PROGRAM BUDGET

In developing a budget for direct marketing programs, there are a number of key variables that need to be part of the planning process:

• *Solicitation cost:* including the cost of space, broadcast time or mailing lists; creative, printing and mailing costs (including postage); agency fees and sales commissions, if any. Remember to add the cost of any telemarketing sales support here, too.
• *Response rate:* both gross (*all* mail received) and net (actual accounts signed up)—but remember, this is a two-step program and there is incremental fall-off in response between these two steps.

• *Cost of fulfillment:* this includes the material sent as the second step in a two-step sales process, and/or the cost of a "welcome" kit for new customers, if you use one.

• *Fee Income for credit products, or Opening Deposit for liability products.* When selling a credit card, do not forget to include interchange, interest and cash-advance fee income. On a deposit product, include additional deposits expected, or percentage of accounts estimated to rollover on a time deposit.

• *Account set-up charge* and estimated cost of customer service programs.

• *Allocated overhead* for the program, determined by the corporation's management.

• *Cost of FDIC insurance:* if applicable.

One last point: remember to list all your assumptions, footnoting them on the front of the profit and loss projections, if possible. This will document your logic and answer many of management's questions. It also provides an audit trail when you are matching actual results against projections. Experience shows that nobody remembers where "the number" came from when it is off-target; but you can possibly save a program with borderline results for another test if, months later, you can prove the initial assumptions were made on a reasonable basis.

MEDIA SELECTION

Once again, the product drives the selection of media. However, equally important factors in the equation are: (1) can you best reach your prospects through this medium? and (2) will you generate enough orders to recoup your advertising cost?

Direct Mail

Direct mail is probably the most versatile of direct response media, and certainly the most easy to target. With the ability to add demographic overlays to direct-mail subscriber and buyer mailing lists, list selection has become so refined these days you probably could target people (as far out as it seems) by the color of their eyes. Just buy a list of buyers of colored contact lenses, segmented by color of lens purchased.

You can sell complicated or simple products through the mail, in one or two steps, with no personal sales intervention, or with the addition of telephone support.

It has been argued that direct mail is too expensive. Package costs (including postage) can range upwards of $1.50 each for an elaborate six-color package in small quantities, to less than 40 cents each for a simpler package in large quantities. If you manage your costs well, an effective direct-mail campaign can be tailored to fit any budget.

Breaking through "mailbox clutter" is a major challenge today. Due to the intense competition for consumers' dollars, more and more marketers are turning toward mail as an alternative distribution source. This has resulted in the average consumer getting two or three unsolicited pieces of mail daily—mail that quickly becomes "junk" when it is untargeted, and therefore unwanted. If you want your piece to stand out, use some well-planned envelope and format techniques. Most important, however, is your *list*, the major factor in directing the right offer to the "right" customer.

Telemarketing

With telemarketing currently in vogue, its pros and cons are being discussed widely among financial service marketers. Most effective as a cross-sell medium, experience has shown telemarketing does not work well for "cold" sales calls. The preponderance of research indicates that people do not like to be called at home by strangers offering them a new product, but are much more receptive when talking to a company with whom they are already doing business.

The personal nature of a telemarketing call can work well with both complicated and simple products. Remember, however, that if you are paying by the length of the call (some telemarketing companies charge an hourly rate, some by the number of closed sales), you will want to keep it short.

In analyzing profitability, remember to track and to factor in the percentage of "buyer's remorse," that is, those people who say "yes" just to get an overzealous salesperson off the phone. There also are people who change their minds between the time of the call and the day they receive the product. This also can vary by vendor. Some sales reps are notoriously more "high-pressure" than others. Generally, the results of a well-managed telemarketing campaign should be at least double that of a comparable direct-mail solicitation.

Space or Print Ads

These include ads on stiff card stock which are bound or "tipped" into the spine of a magazine, as well as free-standing inserts in newspapers.

Print space lends itself to one-step sales of a simple product (like a credit card) or two-step sales, sourcing an inquiry to be followed up by mail or phone.

Space can also be used as a "support" medium, either announcing your mail or reinforcing the message across a wider base. When using space as a support medium, remember that the incremental cost of an ad must be justified by the incremental number of responses received, when measured against a benchmark or "control" ad.

One caution when using space ads for credit products: customers sourced through print media can exhibit somewhat poorer credit performance when measured against the portfolio average.

Television and Radio

Everybody wants to see their product on TV, but because of its cost TV is *very* hard to make pay off as a direct-response medium. For example, a TV commercial tested to boost response to a direct-mail campaign in the Tampa, Florida, market area, achieved an 18 percent increase. In order to make national television commercials cost effective, a 50 percent increase in response would have been required—an almost impossible goal.

When creating such "support" commercials for television, always show the outside of the envelope from the mailing being supported. This provides easy identification when the viewer is told to "look for this offer in the mail." The whole concept of mail support may be lost without this visual key.

As a medium, television also makes it more difficult to target audiences, though the advent of cable outlets has helped in this regard.

Radio can be a much less expensive form of broadcast advertising, and one that mutual fund companies seem to find especially effective for generating leads.

However, radio presents some of its own problems. For example, if you buy "drive time" (during the most popular commuting hours, when most adult radio stations have their largest audiences) your prospects are usually in their cars. This means they are away from a phone when your message and phone number are broadcast. However, with the price of radio time being fairly inexpensive compared to television and even some print media, you have the ability to test inexpensively and get a quick read of the results.

Which medium should you use, when, and how? Test them all, if your budget and product set permit. Some will become permanent parts of your marketing plan; others will provide valuable benchmarks for measuring future results, and add to your own personal marketing knowledge.

DOING IT YOURSELF OR SELECTING A VENDOR

There are two basic ways to approach the "inside" versus "outside" question.

Don't do anything yourself if you can pay someone else to do it for you. If you are being paid to bring marketing expertise to your company, you are *not* being paid to write copy, do paste-ups and mechanicals, or film TV commercials. Some financial institutions seem to confuse the "marketing" function with more tactical, executional duties. Just because you are responsible for seeing that a project is done well does not mean you and your staff should actually do it yourselves.

This means simply: do what you do best, and hire someone else to do what they do best. Hiring outside help need not be expensive, and even small budgets can accommodate the use of most free-lance talent.

In addition, managing outside staff rather than internal staff gives you more control: you can pick and choose the best ideas and performance, get fresh perspectives or test the newest techniques—all without hiring or firing.

The other approach is to bring the function inside when you know the business so well it is cheaper and more effective to manage it internally. It also may make sense to do the work internally when you are ready to expand your own area of responsibility within the organization.

Choosing a new vendor is not a particularly difficult process. Of course, you want a company that has demonstrated it has good people, is price-competitive, has high standards of quality, has performed similar work, and is eager enough for your business to dedicate staff to your projects.

But you also want a company from which you can learn something. Most people love to talk about what they do and how they do it. Your current suppliers will have most likely worked for your competitors at one time or another and will have learned from that experience. So encourage them to talk about the business and be receptive to their ideas even if they are not in businesses generally thought of as "creative." Some of the most successful promotional ideas have evolved from conversations with data processors, list brokers or printers.

REACHING YOUR CUSTOMER

When your customer cannot see you and you cannot exercise your selling skills in person, creative communication becomes even more important. Creativity in direct response is still often considered a "poor stepchild" in the advertising world.

Art directors love to make fun of its simple words and plain graphics. While you may not win any design awards with your direct response ads, the truth is that *simple* sells...*plain* sells...and, sometimes, what's downright *homely* sells.

So resist the impulse to make your advertising beautiful for art's sake alone. Instead, design copy and graphics that communicate your message clearly and accurately and put all that extra "creativity" into structuring an *irresistible* offer.

The following techniques, broken down by media, are tried and proven.

Space Ads

Use space to sell simple products, or as a lead-generation source for two-step sales. One-step sales usually require a full-page ad, while lead-generating ads (for two-part sales) can be smaller. Visuals should be simple, with graphs or charts used as the best way to illustrate the earnings (or savings) potential of a product. It also helps, especially in a direct-mail brochure where you have more space, to show average consumers actually using your product (buying with a credit card, writing a check, and so on). If you cannot show your product actually being used (how do you use mutual funds?), show the benefits (long- or short-term) of owning it (for instance, a college graduation or retirement party, on a vacation trip, or a new home). Always make the attempt to "tangibilize" the product by putting it in a real-life context.

In either case, when using a reply coupon for response (instead of a 1-800 phone number), make sure the coupon is well-differentiated from the body of the ad so as to make cutting it out easy. Remember to leave enough space for the customer to fill in all required information, and give clear instructions about how and where to return it. (See Figure 1.)

Figure 1

☐ Yes, I want to help my money grow. So please send me more information on your Professional Money Management Account. I understand that if I reply by January 1 I will receive a $20 bonus just for taking advantage of this special offer.

Name

Address

City State Zip Code

Send to: The Bank
Post Office Box 0000
City, State, Zip

Attention: Investments

The most effective way to maximize response is to make the coupon itself into a postage-paid reply device. But due to postal weight requirements, the only way to execute this in magazines is to use the heavier paper stock of a bind-in format. Free standing inserts can often be designed to accommodate a postage-paid reply device, and remember, any additional media costs will most likely be offset by the incremental response.

Direct-Mail Packages

The traditional direct-mail package consists of an outside envelope with or without "teaser" advertising copy, a one- or two-page letter, a brochure, reply device (coupon) and postage-paid return envelope. Historically, this has been the most successful creative mix overall. However, other variations often prove successful, including:

- Longer letters (as many as 5 pages), no brochure.
- Short letter (l page), no brochure.
- Self-mailer—where all the elements are combined into one piece.
- Combining the reply device and the letter into one page (the reply device is perforated and gets detached and returned in the reply envelope).
- Making the reply device into a self-mailer (no reply envelope).

Outside Envelope Formats

As mentioned earlier, direct marketers today are facing the challenge of breaking through "mailbox clutter." One of the ways to do it is with envelopes that stand out. Descriptions of some of the successful formats you can test follow:

"Kraft" Envelopes. These are those brown paper envelopes that look as if they contain a utility bill. Everyone opens them. To reinforce the impact, do not use your company name or logo on the outside.

Snap-Packs. These are self-contained carbonized packages that require the recipient to rip off a perforated strip on the end in order to open them. Once opened, they reveal forms that look like a reprimand from the IRS, a rent bill, a collection notice, and so on. Whatever they trigger in the mind of the consumer, they get opened. And, they get a reply too—up to twice as many as your control package.

Larger Envelopes. Envelopes larger than the standard #10 business envelope, closed-face or with one to four windows, or even envelopes designed to resemble overnight mail, are also used successfully.

While there are many options, no one format is always better than any other; some work better for certain products; test as many as you can to determine which is best for your specific purpose.

There are other techniques that can boost the mail response, and we now turn to a discussion of these.

The "Yes/No" Box

Your reply coupon should always contain a check-off box next to copy that reads something like: "Yes, I've decided to accept this once-in-a-lifetime offer... " Right below this should be a smaller box with, "No, I've decided to pass up this once-in-a-lifetime offer. Please give the account (or credit card) you've reserved for me to someone else."

The "Yes" should always be larger than the "No," and the "No" copy should strongly imply a missed opportunity. This is what will happen: you may receive as many "No" replies as "Yes" replies, but your "Yes" replies will be anywhere from 20-50 percent higher than your control. Experience shows that if you save the "No" responses and mail these people again, they will respond up to 50 percent better than your best list. Why? Probably because (1) the prospect has proven they're mail responsive, (2) they read your offer and understood it, or (3) maybe they just weren't ready to buy at that time.

Long Copy Versus Short

If you ask consumers in a focus group what they prefer, they will *always* tell you they want short letters, two-panel brochures—just the unadulterated facts with no advertising "hype." The truth is that people do not read everything. But because you cannot be there with them, the mailing piece must tell them everything they need to know to make the buying decision. Plus, each element of the package must stand on its own. If the recipient is a letter reader, the letter should be able to close the sale; if a brochure reader, the brochure must tell him enough to convince him to buy. And, even the reply device should be a selling piece. The point is that you must use as much copy as you need to sell your product.

You are often asking a customer to send their money away to a place that might be hundreds or thousands of miles away from their home. You need to use every technique you can to make them secure in that decision. Let the consumer pick and choose what and how much they want to read;

make certain to give them enough information to make an intelligent decision.

Long Applications

As mentioned earlier, response falls in direct proportion to the length of the application. But if your credit people need to know more about your prospects than you would like to, there *is* a way to handle it. (See Figure 2.)

- First, break up the information into logical categories: personal information, employment information, financial information, and such.
- Each category can be visually linked by the same background color—preferably surrounded by a contrasting color—thus grouping each category into a visual whole.
- Number each section with a large numeral: 1, 2, or 3 so that each section appears short, and easy to fill out.
- Use a roll-fold format (that is, one that unfolds panel by panel) so that the actual length of the application is only revealed as the form is completed and unfolded.
- Intersperse the sections with sales copy so that you actually reinforce the benefits of the product as the applicant is completing the form.

Personalization

Computer personalized letters, while more expensive, generally pay off in increased response. But remember to use personalization to bring the customer into the selling process. For example, you can partially pre-complete an application with such entries as the customer's name, address and phone number. This is far more effective than just showing off the technology by, for example, repeating the customer's name throughout the text.

Business Reply Envelopes

Some marketers try to cut corners by not paying postage on the reply envelopes containing their orders. Their rationale is that the types of customers who buy their products have enough money to pay for a stamp. The real reason is usually that they or their management have reviewed the

Figure 2

1. Tell us about yourself

Name (Last) (First) (Middle Initial)			No. of Dependents
Social Security No.	Birthdate	Home Telephone No. ( )	
Home Address		How Long Yrs. Mos.	
City	State	Zip	
Previous Address		How Long Yrs. Mos.	
City	State	Zip	
☐ Own Home ☐ Rent ☐ Other ______	Monthly Rent/Mortgage $	Original Mortgage $	
Present Balance $	Estimated Value $		

2. Tell us some financial information

(if you need more space, please use another sheet.)

Checking (Bank Name and Address)			Account #	Balance
Business Checking (Bank Name and Address)				
Savings (Bank Name and Address)				
Other (Money Mkt., Stocks, Bonds, IRA, etc.)				
Real Estate (Type of Property/Address)	Date Acquired	Mo. Mortgage Payment $	Annual Income from Asset $	Present Value of Asset $
		$	$	$
Stocks and Bonds/Issuer			Annual Income from Asset $	Present Value of Asset $
			$	$
			$	$

FOLD HERE

3. Tell us about your work

Business or Employer		
Business Address		
City	State	Zip
Business Telephone No. ( )		
Position		How Long Yrs. Mos.
Type of Business		Annual Salary $
Previous Business or Employer		
Previous Business Address		
City	State	Zip
Annual Salary $	Position	
How Long Yrs. Mos.	Previous Business Telephone No. ( )	
Other Income $		
Source of Other Income		

Questions? Call toll-free 1-800-000-000

FOLD HERE

4. Tell us about your co-applicant

(if any)

Name (Last) (First) (Middle Initial)		Birthdate
Social Security No.	Home Telephone No. ( )	
Home Address		
City	State	Zip
Business or Employer	Business Telephone No. ( )	
Business Address		
City	State	Zip
Position	How Long Yrs. Mos.	
Type of Business	Annual Salary $	
Other Income $	Source of Other Income	

PLEASE SIGN HERE: Applicant and Co-Applicant (if any):

X ______________________________
Applicant Signature Date

X ______________________________
Co-Applicant Signature Date

marketing budget with a view toward cutting costs, and their red pencils have stopped at the line for postage, usually a large up-front expenditure.

This is, to say the least, a false economy. The point is not that your customer does not have the money to pay for the postage, but that if your prospect waits until he finds or goes to buy a stamp, there is a good chance that the sale will never get completed.

Telemarketing Scripts

The most important factor about telemarketing scripts is that you definitely need one, and the second is that your script should sound so natural that no one knows your salesperson is using it. This sounds easier than it is, because learning a script so well that it sounds like normal dialogue takes considerable practice. You should make sure that your sales reps get ample opportunity to "role play" and get appropriate feedback before they go live on the phones. In telemarketing, confident attitude and smooth delivery is the name of the game.

A good telemarketing script will contain all the answers to a prospect's questions about the product and its pricing. And in the end a good script has to *go for the close*: if a sales rep does not *ask* for the order, he may have had a pleasant conversation, but he hasn't done his job.

Broadcast Commercials

Both TV and radio commercials have to grab attention, be intrusive, create desire and inspire action—not an easy task to accomplish in 10 or even 30 seconds. Traditional direct response commercials can run as long as 120 seconds, but if you are paying for the time up-front (rather than on a P.I., or "per inquiry," basis), there's probably little cost-effectiveness in a "120."

The main fact to bear in mind about radio or TV is that the message must be driven home in a short amount of time. So keep that message *very* simple. Also, allow time for enough repetition of the 1-800 phone number so that the customer is able to write it down; four to five times is standard.

When using TV to support a mailing, make sure you show the mailing envelope long enough for it to become recognizable to the customer. For example, print a blue bar across the lower corner of the envelope, point it out to the customer as the key identifier, and make sure your mail carries it. Be careful to time your mail so it is delivered on the third day the commercial is running. If you miss this window, you may lose the effect of the "support."

It is important to remember that direct response ads are written to produce a response, and for no other reason. If, therefore, you use a commercial produced for another purpose and "doctor" up with a 1-800 number, do not expect the same results.

There's a lot of talk now about using broadcast media, particularly for creating an "image" for a financial institution and its products. While this may *sound* like a great idea, remember that brand identity is very difficult to establish, especially in financial services. Unlike many consumer products, checking accounts or mutual funds or credit cards can seem very much alike. Because they are not visually or functionally distinct, and the major product differentiation is intangible (and usually only realized over time), one does not clearly stand out from others. And, unlike cereal or toilet tissue or razor blades they do not have a defined product life, so a customer is not regularly faced with a buying decision.

Creating an image in financial services is a long-term commitment and will not be accomplished by a one-shot ad campaign. Although the image is also helped by some degree of local presence, the key is consistency of message, delivered over time through all communications literature, not just advertising. In order to do this, you must first define who your consumer is and what he or she wants that you alone can offer.

YOUR MOST IMPORTANT MARKETING TOOL: THE DATABASE

The key difference between direct response marketing and general marketing is the opportunity direct response marketing gives financial institutions to build and use a database of original and extrapolated information for help in targeting an offer to the most responsive customer.

This is what makes direct marketers different from other marketers who do not have the ability to precisely discriminate by a prospect or customer's behavior, track orders by source, or establish individual customer profitability by performance. The database that makes it possible for direct marketers to maximize success, cut losses, pinpoint pockets of profitability and build whole new categories of customers.

Benefits from a database include:

• *Stabilizing and expanding your customer base.* Database marketing can help deepen product penetration among current customers and help expand market share. Use it to target new customers, select mailing lists, lower the cost per account acquired, obtain response reports, cross-sell current customers, manage against sales "overload" (making too many offers to the same person), and for customer surveys and research results.

• *For strategic planning.* Spot changes in buying trends and the emergence of new customer segments *before* the competition, or identify the emergence of new customer segments.

• *A new source of income.* Many marketers create a new profit center by making their customer lists available for non-competitive offers. These lists are products with no overhead, since your organization maintains its customer lists and updates them for its own billing purposes—anything you make is pure profit.

Should you build your own database, let an outside vendor do it for you, or buy a "canned" program? The decision depends to a great extent on your budget and where you are in the direct marketing process. Generally, building your own database is best when you have the in-house resources (budget, equipment, and equally important, manpower) to build and manage it. Remember too, that building the database is only part of the story: in order for it to be an effective marketing management tool, it needs regular data updates and maintenance.

If you do not have these resources available to you, or you do not have the knowledge to build your own database, it is advisable to go to an outside vendor. The vendor presumably will have experience you lack, and initially this may even be a cheaper, as well as a more practical, approach.

Do make sure that any contract you sign stipulates that *you* own the program and the data. This will permit you to insure the integrity of the data if you wish to take it inside at a later date or switch your business to another vendor.

"Canned" or pre-written software is available from a few vendors, especially in the credit scoring area. While this may be effective in the short run and may serve as a bridge until you develop your own program, it is rarely as good a tool as a program developed from your own data.

After you have built a database, where do you want to go with it? The whole reason for this exercise is, of course, to build a statistically valid model that can help you market smarter, that is, to spend less money to get better results. The ultimate application is a predictive score to forecast what prospects will buy and how they will use your product. Although this may seem complicated, many organizations are using models every day to target potential customers and forecast their financial behavior, to spot who will most likely attrite, or who is most likely to go to collections, or who will become a write-off account. This is done by tracking the customer's credit performance, overlaying appropriate demographics, analyzing actual buying behavior (both with your institution and with others) and then patterning, or "modeling" the information. This model is then used to select the mailing list from the millions of names available.

Database marketing is, without a doubt, where marketing generally and financial services marketing specifically are headed. If your organization is not yet involved in it, it may soon lose market share to its more far-sighted competitors.

CUSTOMER SERVICE

When the customer cannot see your institution, its staff or its product, the strong support of a well-trained, professional customer service unit becomes critical. Customer service people may be the key to your firm's success as a "remote" financial services provider. One of the most prevalent complaints about financial services companies today is the lack of "personalized" service. The average consumer feels (and in many cases, rightly so) that financial services providers are abandoning him to a world of machines. But a well-trained customer service area can go a long way toward defusing this issue, even over the phone, *if* they know how to answer questions, are courteous, well-trained *and* accessible.

Customer service may not be the responsibility of the marketing department. But since marketing is responsible for the ultimate success of the product it is very much in marketing's interest to get involved in helping customer service people do their job better. Begin by preparing and distributing product fact sheets, including possible customer questions, before initiating a promotion. Be present at training sessions. Monitor calls, or even answer the phones for an hour or so to get the real feel for your customers and their concerns.

Not every customer service representative can be trained as a salesperson. But by the very nature of the work they perform—helping customers solve problems—customer service personnel can be trained to spot a need which can be helped by your other products. Therefore, include them in training sessions for new products information and make certain they understand which other parts of your company's product line can be logically cross sold along with those new products.

CONCLUSION

Direct response marketing has been gaining acceptance in the financial community for several years and though it still has a way to go in that regard, direct marketing programs play key roles in the overall marketing programs of many institutions.

Direct marketing is a mixture of advertising creativity, computer technology and good, old-fashioned selling.

More importantly, it responds to the changing needs of important consumer market segments, those people who have the ability to buy but have neither the time nor the inclination to "window shop" for financial products. That is why financial services companies will increasingly use direct response marketing to sell customers their products. Never lose sight of the fact that direct marketing is a *sales* tool, not just a communications vehicle.

Chapter Eleven

Gary H. Raddon

Gary H. Raddon received his Masters Degree in Business Administration from Brigham Young University in 1965. In 1966 he was appointed Special Assistant to David M. Kennedy, Chairman of Continental Bank, Chicago, Illinois. Following this special assignment, he was assigned New Product Development Manager, and in 1970 he was promoted to Commercial Marketing Manager. In 1974 he graduated from the Stonier Graduate School of Banking.

In 1983 Mr. Raddon formed his own company, the Raddon Financial Group. His firm specializes in consulting and new product development for the financial services industry. Its clients are currently comprised of over 300 financial firms nationwide.

Mr. Raddon writes for the Bank Marketing magazine, and he is a frequent speaker for the Bank Marketing Association. He also participates in management conferences with the U.S. Leaque and Financial Institutions Marketing Association, and since 1982 he has been on the faculty of the New Mexico School of Banking.

Robert L. O'Meara

Robert L. O'Meara began his career in accounting, with Home Federal Savings of Chicago in 1978. His responsibilities included servicing mortgage loan accounting, corporate account reconciliations, and regulatory reporting.

In 1980, he moved to the marketing department of Talman Home Federal Savings and Loan in Chicago. As Research Analyst, Mr. O'Meara's responsibilities included primary and secondary market research, industry analysis, competitive tracking, and branch performance evaluation.

Currently Director of Market Research for the Raddon Financial Group, Mr. O'Meara is responsible for consumer and commercial market research, pricing studies, financial analysis, and market location evaluations.

Mr. O'Meara received his B.B.A. degree in Marketing from Western Illinois University in 1978. He received his M.B.A. from DePaul University, Chicago, Illinois.

MARKETING INDIVIDUAL RETIREMENT ACCOUNTS

Gary H. Raddon
President
Raddon Financial Group

Robert O'Meara
Vice President
Raddon Financial Group

Certainly, the market for individual retirement accounts is changing. But, despite some arguments to the contrary, it will remain a strong and profitable market in the foreseeable future. It is important that financial services institutions maintain their IRA business and structure marketing programs that will allow them to continue to grow in this area.

An IRA is a major relationship-building tool, and therefore also has a marketing application far beyond its own product-profitability. IRAs have been called the core accounts of the future. Research by Raddon Financial Group and others indicates that as a family or single person's IRA account grows and as the percentage of liquid assets is invested in an IRA, the location of that retirement account is a strong indicator of which institution holds the household's primary financial relationship. In short, as more institutions offer many of the same types of products and services, the location of the IRA plays a great role in establishing the strongest customer-financial services provider relationship.

A financial organization must, then, continue to meet its competitors with timely, efficient products that allow them to retain their IRA customer relationships and develop new ones.

But IRAs present some unique marketing problems because a firm is not marketing a single product but rather a number of different products, many of which may not fit comfortably into your customers' recognition of your product line. An example is a bank marketing a mutual fund as part of its IRA program.

Also, keep in mind that IRAs are a classic example of "need-driven" investment sales. In order to successfully compete in the IRA marketplace, an institution's salesforce must be trained to understand customers' individual needs and objectives.

Furthermore, it needs to be recognized that IRA investors are *shoppers,* and they routinely select the services that meet their needs, often from a variety of product providers. They also reject services and products that do not measure up to their objectives, even if those services are offered by institutions with which they already have relationships.

To attract and retain IRA business, financial institutions must not only be able to offer value, but offer the *right* value. Consequently, they must keep abreast of their clients' needs through market research. They also must maintain a competitive position through constant review of the products that are being offered by competing firms locally and nationally, whether they are banks, savings and loans, brokerage houses, mutual fund companies, insurance companies or financial planners.

In short, successful IRA programs comprise a firm which aggressively goes after this market, a salesforce that understands how various products can fit into their customers' retirement plans, and products already on the shelf when the customer says "Yes."

Obviously, the Tax Reform Act of 1986 (TRA-86) has made IRAs more complicated for both issuers and consumers, which also complicates IRA marketing programs. However, the popularity of IRAs continues to increase, and IRA providers will find their new marketing efforts well worthwhile.

Tables 1–3 demonstrate how IRA usage increased from Fall 1985 to Fall 1986.

Table 1: IRA Usage By Age

Age Group	*Fall 1985*	*Fall 1986*
18 to 34	17%	24%
35 to 44	37%	43%
45 to 54	37%	50%
55 to 64	41%	48%
65 and over	10%	20%
TOTAL	24%	34%

(Source: National Consumer Research, Raddon Financial Group.)

The fact that 34 percent of all households had IRAs in 1986 represents a 41 percent increase over 1985.

Further, this study indicates that the reasons people open or add to IRAs will be largely unaffected by TRA-86.

Table 2: IRA Investment Goals By Income Group

		Annual Income	
Major Reason for Investing	*$25K or Less*	*$25–$50K*	*$50K–Over*
Build for Retirement	48%	42%	31%
Save on Taxes	27%	33%	45%
Defer Taxes on Income	13%	19%	17%

(Source: National Consumer Research, Raddon Financial Group, 1986.)

This bodes well for the continued interest in IRAs. Those people who are investing to build capital for retirement can be expected to continue their contributions. People whose primary IRA strategy is deferring taxes will be unaffected by TRA-86.

Table 3: IRA Investment Goals By Age Group

Major Reason for Investing	*Age Groups* 18-34	35-44	45-54	55-64	65 and Over
Build for Retirement	52%	39%	36%	34%	24%
Save on Taxes	32%	35%	39%	38%	30%
Defer Taxes on on Income	12%	12%	18%	24%	27%
Other	4%	14%	7%	4%	19%

(Source: National Consumer Research, Raddon Financial Group, l986.)

Again, the combination of building for retirement and *deferring* taxes presents ample evidence of continued IRA use.

But this survey also fuels consideration of new marketing strategies to keep up with the changes caused—or likely to be wrought—by the new federal tax law. For example, many of those who judge their primary IRA goal to be tax savings during the current tax year will likely be interested in saving on taxes *each* year. So IRA marketing plans should include a strong educational effort to reach people who have much to gain by deferring taxes on income, even at the new lower tax rates.

IRAS IN THE NEW MARKETING ENVIRONMENT

It is not enough to judge the new marketing environment for IRAs solely on the basis of a new tax law. The ever-increasing number of competitors, the cycles of investment markets that make one type of instrument more attractive than another and the demographics of an IRA issuers' natural market all play significant roles.

Currently, commercial banks still hold the largest market share of IRA funds, but they are slipping in that role, as shown in Table 4.

Table 4: IRA Market Share of Financial Institutions

	Market Share 1985	*Market Share 1986*	*Gain/Loss*
Commercial Banks	28.9%	26.9%	-6.9%
Savings and Loans	22.5%	21.5%	-4.4%
Mutual Funds	14.0%	18.3%	+30.7%
Stockbrokers	11.6%	14.9%	+28.4%
Life Insurance Cos.	9.5%	7.4%	-22.1%
Credit Unions	7.5%	7.1%	-5.3%
Mutual Savings Banks	6.0%	3.9%	-35.0%

(Source: *IRA Reporter*, 1986.)

The growth of mutual funds and the products normally offered through brokerage houses grew at the expense of every other type of financial product line. Part of this surely is the result of the continuing upward movement of the equities market. Yet, it indicates that IRA investors are willing to be more aggressive.

With the new tax law changes in effect, tax savings will be negated for many investors, so there will be an ongoing emphasis on return.

Not all IRA holders are willing to take on the risks inherent in purchasing mutual fund shares. But many more of your customers are, and the impact is real. The proverbial "little old lady in tennis shoes" is now purchasing Treasury Bills, buying into mutual funds, or taking the interest from her bank CD and buying bonds.

The trends expressed in the *IRA Reporter* market share data also show the growing national scope of customers' pursuit of profitable IRAs. An institution can no longer measure its success by looking at its market share against the other traditional financial institutions in its area, such as banks, savings and loans and credit unions. All your traditional competitors may be losing deposits or growing at a slower rate than your new competitors.

The easy answer is to offer every conceivable product to be all things to all people. This is not practical, and it is surely bad business judgment. The next best thing is to understand what your customers want and structure programs that meet their needs.

If you have a broad spectrum of customers in terms of age, income and liquid assets, a broad product line becomes a necessity. If your organization has a fairly well-defined and limited customer base, a smaller set of well-chosen, solid performing instruments can make a profitable IRA product line.

Tables 5–7 break down by investments who uses what instruments in their IRAs.

Table 5: IRA Users By Age Groups

Investment Type	*Total*	*18–34*	*35–44*	*45–54*	*55–64*	*65 and Over*
Certificates of Deposit	40%	35%	35%	43%	42%	57%
Money Market Account	27%	24%	28%	23%	32%	27%
Regular Savings	22%	24%	18%	21%	25%	22%
Stock Mutual Fund	22%	18%	33%	21%	14%	16%
Self-Directed	18%	22%	18%	15%	20%	11%
Bond Mutual Fund	6%	8%	6%	5%	3%	8%
Other Fund	8%	5%	10%	13%	9%	3%
Ginnie Mae Fund	3%	1%	2%	6%	4%	0%

(Source: National Consumer Research, Raddon Financial Group, l986.)

In applying this information to the design of marketing programs, products promotion should be matched to targeted areas of interest or lack of interest.

For example, if a stock mutual fund is looking for its heaviest concentration of users, it will find them in the 35-44-year-old range. Perhaps it can position stock funds as an opportunity for higher yields than those available from CDs, this group's most popular IRA investment. Similar types of analyses should be done according to income, liquid assets and lifestyles.

Table 6: IRA Users By Income Groups

Investment Type	*Total*	*Less than $25K*	*$25–50K*	*$50K and Over*
Certificates of Deposit	41%	39%	38%	42%
Money Market Account	27%	30%	25%	29%
Stock Mutual Fund	22%	16%	19%	35%
Regular Savings	22%	27%	20%	22%
Ginnie Mae Fund	3%	--	2%	6%
Bond Mutual Fund	6%	7%	4%	8%
Other Fund	8%	4%	10%	11%
Self-Directed	18%	23%	17%	19%

Table 7: IRA Users By Liquid Assets

Investment Type	*Total*	*Less than $10K*	*$10–25K*	*$25–39K*	*$40K and Over*
Certificates of Deposit	44%	21%	24%	31%	25%
Money Market Account	30%	27%	19%	31%	23%
Regular Savings	22%	25%	25%	31%	20%
Stock Mutual Fund	25%	22%	28%	28%	21%
Ginnie Mae Fund	3%	21%	7%	36%	36%
Bond Mutual Fund	6%	23%	31%	23%	23%
Other Fund	8%	33%	23%	26%	18%
Self-Directed	18%	42%	18%	23%	17%

Charting lifestyles can be a little more tricky, and certainly requires more analysis of interview data. Our research, presented in Table 8, divides the customer market for financial services into eight distinct types of customers. These segments are created by grouping people of similar lifestyles, values and attitudes toward money and banking.

Table 8: Lifestyle Profile of IRA Holders

Lifestyle Groups	*% of U.S. Households*	*% With IRA*	*% of IRA Holders*	*Average IRA Balance*
Accumulator Leaders	14%	60%	25%	$9,330
Price Alert	13%	36%	14%	$5,960
Institution Dependents	13%	31%	12%	$8,740
Ambitious Security Driven	13%	30%	12%	$6,280
Traditionalists	13%	28%	10%	$7,820
Service Seekers	8%	28%	10%	$6,640
Convenience Driven	9%	27%	7%	$7,290
Trendy Credit Buyers	15%	26%	11%	$7,280

Lifestyle and personal attitudes obviously affect purchasing behavior, and this can be especially true of investments. Consequently, whether for IRAs or for just general information, it is extremely helpful to have some type of lifestyle survey taken to determine how an institution's customers will react to new economic circumstances and to new products.

Table 8 provides examples of the types of customer groups that can be established and the characteristics that allow market researchers and analysts to group them. This type of breakdown is especially useful in marketing investments such as IRAs, where so many different instruments are offered over such a broad range of prospects.

Accumulator leaders are people with above-average incomes, over 35 years of age, white collar, outgoing, and active in their communities. They believe they are better off financially now than a year ago.

Price alert people are slightly younger than average, have high incomes, active in personal money management.

Institution dependents are older than average, have high incomes, place a strong emphasis on financial safety and look to financial institutions for advice.

Ambitious-security-driven people are older people with slightly less than average incomes who place a great deal of emphasis on investment safety.

Traditionalists are the largest cluster group, the oldest in average age. They place great importance on personalized service.

Service seekers want fast accurate handling of their accounts. They are slightly younger than average and generally hold higher-than-average liquid assets.

Convenience-driven people are people just starting out—young, lower-than-average incomes, with a heavy emphasis on access to services and to their funds.

Trendy credit buyers are the second largest group. They are spenders, not savers, and have average incomes but the lowest liquid balances.

By cross-referencing these groups with age, income and liquid asset information, accurate market segments can be developed so specific products can be targeted to specific types of consumers.

THE NEED FOR INVESTMENT ALTERNATIVES

With so many types of IRA investments competing for the dollars of so many diverse consumers, the structuring of product lines and the design of marketing programs obviously can be complex. However, there are some general observations that be made about the IRA market. All point to the desire of consumers for a variety of investment alternatives.

A Willingness to Shift Assets

IRA investors consistently indicate a willingness to move their IRA funds to other investments. This willingness is most pronounced (one-in-four) in households with higher liquid assets and higher income, in which the head of the household is 35 to 54 years old.

Rate Sensitivity

Another factor is the desire for greater returns. How much added interest is required to get an investor to move his or her account? When questioned about their rate sensitivity, between 20 and 31 percent of the respondents to Raddon's 1986 survey indicated they would be willing to move their IRA for an additional 1 percent. A 2-percent differential could move up to 52 percent of customers.

Willingness to Take on Risk

A substantial percentage of people have indicated that they are willing to put at least some of their IRA assets in instruments that carry an inherent risk. Overall, in our research, nearly half the respondents expressed a willingness to assume risk for the opportunity of greater return. The group most willing was again, the 35–44-year-old group. They were followed closely by those in the 45–54 age bracket.

UTILIZING INFORMATION SOURCES

Where should advertising and promotion dollars go to generate the greatest amount of interest in an institution's IRAs? Decisions about where IRA contributions will be placed are often made in a brief period just before federal tax forms are filed. Consequently, promotional efforts should utilize a wide range of media and techniques, and should provide prospects with convenient access to rates/returns and product features.

Particular emphasis should be paid the staff; the lobby "point-of-purchase" advertising (including rate boards); and the local newspapers, both in terms of advertising and inclusion in IRA news reports.

Research conducted by Raddon polled investors on where they get their IRA information. Results are shown in Table 9.

Again, IRA providers should take a broad-brush approach in promoting the rates and features of their IRA products. Sales staff should be trained to provide all the important information about each product that customers require, whether by phone or in person. Firms should consider preparing

Table 9: Sources for IRA Information

Source	Percent
Comparison Charts in Newspapers	41.4%
Newspaper Advertisements	40.2%
In-Person Visits to Institutions	35.8%
Discussions with Friends	29.8%
Phone Inquiries to Institutions	29.1%
Interest Rate Hotlines	8.5%
Others	16.0%

(Source: Raddon Financial Group, 1986.)

special information packages on their products for local newspapers and for financial reporters on local broadcast media. And they should advertise IRA products with both signs and literature in their lobbies.

RETIREMENT MANAGEMENT ACCOUNT

A relatively new way for institutions to attract and hold IRA funds is through Retirement Management Accounts (RMAs). They fulfill a variety of marketing needs by enabling financial salespeople to offer customers broad-based services and a variety of products. They also provide them with the opportunity to influence purchasers' choices. Furthermore, an RMA can be sold for its overall benefit, rather than the rate or past return on any one instrument purchased through it.

RMAs can be marketed in ways, but certainly one way is to promote their convenience. Many customers who are in the habit of opening a new account or buying a new CD each year will welcome an RMA because it will place all their records and investments in a single account. RMAs currently being offered provide each customer with a consolidated statement of their full IRA position on a quarterly basis.

RMAs require that an institution arrange for accounts to be set up for its customers through the growing number of third-party firms (usually large banks, brokerage houses or mutual fund companies) that structure such accounts. The third party handles the transactions, keeps the records and provides the customer with a personalized statement on your corporate letterhead listing all the customer's IRA investments and the value of each.

Whenever your customer wishes to purchase an investment from your product line, the deposit is placed in your institution, and a record of the deposit is sent the third party.

As your customer's balance increases, you have the opportunity to introduce additional products to the account—yours or those of other firms.

Bear in mind that even if the RMA includes substantial investments in other firms' products, you retain the account and the customer relationship. You also stand to gain sales commissions on those dollars going to other firms' products.

Many financial organizations already have "clubs" for customers aged 55 and over. These are excellent vehicles for introducing Retirement Management Accounts.

CONCLUSION

The popularity of IRAs will diminish somewhat due to the reduction in deductibility of contributions from some types of investors. However, the market will remain strong, and the account will remain an important vehicle for establishing and maintaining core relationships with a broad range of key customer groups.

This market also will continue to be competitive. Therefore, an institution should seek to offer a broad range of IRA products. If it does not now, it should move quickly to develop the ability to offer a range of investment alternatives. Otherwise, its customers will most certainly find those products elsewhere.

Financial institutions must base their IRA marketing programs on an understanding of customer needs, and sales personnel must be trained to understand those needs and to recommend products that meet those needs. This sounds a lot simpler than it is. IRA investors are shoppers, and many sales are made on the basis of phone inquiries and lobby visits. If prospects do not get the answers they are looking for the first time around, there may well not be a second chance.

Finally, because IRA contributions are often made within a tight timeframe just before tax filing, promotional and informational efforts should take advantage of a wide range of techniques.

Chapter Twelve

James V. Shafer

Mr. Shafer is Director, Financial Products/Financial Planning for the Equitable Life of New York. He has been with the Equitable for thirty-four years and is a member of the National Association of Life Underwriters, the American Society of CLU and ChFC and the International Association of Financial Planners.

He has written on topics related to insurance and financial and estate planning.

Mr. Shafer is a graduate of Carroll College, Waukesha, Wisconsin.

Nancy R. Scheck

Nancy R. Scheck is Associate Director, Advanced Underwriting, for the Midwest Operations of the Equitable. Ms. Scheck is a graduate of Northwestern University and Loyola Law School. Prior to joining the Equitable, Ms. Scheck was in private practice, dealing with several aspects of estate planning including wills, trusts, buy-sell agreements and estate and gift tax. She is a member of the Illinois State Bar Association Section of Estate Planning.

Ms. Scheck joined the Midwestern Operations Underwriting Staff of the Equitable in 1985. She is responsible for consultation and technical assistance in estate planning, retirement planning, business insurance and taxation. She has developed and presented workshops on estate planning, business insurance, and retirement planning.

MARKETING LIFE INSURANCE PRODUCTS FOR ESTATE PLANNING

James V. Shafer, CLU & ChFC
Director, Financial Planning/Financial Products
The Equitable

Nancy R. Scheck, JD
Associate Director, Advanced Underwriting
The Equitable

The need for life insurance may seem clear to those of us who work in the field, but the marketing process for life insurance products must be based on helping customers realize that they have this need.

Life insurance is the one vehicle that can guarantee the exact amount of money necessary at the exact time it is required. Because of this unique feature, life insurance has a strong position in estate planning. In fact, it stands alone as the one tool in personal estate planning that can effectively fulfill the need for cash that will be created by the death of an individual.

A person's requirements for life insurance vary according to such factors as income, source of income, family situation and personal financial goals. The various life insurance products that have been developed over the past 20 years represent the industry's attempt to give its salesforce the equipment to offer the type of policy (or policies) that meet customers needs and fit into their overall financial game plan.

Market segmentation, then, is a key element in life insurance product development. However, product use is not often easy to predict based only on broad demographic segments. Life insurance is a highly personalized need. After product development, the most important part of a successful marketing effort is training agents to work with each customer and match the proper product with his or her specific needs.

Generally, as a person's wealth increases, so does his or her need for life insurance and other elements of estate planning. For example, not everyone will have an estate large enough to incur federal estate tax liability. Those who do, however, need help coping with very high estate tax rates (currently for estates in excess of $3 million). Very wealthy clients will need life insurance products that provide liquidity to pay taxes and replace the dollars that will be lost from the estate because of tax liability.

But good estate planning and a sound life insurance program are not limited to the wealthy. Those individuals without substantial wealth may require life insurance to provide income for their surviving spouses or to help replace their earnings for major expenses, such as their children's education.

However, as a practical matter, wealthy individuals—particularly those entrepreneurs who own and run successful businesses—require more and more varied types of financial services, including life insurance products. As Table 1 (from the Life Insurance Marketing and Research Association, Inc.) [LIMRA]) indicates, the policy sizes and premiums vary greatly according to income groups.

Table 1: Life Insurance Sales By Income

Income	*% of Policies*	*% of Sales Volume*	*Average Policy Size*	*Premium Per Policy*
$50,000 and over	11%	28%	$185,250	$1,951
40,000–49,000	6	8	106,480	993
30,000–39,999	15	17	82,590	705
20,000–29,999	29	25	62,680	530
10,000–19,999	33	20	43,350	350
Under $10,000	6	2	26,490	249
	100%	100%	$ 72,840	$ 660

Source: *The Buyer Study*, LIMRA.

PRODUCTS AND THEIR APPLICATIONS

Whatever market is targeted, the company must decide what product it would like to sell to that market. In this decision, administrative and marketing personnel must consider which products they will design in-house and which they will "import" from other companies, and resolve any questions as to feasibility and profitability. The most popular current products fall into the following general categories:

A standard *whole life* product may be the answer to many estate planning problems, since it has a level premium and is a guaranteed source of funds upon the death of an individual. The new whole life policies now issued by many life insurance companies have "Vanish Provisions" which enable policyholders, because of the greater amount of interest credited to the policies, to terminate the out-of-pocket payment of premiums.

In *level premium* policies, an annual premium is established. This premium never varies and will buy a guaranteed amount of death benefit. These policies are very attractive to those in more advanced age brackets.

In *single premium* policies, all insurance costs for the rest of the insured life are paid at one time. This is an attractive option for those with a large amount of ready cash.

Universal life policies have "flexible" or "adjustable" premiums, and the cash value buildup depends on the premiums paid. These policies appeal to younger individuals who are able to buy the life insurance they need at term costs with the ability to increase their policy value as their needs change (see Table 2).

Variations on these products are targeted to customers' personal needs. For example, some *flexible premium* variable policies will appeal to those who want inexpensive life insurance combined with investment options. This product is a marriage of universal and variable life insurance. Like universal life, there is no set premium. The policy is structured as a term plan with investment of the balance of the premium through the insurance company. As in a variable insurance contract, the insurance company offers a number of investment options in which the extra money can be placed, such as a common stock account, an aggressive stock account, a balance account or even a money market account. Of course, funds are currently being developed to take advantage of high-yield investments or international stock markets.

Table 2: Product Sales By Agents (in percent of policies)

	Cash Value	*Term*	*Universal Life*	*Variable Life*
Distribution of Sample				
Adult male	46%	68%	65%	67%
Adult female	33	31	26	21
Juvenile	21	1	9	12
	100%	100%	100%	100%
Size of Policy				
$300,001–$500,000	1%	4%	1%	3%
100,000–300,000	10	46	30	25
50,000–99,999	18	28	40	30
25,000–49,999	24	16	25	39
Under 25,000	47	6	4	3
	100%	100%	100%	100%
Age of Insured				
55 and over	7%	4%	7%	6%
45–54	9	11	12	11
35–44	17	32	26	25
25–34	28	43	33	34
15–25	18	9	13	12
Under 15	21	1	9	12
	100%	100%	100%	100%
Marital Status				
Single	38%	10%	26%	30%
Married	46	77	68	58
Widowed, divorced, or separated	4	3	4	2
Unknown	12	10	2	10
	100%	100%	100%	100%
Income of Gainfully Employed				
$40,000 and over	15%	23%	19%	34%
30,000–39,999	13	18	19	14
20,000–29,999	29	30	30	33
10,000–19,999	37	26	28	17
Under 10,000	6	3	4	2
	100%	100%	100%	100%

Table 2 (continued)

	Cash Value	*Term*	*Universal Life*	*Variable Life*
Occupation				
Professional/ executive	31%	56%	45%	54%
Nonprofessional	33	32	35	25
Student aged 15 and over	6	2	4	3
Homemaker	8	9	6	6
Juvenile	22	1	10	12
	100%	100%	100%	100%

Source: *The Buyer Study*, LIMRA.

This product generally is targeted at an upscale market, 35 to 45 years old and earning between $35,000- $50,000 annually. This market is likely to consist of married, non-traditional risk takers willing to assume the risk of the investment. Looking closely at this profile, it is easy to see how flexible premium variable life might appeal to the young and upwardly mobile. There are over 77 million "baby boomers," those born between 1945 and 1965. This is by no means a homogenous group, but it certainly is a large market.

There are no formal statistics on the sale of flexible premium variable life, but early readings show the sale of this product has not been restricted to "baby boomers." The investment portion of this product has appealed to people in all ages who are interested in taking advantage of the stock market's rise.

One product designed specifically for the estate planning market is the joint or "second to die" policy. This policy insures two people and only matures at the death of the second. Because of the unlimited marital deduction, estate tax liability can be deferred from the first death to the second death. But at the second death, all taxes will be due. The second to die policy will take care of federal estate taxes that will be due on the death of the surviving spouse.

New products may be developed to fit the estate planning market, but for the most part the last couple of years have seen a boon in product development, with the distribution force being drawn to each new product as it came out. In fact, according to a LIMRA survey of the life insurance industry in 1985, 47 percent of new premiums of the companies surveyed came from new policies replacing old ones. This dropped to 43 percent in 1986. Previously, 15 to 20 percent of new life insurance premiums typically came from replacements. This is an indication of what has been happening in the life insurance industry. However, it should be pointed out that once the development of new products slows down, there may well be a large drop in new sales unless agents go back to the basics of "need selling." Need selling is simply selling the client what he needs, taking into account the clients goals and objectives, not just the agent's attempt to sell the "product of the week."

New products, of course, will still come out, although they may largely be refinements of existing products, such as a single premium variable that takes advantage of the popularity of single premium and gives the consumer the choice of investment decisions.

Existing products will also be revamped to adjust to new needs and tax changes. An example of this is the move away from the minimum deposit, which allowed payment of the least amount of premiums so that loan interest was deductible. Since interest paid to the policyholder is no longer deductible under new tax laws, these products will be re-designed to include a vanishing premium, which allows the payment of the premium for the least number of years while still allowing the policy to sustain itself.

Aside from changes of this kind, product development should slow down in part because it is too expensive to continue to develop new products at the current rate and because certainly some of the premium dollars attributed to these policies have come from existing business.

The next few years should give the distribution force a chance to evaluate all the new products and choose the product that best fits the need of the particular client.

It is only after these decisions have been made that the company can consider how to market their life insurance products. There are two groups to consider in any discussion of marketing life insurance products for estate planning: the salesforce and the customers.

MARKETING TO THE SALESFORCE

The first step in marketing insurance is marketing to the distribution network. The distribution network can be made up of the following, either alone or in any combination: insurance agents, investment brokers, banks and other savings institutions, financial planners, national retail chain stores, and of course the insurer's own direct marketing efforts to consumers. For ease in referring to this group and because, for many of the major life insurance companies, the strongest distribution network is the agency force, we will refer to this first level as marketing to the agency force.

In order to market to the agency force, the life insurance company must provide product materials and information. Also, good agent training on products and on estate planning is necessary. Part of this training should involve sales ideas and suggested funding ideas. The company also should provide market information, detailing to whom this product is targeted, why this particular segment of the population needs this product, and how the agency force can reach this market.

MARKETING TO THE CUSTOMERS

The second level is marketing to the public. We already have shown that the need for life insurance is clear; once we have demonstrated this need to the public, sales should result, as long as we have a good product.

Within his or her own sales market, the agent must establish a target market for specific products and decide how to reach those markets. Any successful marketing strategy in the estate planning area is necessarily tied to the *education* of the market, which will demonstrate the need for the products, and also to relationship building between the agent and client.

Prospecting methods that incorporate these two factors include seminar selling, direct mail and telemarketing. These methods work well in combination. For example, seminar selling is an excellent way of finding prospects, educating them and building a relationship, but direct mail or telemarketing may be the tool that helps find many seminar invitees.

The more times an agent has his name in front of the public in reference to estate planning, the easier it will be for that agent to build a reputation as an estate planner, in the eyes of the public and in the eyes of other professionals involved in this area.

The life insurance company can certainly aid the agency force in marketing by developing mailers, helping agents locate lists, providing seminar selling information to the agents and making materials available as slides or video tapes suitable for presentation. It is very important that a life insurance company endeavor to have its name out in front of the public and to have a reputation as a good company.

The Agent-Client Relationship

The agent also must provide some value-added services for the client. Anyone can attempt to sell life insurance, but the agent who does well works hard at it and gives his clients a reason to buy from *him*. Many agents do financial/retirement/estate planning so that they can help their clients make specific plans meeting their individual needs and goals.

Many agents combine all these services together with products in a financial planning package. This may help supplement what other professionals do for their clients and help reduce clients' accountant's or attorney's fees. The insurance company can assist the agents by providing or locating good software systems for them to use.

A life insurance agent, in order to be competitive in today's financial services marketplace, must be very capable of selling both life insurance and investment products. Most life insurance companies now have their own broker-dealerships which allow their agents to sell both mutual funds and an assortment of limited partnerships. As companies create their own broker-dealers, they often sell their own proprietary limited partnerships and mutual funds, and the products of other sponsors as well. Thus, the agent and the insurance company have the opportunity to control the dollars of the clients whom they serve. By building a solid relationship, the agent (and the company) have the means to make repeat sales. For example, as a client's children finish their education and he begins looking toward retirement, he is not only interested in various annuities but also in investing in mutual funds and limited partnerships. These new products can help create a much tighter bond in the relationship between the client and the life insurance agent, while providing the agent with more opportunity to be in contact with his client.

Life insurance agents traditionally develop much closer relationships with their clients than do average stock and bond salesmen because they go out to see their clients or have them in their offices for in-depth interviews in order to determine the type of policies which will best serve their clients' needs. In the process of the fact-finding interview and in the fulfillment of commitments to the client, the bond becomes stronger. This, in turn, allows the life insurance agent to turn to non-insurance products to meet the savings and retirement needs of clients.

CONCLUSION

Consumers today are well educated, and they like comparison shopping. In the competitive financial services industry, the marketing of life insurance products must include added service and value for the clients. Insurance companies are now marketing through credit card companies, banks and department stores. Consequently, in order for agents to be an efficient salesforce, they will need more time to do what they do best—sell. To aid their salesforces, insurance companies of the future will be required to provide a full staff to perform support functions, prospect, prepare sales presentations and provide technical advice from legal and accounting professionals. In this way, the agents can give clients the extra value of a team approach, while at the same time keeping their sales productivity at a high level.

Chapter Thirteen

Stephen A. Kerns

Stephen A. Kerns is Vice President of the Weiser Group, a consulting firm that provides marketing advice to a wide range of banks, brokerage houses, insurance companies and other financial service organizations. Mr. Kerns has had extensive experience in developing and implementing financial marketing strategies in his present position with the Weiser Group, as well as in his earlier position with the Chicago Board of Options Exchange.

MARKETING TO CORPORATE TREASURERS AND ASSET MANAGERS

Stephen A. Kerns
Vice President
Weiser Group

Marketers of financial services to corporations and institutions face many of the same problems as their retail counterparts. However, the competitive situation is even more complex.

To begin, many types of financial services have changed substantially. The days when corporate lending meant a "plain vanilla" commercial loan are gone. Likewise, a solid track record in equity or AAA bond markets qualifies an investment manager as only a *niche* player in these days of stock index options, junk bonds and fungible securities and futures products.

In addition, the number of competitors in the market is increasing rapidly, and even the newest market entrants find financial managers within corporations and institutions willing to listen to their marketing message. The past 10 or so years have shown that most new financial products and services are in fact good ideas. Also, treasury officers and inside money managers are in large part receptive to new ideas and new approaches to old problems.

Many of these changes, of course, are the result of deregulation. But others are the result of new regulations. For example, the Monetary Control Act of 1980 gave the Federal Reserve the power to crack down on "float." This in turn made banks offer more near-market rate products, such as interest-bearing checking, money market accounts or zero-balance accounts with such features as unlimited sweep arrangements.

Suddenly, the mundane question of handling short-term funds turned into a major product-design and marketing effort.

The biggest change in corporate funds management is, however, technological. With the increasing capabilities of mini- and micro-computers and more sophisticated and flexible software, corporate treasury operations have become a much more integrated package for most companies.

Instead of a number of functions operating more or less independently, the principal areas of corporate financial management are now part of an integrated treasury management system (ITMS). Cash, collections, payments, debt, investment returns and operating funds all can be part of a single integrated picture that allows treasury personnel to know on a day-to-day basis what financial services are needed and whether necessary cash is available. (See Figure 1.)

An ITMS also provides information for long-range planning. The information collected from the cash management, debt, investment and accounting systems comprises the databases upon which corporate financial officers decide such issues as where and how to place investment funds or what sort of debt the company is willing to undertake.

From a marketing perspective, ITMS has internalized some of the functions that used to come from the outside. However, as more commercial financial services are fee-based, new opportunities have been created for both multi-service and *niche* players.

At most companies, internal financial managers have a greater awareness of their financial status and needs. In their external relationships, they seek companies with broad enough expertise to be part of their planning process and specialized financial firms who provide above-average service in specific areas where the client company needs help.

The key, then, is to demonstrate *value.* As a rule, today's corporations are very well-equipped and willing to engage in a number of different relationships with providers of financial and investment services. Differentiating your services from others is a function of proving you can do it better. This is obviously very relative to specific types of financial institutions engaged in different types of business. (Specific marketing efforts within banking and investments are discussed in later chapters.)

There are, however, common threads running through corporate/institutional financial services that affect marketing programs. Too often in the past, marketing considerations were rarely taken into account in developing either individual products or overall product lines. Once they were developed, someone asked, "Now, how do we sell these things?"

Figure 1

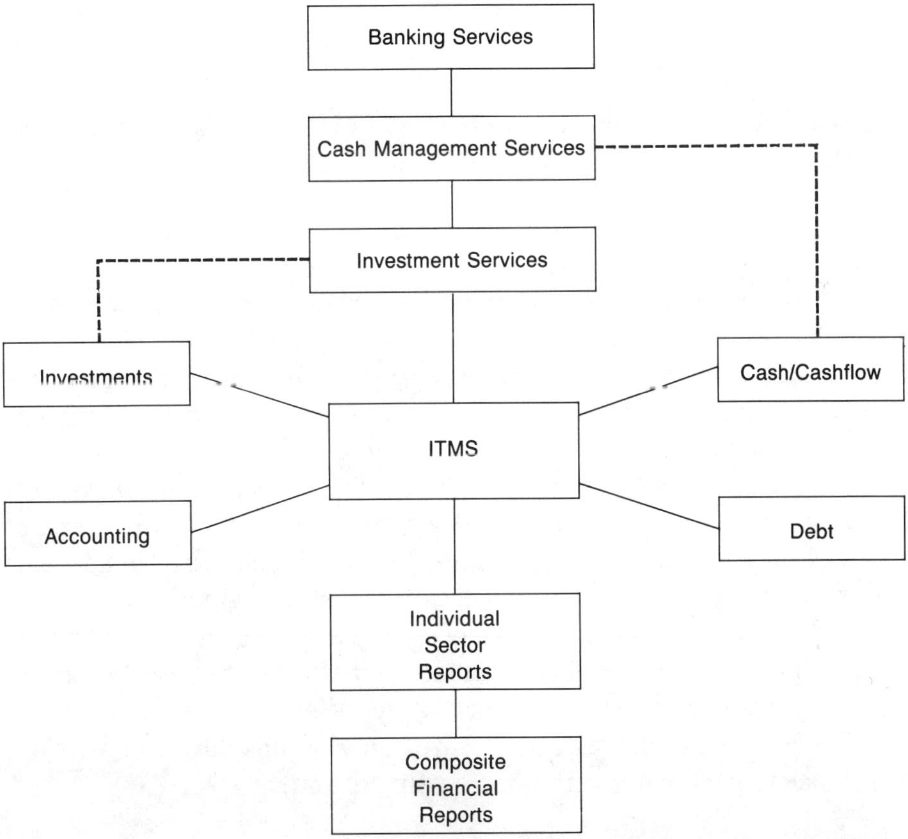

Furthermore, products or services often were offered because the competition offered them. Though this can be a very legitimate reason for including them in a product line, little thought was given to designing features that would make new products work in tandem with the existing product line.

Product lines were often developed around existing clients. Product features, then, are fine for the current client base, but are they going to help that bank, commercial financing company, asset manager or mutual fund company grow to meet its long-term goals? Such companies are relying more and more on their marketing departments to determine what product relationships can help overall customer relationships grow and grow profitably.

DEVELOPING A CORPORATE/INSTITUTIONAL MARKETING PLAN

As commercial financial services and institutional investments become increasingly transactional and sectored businesses, it is not an oversimplification to say that marketing plans should be based on what business can be transacted profitably with which customers. The failure of many marketing efforts is that they seek to sell the same products to everyone without targeting sales efforts. The result can be a mixture of wasted time and effort and missed opportunities.

As financial service generally becomes a fee-oriented business (as opposed to interest-oriented), financial services providers must be certain that the fees they generate within their customer relationships are adequate to properly and profitably cover the expense of bringing in the business. Consequently, a financial services company should deal from its strongest hands. This process begins with some basic questions: What is the company's best performing product? Why? Who is using this service, and why? What other services can the firm provide this customer base? The best place to get the answers is from your customers.

Market Research

The sales process in the corporate/institutional market has been based almost exclusively on the ability of sales personnel to know and service their customers. Large-scale market research is often viewed as unnecessary, and perhaps a source of internal friction between sales and marketing personnel.

However, well-planned and executed market research certainly is an integral part of new product design, refinement of existing products and targeting products to market segments. However, corporate/institutional service needs are very relative to the customer/client—much more so than in the retail market. Also, these needs change quickly and dramatically. Because of this, market research for corporate/institutional products and services must work hand-in-hand with the impressions and information gathered through the salesforce.

The norm in the industry now is a small amount of research. It usually is conducted after the decision to offer a product or service has been made, and sometimes after the product has been designed.

There is a middle ground between mass-market questionnaires and luncheon conversations with customers. Many firms use a less formal type of research that is conducted *through the salesforce* to augment more formal research. Relationship managers and brokers ask customers about their needs, about their relationships with other providers (when possible) and the product or service needs that are not being met. The responses are part of the customer information files (CIF), but also are compiled in larger, more comprehensive reports. Though this approach obviously lacks the precision of a survey with weighted answers and response alternatives, it can provide a general view of marketplace needs and supplement detailed market research.

Resist the temptation to make "seat-of-pants" decisions. The idea, of course, is to determine what products and services are being used, how and why customers select providers, and what ingredients they take into account in determining the value of the service. The answers to these questions are the key to successful marketing, and the anwers should not merely be based on a guess.

Making these sorts of determinations requires a financial organization to segment its markets, study those segments' needs and build relationships based on servicing those needs.

Market Segmentation

Customer information files list information relevant in assessing the customer's current use of financial products and services and determining potential need and desire for additional services.

In the case of a commercial bank or finance company, for example, the CIF should contain information on the company's:

- *Size*, or in the case of larger companies, the size of the unit being serviced.

- Industry group(s), including specialties within their industries.
- *Market locations*, e.g. Northeastern United States; U.S.; Canada and Western Europe.
- *Type of ownership*, such as publicly held, partnership, sole proprietor, and so on.

Targeting Products

Based on responses collected by sales representatives or relationship managers, the institution's list of products should be ranked in order of importance *to the customers within those segments*. This allows the financial services provider to reëxamine its view of what its core businesses are within various market segments. It also can identify potential cross-selling opportunities.

Assume that a commercial bank serves a wide spectrum of corporate customers and wishes to increase market penetration among various types of middle-market and major national companies. Nearly all of its customer relationships include demand deposits and lines of credit. Where does it go from here?

It needs to create new areas of emphasis within its product line that meet the needs of each market segment. Some of these services will be interest-rate services and some will be fee-based. The important thing is to increase the number of products that are comprised in the bank's relationship to the overall segment. As this number grows, so do the opportunities for cross-sales and new product areas.

Using size and industry group as the criteria, products are ranked according what customers say they need. A hypothetical ranking of products for large and medium-sized companies can be as follows:

Middle-Market Manufacturers	*Major National Manufacturers*
1. Term loans	1. Money market services
2. Lockboxes	2. Investment advice
3. Time deposits	3. Deposit transfers
4. Trust services	4. Term loans
5. Money market services	5. Coin and currency
6. Deposit transfer	6. Time deposits
7. Coin and currency	7. Trust services
8. Revolving loans	8. Stock transfers

A hypothetical analysis can be made from the above ranking. For example, in asking themselves how the bank can further penetrate middle-market manufacturers, the marketing staff may conclude that differentiating itself from the competition in the first three service areas (term loans, lockboxes and time deposits) requires modifying or improving these services in some way, since it and its chief competitors offer very similar services in these areas.

If this is difficult to do profitably because of the nature of these products, then perhaps the bank can attract new customers and solidify existing relationships by paying more attention to trust and money market services. These are product areas where the difference between one institution and its competitors is more easily distinguished.

In the case of investment products, the type of fund, portfolio size, investment history, objectives and investment philosophy can all be delineated against specific investment vehicles to create an effective sales model.

Another method for analyzing product demand against a financial organization's current product line is to build a matrix that allows the marketing department to rank products not just against each other, but in the overall scope of customers' financial needs. The relationship managers ask not just what products are most and least important, but *how* important they are to funding the customers' operations and contributing to its entire financial health.

Using the same middle-market banking example, the responses would be delineated in the manner shown in Figure 2.

The bankers now can see what products are likely to be at the core of the relationship with a company in this segment.

The matrix also clearly points to the products/services that will help those relationships grow. In short, it provides information on those areas the bank needs to concentrate on in order to continue its business development among a specific group of current and potential customers.

CONCLUSION

It is important to note that research such as that described here requires a close working relationship between marketing, administrative and sales personnel. This relationship is necessary throughout the product development and marketing process.

Figure 2:

Product/Service	Critical	Very Important	Important	Moderately Important	Usually Not Important
Coin & Currency					X
Deposit Transfers				X	
Lock Boxes	X				
Money Market Services			X		
Revolving Loans					X
Term Loans	X				
Time Deposits		X			
Trust Services		X			

There has been much talk about corporate/institutional sales people providing consultative services to customers. The focus of much of the training these people receive is to equip them to fulfill this role. Training should be initiated to help sales personnel provide similar services *to their own companies.*

With the mass of new products, new competitors and new customer expectations, financial companies must give themselves every opportunity to anticipate changes in the market. Part of the marketing function, then, is to structure the product delivery mechanism as a two-way street through which the customer is served and the provider gains continuing insight into market demands.

Chapter Fourteen

Mary Ann Hagerty

Mary Ann Hagerty is Vice President, Marketing, LaSalle National Bank, Chicago, a member of the ABN/LASALLE group. The ABN/LASALLE group, headquartered in Chicago, is the management company for all of Algemene Bank Nederland N.V. (ABN Bank) North American operations.

Ms. Hagerty has been with the organization since 1968, holding various marketing positions in retail, commercial and corporate marketing. She holds a B.A. in Marketing from DePaul University, and M.B.A. in Finance from Loyola University. She graduated from the Graduate School of Banking, Madison, Wisconsin.

MARKETING BANKING SERVICES TO MIDDLE-MARKET COMPANIES

Mary Ann Hagerty
Vice President
LaSalle National Bank
ABN/LASALLE Group

MARKETING TO THE MIDDLE MARKET: EVERYONE'S SALVATION...OR A MOVING TARGET

To assist in the growth of middle-market businesses, bankers are being asked to analyze and provide advice on various strategies for their clients. The ability to differentiate your institution as the one that offers creative thinking and critical solutions to middle-market companies has become essential for a successful marketing effort.

In the past, middle-market needs were considered "vanilla", in that single product lines were required—credit services or a depository for funds or simple operating services. Today what is required is being that *one* institution that materially adds value to the product offerings. An example of a bank that successfully focused on the middle market is the American National Bank, Chicago's fifth largest institution. While the larger Chicago banks were courting the Fortune 1000 and large multinationals, American National targeted the smaller middle-market firms—those with sales between $5 million and $75 million, located within the Chicago. American National recognized the economic growth and health of these corporations and structured its long-term business strategy around their needs. More recently, large money-center banks in New York, Chicago, Pittsburgh and

Los Angeles also have found the value in middle-market relationships. Some have been successful, but many others have failed. Those that have been successful spent time analyzing their strengths and weaknesses compared to the needs and requirements of mid-size, growing companies. Through a thorough assessment, a bank can set itself apart from its competitors and gain a solid share of the middle market.

From the very largest institutions down to the community banks, the middle market has become a very attractive target. However, a very significant trend has emerged which has recently resulted in a significant advantage for smaller sized banks servicing the middle market.

The largest banks in the United States have shown a marked decline in commercial and industrial (C&I) loans, while the second-tier banks, those in the top 300 but not the nation's largest, have posted significant lending gains. These skewed results stem from both environmental and marketing trends. The sale of loans by the top 50 banks, through participations, has been required by federal regulators' new capital adequacy requirements. Also, the Fortune 1000 clients, the primary clients for the nation's largest banks, have access to national money markets and have turned to the commercial paper market for funds, thereby reducing loan demand. Consequently, the larger money center banks have adopted their marketing push to meet with investment banking- type products.

At the same time, smaller regional or city bankers who service the middle market have enjoyed strong loan demand in the past two years. According to the *American Banker's* annual survey of the top 300 commercial banks, C&I loans declined 6.1 percent at the top 10 banks in 1985 after falling 1.2 percent in 1984. However, business loans at lower tiered banks rose 20.5 percent in 1985 following a rise in 1984.

In addition to these shifts caused by environmental factors, the lower-tier banks have begun to formulate marketing approaches based on a relationship banking philosophy. This philosophy has become a focused objective, a strategy and an outcome, targeted to the middle market.

The strategic approach can be considered as a four-step process involving the following:

- Market Segmentation
- Core Services
- Relationship Management
- Relationship Pricing

Institutions focusing their attention on the middle market face both opportunities and challenges. The opportunities are many and often very attractive: higher loan demand, higher margins, loyalty to fewer banks and the real need to work with a bank for credit and operating services. On the other hand, the challenges are clear, too. How will you organize for maximum market penetration? What core services are required and what types of value-added services need to be considered and ultimately delivered?

Many players are involved in the middle-market game, but the big winners will be those institutions that provide the highest quality and most satisfying financial services to their clients. Bankers that serve this market genuinely need to know their client's business. You need to be an innovative problem-solver, and a creative thinker. You need to be supported by a financial institution that has the resources to deliver specialized services. Because the middle-market customer tends to rely on only one or two banks, it is critical the institution deliver a full range of value-added services.

One way of adding value to your services is to be sensitive to your customer firms' specific needs. In this regard, smaller banks often have the edge on multinational institutions.

MARKET SEGMENTATION

In market segmentation it is necessary to distinguish among industries, but also within particular industries. As an example, a market segment within the steel industry would be companies that manufacture flat rolled steel bars, or specialty steels. The objective here is to be as specific as possible, because an industrial market segment comprises a much more distinct group of companies that may or may not have similar requirements. Making the distinction between an "industry" and a "market" places you in a better position to identify target segments. For example, original equipment manufacturers (OEM), going up against after- market manufacturers, can employ these typical types of segmenting: by four-digit SIC's (standard industrial classifications), by client usage factors, by common buying factors, or by client size.

As a manager, you are going to want to make sure that your market segmentation is deep enough and that there are not too few, too many or unreachable market segments. Check your segmentation strategy against the following criteria to see if it is sound. Each segment should have:

- common customer requirements;
- measurable characteristics (sales, growth rate);
- common sales or distribution system; and
- known key success factors necessary to serve the segment now and in the future.

Market segmentation means making a product commitment in cash management services and investing in equipment and software that will bring flexible and providing creative fund-management solutions to your clients. And it goes without saying that the pure operating services of cash collection, disbursement and mobilization must be performed efficiently. Investments in automated lockbox equipment or treasury management workstations that utilize personal computers must be made. Delivery systems that move money around the country and the world need to be installed and maintained.

Let's look at asset management of employee benefit plans as a product that middle-market companies require. Depending on the company's objective and strategy, a variety of employee benefit plans are available.

A bank relationship manager must be able to match the client with the right plan or plans. This can be accomplished by developing a group of investment products and then mixing the investment funds depending on the client's strategy. This portfolio is constructed according to the client's definition of acceptable risk and expected rewards. Table 1 depicts different funds with different risk/rewards ratios. By developing different funds to match market client's employee benefit objectives, you are employing market segmentation and product segmentation analysis, thereby matching client needs with products.

CORE SERVICES

To make a relationship work effectively, a core service must be built. In marketing to the middle market, this core service must be credit related. Credit is primary because it's the heart of the corporation: it provides the working capital and the necessary liquidity to keep a company solid and, at the same time, opportunistic. The right strategy for structuring credit might involve fixed or floating interest rates, prime or LIBOR, secured or unsecured lending, interest rate swaps or leveraged buyouts.

Table 1

Name of Fund	*Investment Strategy*	*Risk/Results*
Money Market Fund	Certificates of Deposit	Highly liquid Little risk Average return
Short-Term Investment Fund	High Quality Securities	Liquid Little risk Above average return
Income Plus Fund	Life Insurance Companies & Short-Term Investments	Liquid Some risk Better than average return
Bond Fund	Long-Term Government & Corporate Securities	Not liquid Has risk potential Potentially high return
Aggressive Growth Fund	Equities experiencing rapid growth	Holding more than 12 mos. Greater than avg. market volatility Potentially very high return

To further illustrate the importance of a core service, Figure 1 depicts various broad market segments, the associated products they require and the buying factors considered in a banking relationship. The factors have one of three rating points—high, medium and low—indicating the relative significance of each in the buying decision. As can be seen, multinationals as a whole are less relationship-oriented, having placed smaller importance on credit, corporate trust, and operating services as compared to the middle-market segment. Also, multinationals tend to be more price sensitive.

Figure 1

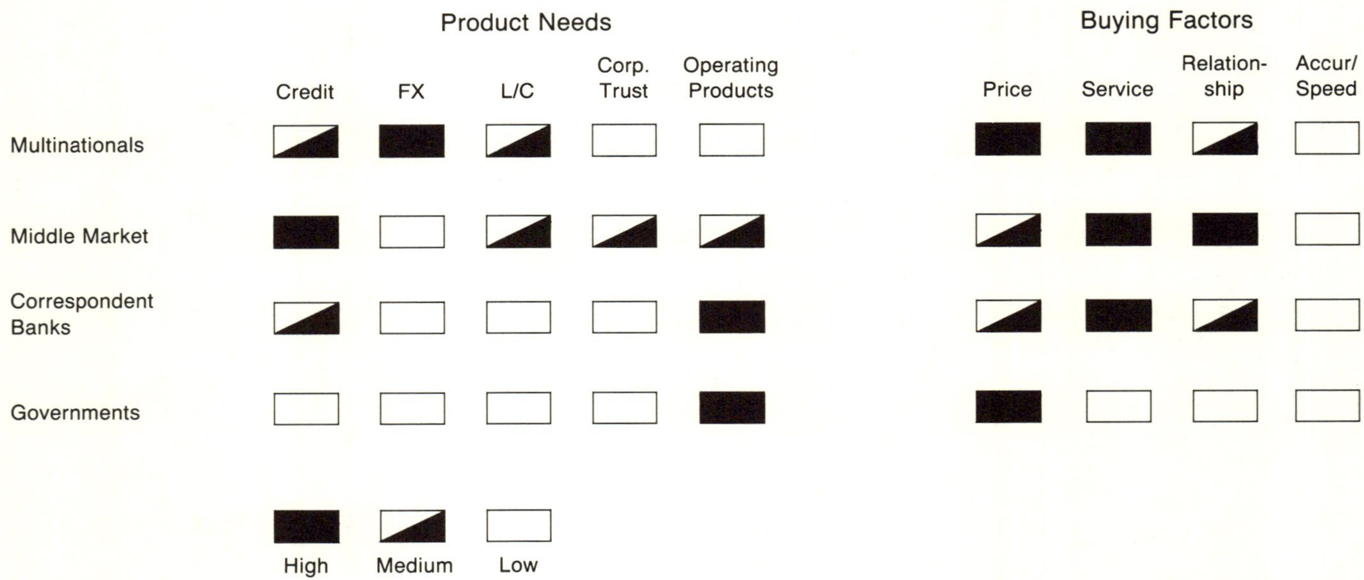

Product Needs
Buying Factors
Credit
FX
L/C
Corp. Trust
Operating Products
Price
Service
Relation-ship
Accur/ Speed
Multinationals
Middle Market
Correspondent Banks
Governments
High
Medium
Low

In contrast, the middle market looks to credit as the primary relationship link and consequently slightly less price sensitive. The credit market considers middle-market clients a greater risk than most multinationals; therefore, a higher price is charged for credit services. Also, other bank products, such as corporate trust and various operating services, are more important to middle-market companies because of their smaller, less sophisticated internal staffs.

However, the core service must also go beyond traditional lending, given the increased likelihood of clients, large or small, becoming buyers or sellers in a merger or acquisition transaction. National papers like *The Wall Street Journal* list numerous mergers and acquisitions daily. Middle-market companies, even though they may be closely held, are not exempt from this process. Middle-market bankers, then, should be prepared to assist their clients in planning and organizing either the merger or acquisition function. Going beyond credit, then, means offering the highest quality non-credit service capabilities available, from simple cash management lockboxes to sophisticated treasury workstations and, to a greater degree, merger and acquisition strategies and international banking services.

International services are another excellent example of consulting-type services now required by middle-market companies. Historically, American corporations have relied largely on domestic markets for the vast majority of their sales. This is especially true for the middle-market companies with rather limited distribution of their products. In today's interlocked international business environment, more and more middle-market corporations recognize the opportunities available through foreign trade.

Companies eager to expand their trading horizons are turning to banks for help in coping with a variety of new and unfamiliar challenges. Assessments of political risk and country risk, trade regulations, sales partners and the nuances of language are obstacles a corporation faces. Bankers need to respond to clients' changing demands and find ways to satisfy these growing and comprehensive export challenges.

Middle-market clients of every size and from every part of the United States are increasingly demanding this international expertise. Community bankers, city bankers, or regional money-center bankers are receiving requests for additional consulting services on international challenges. Middle-market clients have wider markets and need more sophisticated products. Community or city bankers that do not have staff experts in foreign exchange or governmental insurance programs have the option of developing the skill internally or using the expertise of an upstream correspondent bank. Regional money-center banks must have this expertise in-house or risk losing their position of primary bank of their middle-market clients.

However, many large regional banks may find themselves without these specialized disciplines. Strategies of expanding the retail/consumer base or emphasizing certain technological product lines such as automated tellers may have left them unprepared for the changes brought about by internationalization. These trends require a commitment to deliver credit and an ever-increasing commitment to value-added product lines.

RELATIONSHIP MANAGEMENT

One way to enhance a bank's product line delivery is through dedicated relationship management. Relationship management is centered on certain traits that today's banker must possess, such as good conceptual abilities, the ability to learn quickly, sharp reflexes—in short, traits that signify a good mind. But being smart is not enough. Today's relationship manager needs solid common sense and judgment. These come from a sound value system and a mature and balanced view of life's problems and experiences. Stamina and physical strength are also needed. You must therefore take good care of yourself and maintain the capacity to cope and keep a cool head in difficult situations.

Today's relationship manager needs to know products and applications, but they also must have good instincts and timing. Knowing when a product can help a client or when a credit should be reviewed because of problems in the business cycle is critical.

Knowing when a product is correct for a client is a learned experiences. It is an awareness that comes with identification of needs. A banker learns the process through coaching and training. Senior bankers will often take proteges with them on calls. Through this on-site experience, techniques can be taught. Needs are identified, often times prior to the actual visit, and then the banker presents an idea to the clients. The benefits of the idea are mentioned and some form of proof or evidence, such as an example of how a particular service helped a client improve its receivables, is explained. The last part of the technique is asking for the sale. On-site training and coaching are effective, but relationship managers also require additional support in product and sales training. Since credit has been identified as the core service, a thorough understanding of credit and credit analysis is required. Accounting techniques, industry studies and financial statement analysis are skills that really need to be refined. This is most successfully accomplished in a focused training environment similar to a symposium or classroom setting.

One of the most effective techniques is a lecture, an assignment forum, where a group of relationship managers meet on a two-to-three-day basis for one to two hour lectures and then are required to complete homework assignments that complement the lecture material. The trainer needs to be very knowledgeable, but the real key is class preparation. If the trainer is not prepared, the relationship managers will quickly become disinterested and the value of the training experience will diminish. Product training needs to be coordinated throughout an organization, and it works best if one person has responsibility for making sure product manuals are up-to-date, complete and distributed to all relationship managers. Product managers in cash management, trust and foreign exchange then have one person they work with to get their product information distributed.

Another strategy is accessibility. To serve the middle-market client wholly, a banker needs to be available. The middle-market client needs to have a close relationship with his banker—one that promises a true knowledge about the business, trends of the industry and where the business is likely to go in the future. Through this dialogue the middle-market client gains the assurance that credit availability will remain solid. This relationship in many ways resembles a partnership and a partnership demands constant communication.

RELATIONSHIP PRICING

Relationship pricing is another element in relationship banking. It is based on the theory that your best clients should get your best deal. If the relationship manager knows the client's short- and long-term objectives, a good credit strategy which is also cost-effective for the client can be developed. Lower loan rates are one way to say you are serious about developing this middle-market client's business.

Equally as important may be finding ways to keep your client's money earning interest, perhaps by offering "sweep accounts" for excess balances or paying a bonus rate for funds held in your institution beyond a certain amount or date.

Pricing is more than a numbers game—in fact it is one of the more complicated marketing functions. There is no one way, no single mechanistic formula. The approach must be individualized and modified for different relationships.

CONCLUSION

Marketing to the middle market is a process of target identification, analysis of needs and the delivery of the highest quality of service to the client. It is a commitment to excellence. It is not a game of follow-the-leader, but rather one of developing your own paths. There are many steps to success, but the key is to plan, prepare, proceed and thereby pursue the many rewards of middle-market success. The middle market remains a strong, healthy target, but one that is being sought by many banks.

As middle-market businesses mature, their needs become more sophisticated and they require a complete and fully integrated approach to their banking problems. The opportunity for the middle-market banker to stand above the crowd is there, but it requires dedication and constant aiming at and re-focusing on the target.

Chapter Fifteen

William R. Walker

William R. Walker is the President of Balcor Securities Company, the syndication division of The Balcor Company, one of the nation's leading real estate investment banking firms and a subsidiary of American Express. He has been an executive with Balcor since 1978 and has held the positions of National Sales Manager and National Marketing Director. He has been involved in the formation and management of 175 partnerships with real estate assets in excess of $5 billion.

Mr. Walker, a graduate of Brigham Young University, is a leading national expert and popular speaker on investment, marketing and syndication topics.

MARKETING REAL ESTATE LIMITED PARTNERSHIPS IN THE INSTITUTIONAL MARKETPLACE

William R. Walker
President
Balcor Securities Company

THE MARKET FOR REAL ESTATE INVESTMENTS

The employee benefit assets of the nation's 1,000 largest pension funds grew to $1.339 trillion for the year ended September 30, 1986. And that's only the nation's 1,000 *largest* plans; total pension assets are expected to reach $3 trillion by 1995.

Obviously, pension assets are an enormous source of investment capital. Plan sponsor affinity for stocks and bonds is well known. However, as of September 30, 1986, the asset mix of the nation's top 200 funds included only 3.6 percent in real estate equity and 1.5 percent in mortgage-related instruments. Figure 1 clearly shows that real estate constitutes a minimal allocation of pension plan assets among the largest funds. It is safe to assume that most smaller plans have an equal or smaller portion of their assets allocated to real estate.

While some large institutional investors have participated in limited partnerships, real estate investing by multi-million dollar funds usually follows a different course, accomplished via different vehicles or by direct investment. As a result, marketing to these large pension funds will not be addressed at length. However, real estate investments packaged in the form of limited partnerships have many attractive features for the relatively untapped small- to mid-size institutional investors.

Figure 1: Part 1

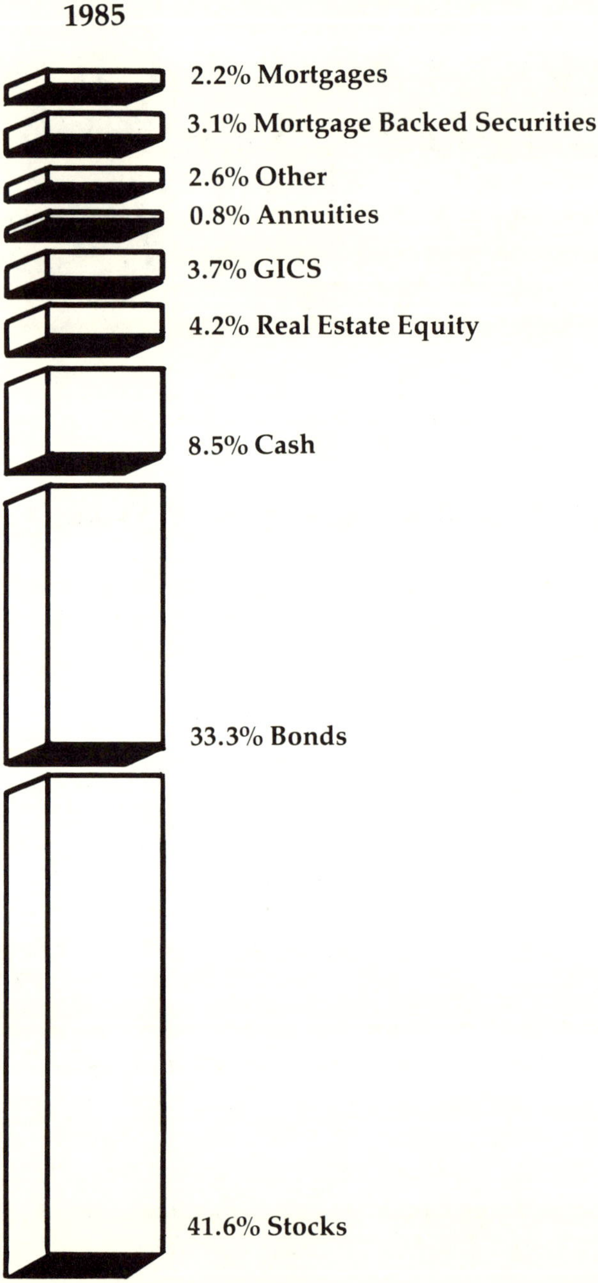

Source: *Pensions and Investment Age*, January 1987.

Figure 1: Part 2

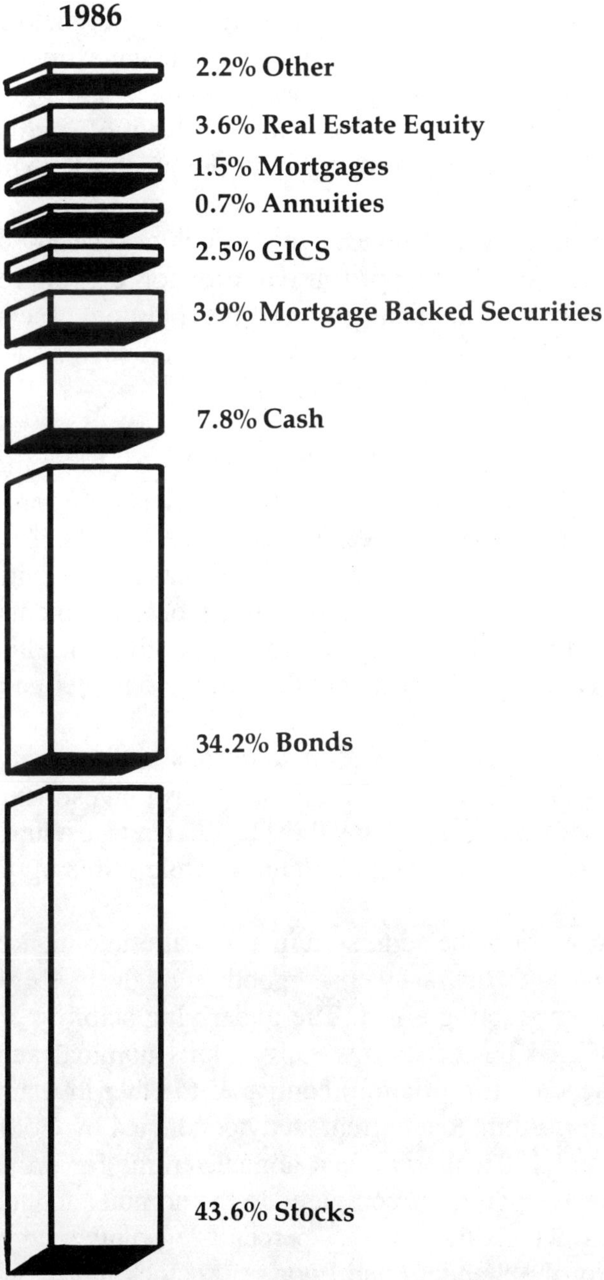

Source: *Pensions and Investment Age,* January 1987.

A VIEW OF THE MARKET

Until the past decade, many institutional investors, particularly pension plan managers, had virtually shunned real estate investments. Though large plans then began allocating a portion of their assets to real estate funds, it was not until the late 1970s, with the advent of syndications, that real estate investments were brought within the reach of small- and mid-size institutional portfolios.

This opposition to real estate investments, which historically have proven to contribute significantly to portfolio profits for corporations and individuals, was probably due in large part to the traditional securities orientation of most pension and trust officers. However, several developments have led to a broadening of sponsor horizons:

- The diversification mandated by the Employee Retirement Income Security Act of 1974 (ERISA) and its "Prudent Man" rule forced sponsors to consider additional investment vehicles.
- With plan contributions shrinking as benefit payments continue to rise, plan sponsors, now more than ever, are focusing on investment returns.
- Real estate's proven ability to produce competitive, and in some cases superior, returns made it an investment that could no longer be ignored.

The fluctuations and uncertainties of traditional investment vehicles in recent years make real estate a desirable long-term investment choice. A key marketing strategy is stressing the fact that real estate investments have the potential to add to portfolio returns while reducing performance volatility.

A question that needs to be addressed in any real estate marketing plan is that of stability, and the answer is good enough to be one of the cornerstones of a marketing effort. The underlying stability of real estate can be demonstrated by the narrow range of its nominal annual returns (unadjusted to account for inflation) compared to other investments over a 12-year period, according to a current study conducted by Goldman Sachs. Between 1971 and 1983, the nominal annual returns for property ranged only 19.6 percentage points, as compared to the nominal annual returns for long-term bonds, which ranged 47.9 percentage points, and the nominal annual returns for the Standard and Poor's 500 stock index, which ranged 63.9 percentage points.

This demonstrates an overall fluctuation range in nominal returns three times greater for stocks and bonds than for real property. Yet, during that same period, the average annual return on real property exceeded those on stocks and bonds by 3.5 percentage points.

The stability of real estate's performance also can be demonstrated by the FRC Property Index, which measures the total return of income property owned by large institutional investors to returns on stocks and bonds. (See Figure 2.)

INSTITUTIONAL CLIENT NEEDS

Every product is designed and packaged to meet the wants or needs of a target market. The first step in developing a real estate limited partnership that will appeal to pension plan investors is to determine what investment benefits they seek.

- Institutional fund managers seek diversification in the sizes and types of their investments in an effort to balance the risks and rewards of their portfolios.
- Investment return is important. Even if not realized in cash, pension plan sponsors want to be able to measure the returns their investments have yielded. Stock quotes serve them well, as do bond yields.
- Primarily, institutional funds, such as pension plans, are investing for a lifetime. The future purchasing power their investments' yield is crucial—thus necessitating investments that offer appreciation potential over the long term.

HOW REAL ESTATE LIMITED PARTNERSHIPS CAN MEET INSTITUTIONAL CLIENT NEEDS

Pension plans and similarly managed funds have been referred to as the most "risk-averse" investors. Obviously, safety is an important consideration in their investment decisions. It is no great revelation that any investment carries a degree of risk. However, a conservatively structured real estate limited partnership can provide the safety, income and appreciation potential fund managers seek in an investment.

Figure 2: FRC Index and Alternatives

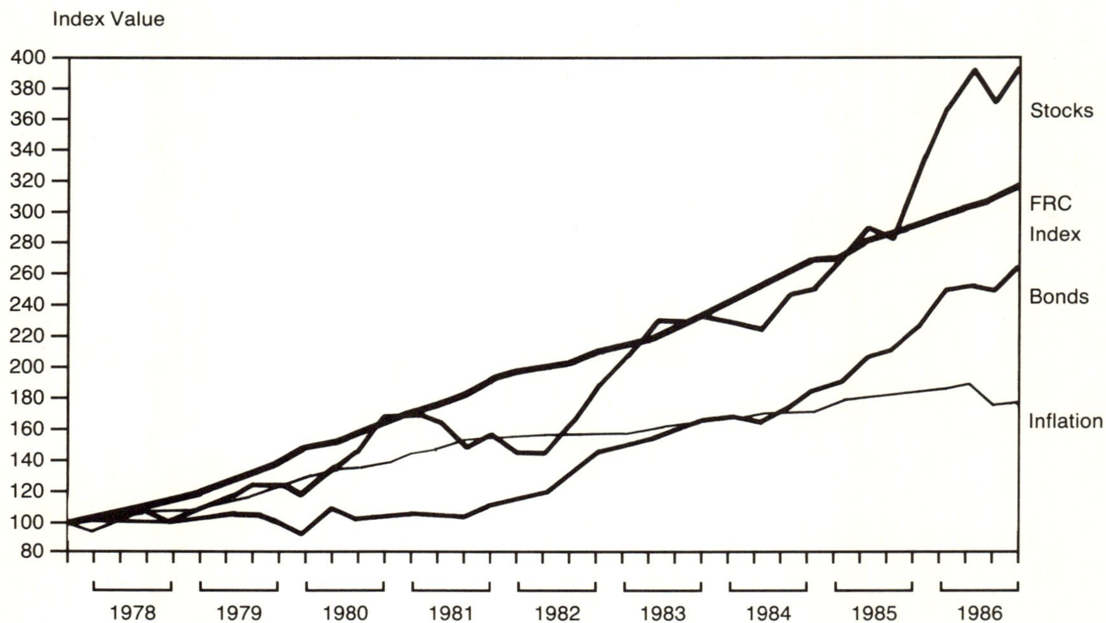

Source: The National Association of Real Estate Investment Fiduciaries and the Frank Russell Company.

Limited partnerships make it easy for institutional investors to include real estate in their portfolios. A real estate limited partnership can provide the asset diversification fund managers seek and also can provide property diversification within one real estate investment by incorporating different types of property located in various geographic areas.

An institution's contribution is pooled with those of other investors, allowing for the purchase of more and/or larger properties and increasing the overall diversification of the partnership's portfolio. Because of the limited partnership structure, the liability of an investor is limited to the amount of the contribution made—no other funds are at risk.

Perhaps the biggest advantage to investing in a limited partnership is the professional real estate management it provides. With a limited partnership, an investor does not have to "know" the real estate business. That expertise should be included as part of the investment. Ideally, the institution's contribution is made to a general partner who is experienced in the disciplines of property acquisition, management and disposition.

MARKETING THE LIMITED PARTNERSHIP PORTFOLIO

Real estate is often called the ultimate inflation hedge, although it has also performed well in periods of moderate inflation.

However, institutional clients also want current returns. The type of real estate acquired for a limited partnership portfolio and how it is acquired have a great deal to do with the timing of receipt of investment returns. There are two types of real estate investments that best suit institutional client needs: all cash equity and mortgage loans.

All Cash Equity

Debt service payments are typically a property's greatest expense. When selling these investments, it should be stressed that by acquiring property for all cash and eliminating debt service payments, a greater portion of the property's cashflow falls to the bottom line and, consequently, is available for distribution to investors. All-cash acquisitions of equity real estate also eliminate a buyer's worst fear: there is no mortgage obligation, so there is no foreclosure risk.

Mortgage Loans

Mortgage pools offer high levels of income because mortgage yields tend to be greater than those from other fixed-income investments. They also offer the stability of consistent returns based on the contractual yields required by the loan documents. If the worst happens and debt service payments cannot be made, lenders are in the favorable position of being able to institute foreclosure proceedings rather than being the object of them.

Participating mortgages offer extra advantages that aid the marketing process. In addition to regular "fixed-income" payments, participating mortgages allow lenders to share in increases in a property's cashflow and/or appreciation in value. In other words, along with contractual payments, participating mortgages include some ownership participation benefits.

PRODUCT DESIGN

As with any investment, there are a number of reasonable concerns your customers will have about real estate portfolios.

Obviously, the most important element in the design of real estate investments are the properties and mortgages underlying them. The following are some considerations real estate companies use in judging properties for portfolio acquisitions. Such criteria also will be of concern to clients, and consequently will impact marketing efforts. The lists are general in scope and are by no means meant to be all-inclusive. They fall into two general categories: property acquisitions and funding mortgage loans.

Property Acquisitions

Successful marketing begins with product design, so every potential acquisition must be carefully evaluated. Economically sound, high-quality real estate should be selected. Property, and thus investment performance, depends on more than just a "pretty face." Many questions should be answered prior to the acquisition of a property:

- What are the short and long-term outlooks for the market area?
- Is the property well-positioned in the market?
- Will property cashflow and appreciation provide investors with a satisfactory return?

Verify all factual data about property operations so that projections of future performance can be made. Review rent rolls, utility bills and service contracts. Interview representatives of taxing and assessing agencies, regional planning commissions, utility companies, building, zoning and traffic departments. Such meetings provide valuable insight into market trends and factors such as construction moratoria, tax reassessments and planned developments. Most important, be prepared to discuss your findings in detail with clients and prospects.

Analyze the competition. Drive through the property's market area. Document rents, amenities, age, location, construction quality, unit size and tenant profiles.

All of this will facilitate accurate projections of a potential acquisition's staffing requirements, operating expenses and occupancy and rent potential and enable your salesforce to accurately answer customers' questions in these areas.

Funding Mortgage Loans

To select economically sound, high-quality real estate, each property under consideration should be physically inspected and the market area in which the property competes should be analyzed. Also analyze the potential borrower by reviewing financial statements, examining other properties owned, and by checking independent business and banking references.

Look for diversification to minimize risk in several different ways. Limit the amount of proceeds that can be committed to any one borrower or property. As with property acquisitions, also diversify by placing loans on different types of properties in different geographical areas. This reduces dependence upon a few properties or locations for a partnership's success.

STRUCTURING THE LIMITED PARTNERSHIP

The structure of the limited partnership is basically a marketing function. Determining the audience, fee structure, sharing arrangements, portfolio make-up, size of the offering, timing and length of the offering and partnership objectives are all marketing considerations. Choices will certainly be influenced by the structure of products being offered by the competition, as well as by the economic, legal and tax environments in which the product sells.

However, several factors need to be kept in mind. First, if the offering is to be accessible to small-and mid-size pension plans, a lower minimum investment amount is desirable. Larger commingled real estate funds set limits for minimum contributions, most often between $100,000 and $500,000. They also usually limit the percentage of a plan's assets they will accept, generally ranging from 10-33 percent. For example, with a minimum investment requirement of $100,000 and a 20- percent limit, portfolios with assets of less than $500,000 are excluded. If a $500,000 minimum applies, a $2.5 million plan is the cut-off point.

A lower minimum investment does not exclude larger institutional investors from a limited partnership offering; it broadens the scope to allow smaller plans to participate.

Second, the illiquidity of real estate investments has long been a negative in the eyes of investors. A real estate limited partnership can be structured to provide limited liquidity in much the same way that commingled funds do. One solution might be to set aside a portion of the general partner's share of cashflow to allow for repurchase of limited partnership interests. Requests can be handled on a "first-come, first-served" basis and honored to the extent funds are available each fiscal quarter.

Liquidity also can be facilitated by structuring a dividend reinvestment program into the partnership. The dividends to be reinvested can buy units of the partnership held by owners wishing to sell them.

Third, all cash acquisitions and mortgage pools reduce the chances of the partnership generating unrelated business taxable income (U.B.T.I.) to tax-exempt investors. Generally, unless realized from "debt-financed" property, certain types of income are exempted from classification as unrelated business taxable income. These exemptions include rents from real property, interest income and gains from the sale, exchange or other disposition of capital assets.

Of course, no tax issue is this simplistic and, conceivably, the IRS could argue for various reasons that some of the partnership's income will be classified as unrelated business income. Opinion letters from reputable accounting and law firms should be sought if the U.B.T.I. issue is a concern. Marketing to sophisticated institutional clients is virtually impossible without such letters.

Fourth, pension plans and similar institutional accounts want valuations of their investments. ERISA requires that pension sponsors periodically set a market value on their portfolios. This allows the plan's actuary to calculate how much must be contributed each year to achieve minimum required funding levels. Most plans prepare valuations annually. However, large commingled real estate funds have set a standard for valuing property holdings quarterly. Quarterly valuations are certainly a client convenience, even though they are not required. But deciding the timing of valuations is the easy part—the most difficult aspect of real property or mortgage loan valuations is that there are no rules as to how they should be prepared.

Most commingled real estate funds use basically the same valuation system: they provide clients with a quarterly "total rate of return" which consists of the cashflow the properties generated plus "unrealized appreciation" based on property appraisals. Ultimately, the choice of valuation methods is left to the discretion of the limited partnership sponsor. So be prepared to help your salesforce explain why you have chosen the valuation method you have and why and how the decision was made. It is an important part of good customer relations.

THE REGULATORY PROCESS

Once the parameters of the partnership have been determined, the regulatory process begins. Again, as with any investment instrument, marketing real estate partnerships goes hand-in-hand with the regulatory process.

Limited partnership interests are defined as securities under the Securities Act of 1933. The public offering of these securities is highly regulated and the registration process is costly and time-consuming. They must be registered with and cleared for sale by the Securities and Exchange Commission (SEC), the National Association of Securities Dealers (NASD) and by each state in which they will be offered and sold.

In addition, those who offer or sell securities on behalf of the partnership must be registered as broker/dealers or salespersons with the NASD and with the proper regulatory agencies in each state in which the offering is to be sold. Sales people also must comply with the requirements of Appendix F to the Rules of Fair Practice of the NASD, which prescribe investor suitability standards, compensation to broker/dealers and organization and offering expenses, among other things.

It is illegal to offer a security prior to the filing of a registration statement. After the effective date of registration, approved sales literature may be used so long as it is accompanied or preceded by a prospectus.

The registration statement (generally Form S-ll for real estate offerings) is filed with the appropriate agencies. The SEC reviews it from a disclosure standpoint. Many states do not formally review registration statements, but more than a dozen states which have a statutory and/or regulatory obligation to conduct a "merit" review to determine whether the offering is fair, just and equitable. In this regard, the Statement of Policy Regarding Real Estate Programs ("Real Estate Guidelines") of the North American Securities Administrators Association (NASAA) is applicable. The guidelines prescribe, among other things: requirements for sponsors; suitability standards for investors; limitations on general partner fees; compensation and expenses; rules concerning conflicts of interest; and investment restrictions, rights and obligations of limited partners and disclosure and marketing requirements.

Guide 5 of the SEC is a blueprint for preparing a registration statement on Form S-11. The key is full and complete disclosure of the terms and risks of the offering, no misleading statements, no misstatement of facts, inclusion of summary information, risk factors and prior performance record.

Once the registration statement is filed, comments are received from the regulatory bodies. Some comments may simply be incorporated, some may require negotiation and some may necessitate visiting a state for a hearing. Some comments may simply not be acceptable or resolvable and will, in some cases, result in refraining from offering the product in a particular state or states.

After incorporating comments previously received and obtaining consents, comfort letters and opinions of counsel, an amendment to the registration statement is filed with the appropriate agencies and the offering is cleared for sale. The prospectus is then printed and the offering is open to the public.

SALES MATERIALS

Using sales materials to present investment benefits to clients in layman's terms, as opposed to the technical "features" presentation given in the prospectus, allows an investment's story to be told.

Regardless of product, clients are motivated to buy because of what the product can do for them, not what the product is. In the sales literature major benefits can be highlighted and the rationale for choosing a particular product can be presented. What makes the product unique? What makes the product better than its competitors? What can the product do for investors? Sales literature is the forum for answering questions such as these.

Under existing legal standards, broker/dealer materials can be more aggressive than those designed for investor use. These materials offer the opportunity to direct the selling of the product by including sales tips, investment comparisons and target audiences.

The regulatory restrictions placed on the advertising and sales literature of real estate limited partnerships are more stringent than those imposed on many other investment products. All advertising and literature intended for investor use must be filed with the SEC, NASD and the applicable states. Materials intended solely for broker/dealer use need not be filed.

The SEC's Rule 134 allows limited partnerships to engage in *limited* advertising which will not be accompanied by the prospectus. Advertisements may not include photographs or reference to investment objectives or structure. Attention-getting headlines are allowed, but only in reference to information otherwise permitted. Use of logos is generally acceptable. Materials which will accompany the prospectus must be balanced in presentation, but can include a much broader range of information.

THE OUTSIDE SALESFORCE

One of the challenges facing any sponsor of real estate programs is building a strong selling group. Most syndicators have the capabilities to acquire and manage properties and to structure them into partnerships. Most, however, do not have an internal salesforce capable of raising all of the money that is required.

The alternative, then, is to find securities firms that are willing to support the product with their selling efforts in return for sales commissions. Finding firms is not difficult: there are various directories listing the members of the National Association of Securities Dealers (NASD). Getting these firms to sign the selling agreement and to sell the product is the challenge. There are several key steps which should be helpful in successfully negotiating and keeping selling agreements.

Talk to the Right Person

The best approach is to start at the top—talk to the decision maker. Call the president of the company or the chairman of the board and tell him your purpose. Have him refer you to the necessary person. All other steps have very little value if you are not talking to the right person.

Meet Face to Face

It is nearly impossible to develop a new business relationship unless the parties have a chance to get to know one another. While part of a broker/dealer's due diligence process involves a close analysis of the specific product, seldom will anyone sign a selling agreement unless he or she is comfortable with the management behind the product. That begins by developing a comfort level with you, and that comfort level is not going to be developed over the telephone.

The Three P's

It is very important to be professional, patient and persistent. Many decision makers have rejected a syndicator out-of-hand because the person who initiated the contact with their firms did not conduct himself in a professional manner. They do not want to subject their financial planners or salesforce to unprofessional marketers.

It is fairly obvious why it pays to be both patient and persistent. The financial services industry is changing rapidly. Firms merge or are acquired. People change jobs. Philosophies of firms change. For all of these reasons, a firm that chooses not to sell your product today may be a candidate to sell it next month or six months from now. Often a firm will set a limit as to how many real estate products it will feature. If the firm is at that limit when you call, it may not sign your selling agreement even if you and your product are impressive. If you have left a good impression, if you have presented your product skillfully, and if you have been both patient and persistent, chances are you will get a call when that firm is back in the market for new products.

Never Knock the Competition

If you criticize a firm that the broker/dealer is currently doing business with, you are criticizing the judgment of that broker/dealer. Sharing a negative opinion of another firm can do nothing to help you, but it can certainly hurt by lowering others' opinion of you and your firm. As Abraham Lincoln once noted, "You can't lift yourself up by tearing another man down."

Always Insist on Compliance

If you have a number of firms in your selling group, you will find from time to time that a firm, or an office of a firm, creates compliance problems when selling your product. They may be using sales literature which is more aggressive than what has been approved by the regulators. They may be "fudging" on customer suitability requirements. Whatever the problem, it can ultimately get your firm into trouble with regulators, clients or both. If you cannot get the firm to adhere to your compliance standards after warning them, your only recourse is to revoke the selling agreement. This is a hard step to take after working so hard to develop the relationship, but a necessary one.

Don't Forget the Person Who Got You in the Door

Once you have a selling agreement, don't forget the person who allowed you in there in the first place. Always maintain that relationship.

Quality and Service

Good salesmanship and good products get selling agreements. Good service and investment performance keep them. It is not your negotiating ability that gets a selling agreement signed. It is the quality of the products you offer and your ability to sell yourself and your firm. Once you have procured the selling agreement, good investment performance will keep the clients happy. Good service to both the clients and the broker/dealer will keep the broker/dealer happy. A selling agreement signed, but not perpetuated, is of little value.

CONCLUSION

Volumes have been written on real estate, limited partnerships, pension fund investing and how to sell anything and everything. It would be impossible in the space of this chapter to incorporate and address all schools of thought, or even all necessary information.

The intent of this chapter is to introduce ways to market real estate limited partnerships to institutional clients by examining how to choose and structure a product that can meet definite client needs, guide that product through the regulatory process and nurture a salesforce. The information provided here can point the way for development of a real estate product that can target a specific investor audience and draw upon the vast source of investment capital that institutional clients can provide.

Chapter Sixteen

Jeffrey C. Paster

Jeffrey Paster is National Corporate Market Manager for Fidelity Investment Institutional Services Company. In this role, he is responsible for nationwide marketing of Fidelity's services for corporations including defined benefit plans, defined contribution plans and corporate cash investment management.

Paster has more than 10 years of experience in marketing financial services to corporations. He holds a Bachelor's Degree in Applied Mathematics and Economics from Brown University.

MARKETING ASSET MANAGEMENT SERVICES

Jeffrey C. Paster
Assistant Vice President and Corporate Market Manager
Fidelity Investments Institutional Services Company

Asset management, with its strong focus on pension products, is in literal terms mostly a market for the retiring. But in today's changing financial environment, asset managers cannot afford to have retiring personalities. Successful asset managers combine the ability to innovate in an ever-changing market with the people skills needed to build long-term relationships with the institutions and corporate clients they serve.

Large players with substantial capital tend to have a leg up in this market, but there are roles for specialists and tailored-service providers, too. The latter managers must expertly target their clients and offer a service component unmatched by larger competitors whose product range, or convenience, will be greater.

Philosophically speaking, asset management is good for the overall economy because it provides a stable pool of funds for capital formation. And asset management can be very profitable. There is large-scale cash-flow and growth, and it is generally stable money. The major focus in this chapter is on asset management for corporations. However, most of the principles to be discussed apply to all types of institutional clients.

A THREE-SECTOR MARKET

Asset-management services for corporations oversee three types of money: defined-benefit plans (pension funds directed by a manager); defined-contribution plans (primarily employee-directed plans and including 401(k) products, thrift plans, profit-sharing plans and money-purchase pension plans) and treasury funds in which non-retirement related corporate money is managed.

Prior to the early 1980s, the vast majority of institutional retirement money went into defined-benefit plans. Usually such funds were set up as one fund per corporation, managed by multiple managers as a single, discrete account. But in the past decade, sweeping changes have produced new trends.

Beginning in 1980, the Internal Revenue Code allowed creation of 401(k) plans (the designation referring to the section of the code covering such plans). These 401(k) plans allow people to contribute a portion of salary, before taxes, to retirement plans.

The 401(k) concept has proved highly popular with corporations—indeed, 401(k) plans are currently the hottest market in the asset management industry. The Washington-based Employee Benefit Research Institute reports that more than 90 percent of Fortune 500 corporations offered their employees 401(k) plans in 1986. Many corporations amended their existing thrift and profit-sharing plans to turn them into 401(k) plans; for others, the 401(k) became their first defined-contribution plan.

For corporations, 401(k) plans—as employee-directed plans, rather than defined-benefit plans—offer a couple of advantages. Because the employee controls his or her contribution, the employee absorbs the risk connected with the investment. There also is a greater element of predictability to employer contributions to such plans; the contributions are likely to be a set percentage of salary or payroll, whereas with defined-benefit plans, such parameters can change with the age of the covered group, and with time.

401(k)'s and similar employee-directed plans provide covered employees a greater awareness of their financial status and a larger sense of participation, of "knowing what's going on." Instead of having some faraway, often anonymous fund manager handling a benefit many workers don't even think about until fairly close to retirement, the employees can keep tabs on their investments over the years and change direction at will.

There is some controversy surrounding the proliferation of 401(k) plans. Some would suggest that lower-paid employees of a given organization simply will not have the income, after covering day-to-day needs, to take advantage of such plans, while their higher-paid coworkers will enjoy 401(k) benefits. Some critics argue that actual at-retirement benefits paid out through 401(k) plans tend to be less than what a standard pension plan would offer. Meanwhile, say opponents, the structure of the plans could cost the deficit-plagued United States Treasury billions of dollars.

Proponents, on the other hand, argue that the older pension plans assume a worker will stay on the job for decades, when the reality for many Americans is otherwise. With job shifts—voluntary or involuntary—workers need a more "portable" retirement plan. And the fact that they can watch it growing and keep close tabs on it makes it even more desirable, backers say.

PENSION PLANS AND EMPLOYEE-DIRECTED PLANS

The times do seem to favor the employee-directed plan. Changing economic conditions since the 1970s have expanded opportunities (IRAs are a good example) with the public becoming more savvy about new ways of placing funds. As a result, people are more willing to take personal investment responsibility; armed with solid information from journalistic and other sources, many feel less fear of failure in the market.

But the institution offering a 401(k), or other employee-directed plan, bears the extra responsibility of providing needed human resources staff support to explain the programs to participants. There may also be added publications or other informational costs. Asset managers may want to consider offering personnel with such skills on a consulting basis.

The tried-and-true method of retirement asset management, pension funds, still offers just what many institutions and their employees want and are an attractive pool of money for any asset manager. Some institutions will offer both pension and employee-directed plans to their staffs.

Changes elsewhere in the investment industry have spurred some of the shifts in asset management. Although mutual funds have existed for years, they have burgeoned in the past decade and account for many IRAs, 401(k) plans and other employee-controlled offerings. Mutual funds offer several pluses. They are easy to follow. Most are listed in newspapers and are easy to invest in and redeem. Also, many have long-established track records and many mutual fund organizations can offer several funds with varying goals and risk levels for investors to move among.

It is noteworthy that, while billions and billions of pension and 401(k) dollars currently are invested in stock- or bond-related vehicles, a large amount of retirement money also goes into guaranteed-interest contracts (GICs) issued by insurance companies. In today's climate, however, no investment is an island. Many fund managers incorporate GICs into their portfolio management services.

TREASURY FUNDS

Asset managers also involve themselves in a sector not associated with retirement investing—the investment of funds of corporate treasuries. Mostly this involves short- to intermediate-term corporate funds that fall into three categories: taxable, tax-exempt and tax-advantaged. The latter designation usually refers to a special federal rule meant to enhance capital formation, allowing corporations to hold each others' stock while retaining 80 percent of the dividend tax-free.

DEVELOPING NEW BUSINESS

Unless you have been doing quite a bit of capital formation yourself lately, chances are you will select a sector of the asset management market in which to start up and expand later, or you will remain specialized. Each of the three major sectors of this market expect particular services from any worthy vendor.

In all three sectors, breaking into the market requires the establishment of a relationship of trust with the institution or corporation considering the services. Asset management has a long sales cycle. While the time span between initial contact and signed contract for a treasury fund may run as short as three months, getting a commitment for oversight of a pension plan or 401(k) could take literally years. Therefore, this is not a business venture for those who must have returns within a short time period to survive. For those who can hang in and hang on, however, the large monetary rewards tend to make the wait worthwhile.

A TEAM OF EXPERTS

Breaking into pension funds or treasury funds requires two types of players working in concert: skilled investment managers and skilled trust-builders for the direct sales contacts. If these individuals have excellent past track records that have developed client trust, so much the better.

More overhead tends to be attached to the offering of employee-directed plans. The fund-management expertise and skilled sales personnel needs are the same as those of pension funds or treasury funds. But because the real end-users of such services actually are employees, under the aegis of their institution or corporation, the employees need enough information to make intelligent choices. This usually requires the asset manager to provide personnel who can explain the plans and answer questions. Also standard for this market segment is a greater need for printed information, audio-visual aids and other employee communications. One might also consider offering such additional services as recording keeping, trustee services, plan administration and document preparation in order to facilitate the sale of investment management services.

In the management of corporate cash, ancillary services a company might provide to chip a niche include reporting, control and disbursement and related functions.

DETERMINING THE CLIENT'S NEEDS

Two factors are indispensable in determining a prospective client's asset management needs: consultation and patience.

A third factor is indispensable in meeting those needs: one has to have the range of products to do so. You cannot very well offer "one from column A, one from column B, one from column C and one from column D" if the last three columns do not exist in your organization. Clients can see through the asset manager who attempts to bluff these issues.

What that means for the more focused asset manager is that in order to get the jump on bigger players, uniqueness of product or unusual intensity of service will be required.

Larger players will have the advantages that size and accompanying capital afford. They will be able to offer multiple services, or a smorgasbord from which clients can pick and choose. They will have certain economies of scale. They will likely be better able to weather storms in certain segments of their business as a result of diversification. And they will be positioned to garner more of a client's business after getting a foot in the door through those months or years of relationship-building.

In determining a client's needs, ask broad questions. Often, more is at stake in the creation of a pension fund or 401(k) than who will get what at age 65. A corporation's image as a generous employer and a desirable place to work may ride on its benefits. Its demographic mix may be in flux. Or the client's employees may be a changing group of people, and that may affect the sort of retirement goals your client is prepared to establish.

In pension asset management, one recent development requires corporations to put their pension liabilities on their balance sheets. It is wise to keep this in mind, as it may affect some corporations' willingness to accept volatility in their retirement portfolios.

When assessing client needs, there are no easy answers. Only time and full discussion will bring you the understanding of the client's business that will allow you to make a reasoned offering of service. It may well be a large investment of your time—but once a decision is made, it is unlikely to be changed for quite some time.

DEVELOPING ASSET MANAGEMENT PRODUCTS

Clearly, one does not just hang up an asset management shingle and watch clients line up at the door. A likely first step might be managing thorough market research.

But the argument is often made that institutional research need not be *too* thorough. Trends in this industry come and go so speedily that, by the time your statisticians determine what's hot, hotter and hottest, the hottest segment may already have cooled down.

Pay attention to the changes at your end of the spectrum. Are new investment vehicles being devised? Are the laws changing in ways that create opportunities or require regrouping of existing arrangements?

Be selective about your client base. Instead of constantly chasing all prospects with a single product, target clients who are large enough now, or are growing, and expand with them.

Also, don't ignore changes and developing needs within your existing client base. For example, do you offer products that might be of interest to retirees when they begin to take their retirement distributions? Wherever there is a money turnover, a new opportunity is created.

FAMILIARITY BREEDS RESPECT

Asset management choices are major life-affecting decisions—not unlike the contemplation of marriage. And, to carry that analogy further, even the most romantic of courtships won't keep the relationship alive if the partners stop communicating once the vows are exchanged.

So *be there* for your clients. Meet with them face-to-face on a regular basis, at least quarterly. Review the status of their assets, even if the news is not always positive. Over a very long time, there are likely to be dips in the curve of performance even for effective managers. If your client knows and understands your management style, he or she will better understand your approach. It also will help both of you decide whether to adopt one another.

Listen to your clients. Have their objectives changed over time? Perhaps their business has new aspects you could service. If they already know you and understand your approach, selling them on a new product will be less complicated than it would be starting from scratch. Remember, your best source of new business is often your current client base.

Consider asking your clients to come to your home office and meet with your team. This will help the clients understand your approach to managing their money and servicing their account.

It takes so much time and effort to win an asset management client that losing one can be an incredibly painful experience. Never slacken up on consultation, even if your message sometimes is negative—because if you haven't built up a relationship of trust already, you certainly won't when the chips are down. And if a client trusts you, that client may well trust you to point the way to a different approach that will work better.

COMMUNICATING ON TWO LEVELS

Winning the confidence of the rank-and-file employees in a sponsoring organization also is important to the success of your client's 401(k) plan, because of tough anti-discrimination rules connected with establishment of such programs. These rules, set by the IRS and amended by Congress in its 1986 rewrite of the federal tax laws, are meant to further ensure that special institutionally supported programs don't provide perks for higher-echelon employees at the expense of their rank-and-file associates. For the plan to work for your corporate or institutional client, you must offer a high-quality "lowest common denominator." For many organizations, this has meant structuring the 401(k) plan to serve more immediate needs of younger participants—allowing them to borrow against their 401(k) plans, for example.

TIME KEEPS ON TICKING

If the younger employees are not concerned about retirement saving, they should be. "Baby boomers" now elbowing each other for jobs are financing the Social Security payments for a pool of retirees currently small, relative to the people footing the bills. When these younger employees retire, demographic trends show that their Social Security program will be kept alive by the payroll taxes of a much smaller group of Americans.

The post-retirement future could be another place where the ascendant generation may find life less bright than it has proved for people in their 60s or older today. Just how bright it turns out to be will be in the hands of individuals.

CONCLUSION

Asset management is an excellent field for those willing to provide superb service within the realm of financial services. Although those starting out in the business must be selective about their clientele and take on only as much business as they can reasonably cover, properly laid groundwork can lead to personal and professional rewards over the long term.

Chapter Seventeen

Joseph T. Grause, Jr.

Joseph Grause is Vice President of Fidelity Investments Institutional Services Company. He has overall responsibility for all Fidelity products marketed to large and mid-size ranks, including Fidelity Institutional Cash Portfolios, Fidelity Trust Portfolios and several other institutional products.

He joined Fidelity Investments in 1976 as a Senior Security Analyst for Fidelity Management and Research Company. In 1980, he advanced to the marketing research group of Fidelity Marketing Company as a Senior Analyst for new product development. Mr. Grause received his undergraduate degree from Brown University of Pennsylvania - Wharton School of Business Administration in 1976.

Mr. Grause is a member of the Boston Security Analysts Society and the Financial Analysts Federation. He is also a Chartered Financial Analyst.

MARKETING MUTUAL FUNDS TO INSTITUTIONAL INVESTORS

Joseph T. Grause, Jr.
Vice President
Fidelity Investment Institutional Services Company

Marketing mutual funds to institutional investors is not unlike other marketing challenges. That is to say, there are opportunities to exploit but also pitfalls to avoid. But before we look at specific programs, it will be useful to examine the current state of the market.

For the marketers of mutual funds, the news is very good. Institutional investors, the people who manage large blocks of money for banks, corporations, public agencies, universities, endowment funds and the like, are pouring money into mutual funds at a record pace.

In fact, they have actually outrun their retail counterparts in the race to add mutual funds to their portfolios. That is especially heartening when one considers that the retail market has certainly not been static. "Explosion" is the word most often used to describe the upward spiral of assets into mutual funds, and for once there is not an ounce of hyperbole involved.

How, then, does one characterize the even greater flood of institutional money into mutual funds? Perhaps as an explosion *and then some*. In 1970, according to the Investment Company Institute, institutional investors were lukewarm on mutual funds, investing only $6.2 billion in them. By 1986, a decade and a half later, that sum had risen to $252.9 billion—a more than fortyfold increase.

A glance at market share lends further evidence of the popularity of mutual funds among institutional investors. Between 1960 and 1986, institutional assets in mutual funds rose from 10.6 percent to 35.3 percent of he total market. In just one of those years—1986—the institutional assets in equity, bond and income funds rose from $62 billion to $117 billion.

The surge in total accounts is equally impressive. Between 1984 and 1986, institutional mutual funds accounts nationwide more than doubled—soaring from 2.9 million to 6.1 million.

Does this make the picture rosy henceforth and forever? Well, not necessarily. Evidence is beginning to mount that this explosive growth may be coming to an end. Yet there is no unanimity of opinion here, and because we are talking future rather than past, it is a much trickier proposition.

Still, a slowdown may well be in the cards, which means the techniques and procedures that work in the marketing of mutual funds may soon be put to the test in ways that will challenge us all. This, of course, begs the question: What are the techniques? They include flexible product and service configurations, responsive customer service, quality and deployment of the salesforce, the quality and placement of advertising, and skillful use of a speakers' bureau. Client newsletters, client conferences, attendance at trade shows and, to a lesser extend, the use of direct mail pretty much round out the agenda.

These will be discussed separately, but it is worth noting beforehand that the sum here is greater than the parts. In other words, mutual funds sales and marketing executives should use every available avenue in their attempt to penetrate the institutional market.

FLEXIBLE PRODUCT AND SERVICE CONFIGURATIONS

Having more than one way to deliver the product will increase its attraction to the widest number of institutional investors.

This is very important because these markets are not monolithic. They are divided into various segments, each with its own product and service needs. Some are dictated by market considerations, others by regulatory mandates. Commercial banks, for instance, are often limited in what they can do with mutual funds because of regulatory hurdles; savings banks and S&Ls even more so. Mutual fund companies must consider this fact as they go about fashioning products and services that will attract institutional investors.

Mutual fund marketing executives should also keep in mind that even the various segments of the market are not uniform. Take, for instance, banks—a major portion of the institutional market. Different *size* banks have different needs which mutual fund companies must take into account.

There are private fund relationships, which are especially popular with large banks because the institution can use its own investment advisors to run the fund—and thus leverage the bank's name and reputation.

A medium-sized bank, for its part, may want to offer funds distributed by a company such as Fidelity to some of its trust account clients.

The idea is to offer products for every size bank. Many will want to use more than one of the services a mutual fund company offers, and, of course, that is so much the better. Cross-selling products within a customer organization helps cement the relationship.

That is not to say a mutual fund company should try to satisfy every part of the institutional market. In fact, small-and medium-size mutual funds companies often do very well as *niche* players, serving the part or parts of the market they are best suited to serve.

Finally, don't try to drive the process. That is the client's responsibility. Listen to his needs and try to meet them. Do not try to serve the same "off-the-shelf" product and service capabilities to every client. That's a prescription for customer dissatisfaction.

CUSTOMER SERVICE

It has been said before, but it bears repeating—do not ignore your existing customer base. If you do, you will not only lose existing business, you will lose an important outlet to *new* business as well.

Half—or more—new business for many mutual fund companies comes from existing customers who either increase their own investment, invest in different products or refer new customers. Institutional marketing is a relationship business and existing clients represent the most fertile source of increased business.

THE SALESFORCE

The ability to develop strong customer relationships is a crucial element of any successful salesforce. A mutual fund company's salesforce must be experienced and well-trained. Salespeople must not only be able to explain very complex products, but to serve clients in a consultative capacity as well.

In short, they must be problem solvers: it is the surest way of establishing a lasting bond with clients.

To be effective in the mutual fund business, a sales representative must assume the consultant's role. The market today is not like selling the proverbial Ford Model "T"—which came in any color the buyer wanted, as long as it was black.

Large mutual fund companies have roughly 125 funds to offer. The options and combinations are virtually limitless. Even smaller mutual fund companies provide a range of choices. Factor in the complex and changing needs of clients, the everchanging stock and bond markets, the thicket of state and federal regulations that must be taken into account, and it is easy to see why a consultant really is the appropriate role for a sales rep.

As an organization grows, it also is important to develop a specialized salesforce. For example, a foundation located in a major city requires not only a regional sales office that, if not located in that city, can adequately service clients there, but also a sales rep serving that area who specializes in working with foundations.

The other major market segments—banks, corporations, universities, public sector agencies, and so on—should similarly have an assigned specialist in each regional office. In a complex business such as mutual funds, it is inefficient to try to make a sales rep an expert at everything.

ADVERTISING

It is not a question of whether or not to advertise, but how a mutual fund company goes about it. In short, how do you get the most for your advertising dollar?

Broadly speaking, image and awareness advertising seem to work best with institutional investors. They are, after all, savvy customers and the products are complex.

For the institutional market, trade publications seem to be most effective. The higher the circulation and the higher up the corporate ladder the readers are (you want to reach decision makers), the better off you will be.

Regardless of where you place the ad, its effectiveness will be enhanced by tailoring it to the segment of the institutional market you are trying to reach. Getting the attention of a money manager at a major foundation, for example, requires a different ad from the one you hope will get the attention of his or her counterpart at a money-center bank.

There can even be variations *within* segments of the market. For example, one month an ad might run in a banking trade publication that targets trust officers; the next month an ad geared toward retail bankers might run in the same journal.

Advertising in special supplements is also helpful. Retail ads in publications like *The New York Times* and *The Wall Street Journal* help, too. They are not aimed at institutional money managers *per se*, but the indirect effect can still support institutional marketing.

The most effective institutional ads often are those that stress performance, investment management expertise and the service capabilities that can make a mutual fund company particularly attractive. Superior investment management is of interest to all investors, of course, but to none more than institutional clients. Remember, they have a fiduciary responsibility to manage money soundly.

TRADE SHOWS

As with ads, this isn't a question of whether to do it but of deciding which ones are worth attending. What criteria does a marketing executive use?

Cost is a consideration, of course, but beyond that there are some questions that need to be asked. Make a checklist to help evaluate such events:

- Is the theme of this show likely to attract the customer base you are trying to court?
- Is it likely to be well-attended?
- What segments are likely to show up?

It always is important to evaluate the attendees. It usually is better to be represented at a trade show with 2,000 attendees who are decision makers—those people actually making the investment vehicle choices—than one with 5,000 or even 10,000 if the attendees can only *influence* the decision-making process.

CLIENT CONFERENCES

This is sort of a trade show in reverse. Instead of travelling to a site to meet the client, you invite the client in. Fidelity, for example, has held both regional and national conferences.

The agenda varies, of course, but several things are essential. First, do your homework. If you are going to go through the expense of putting on a first-class conference—and that's the only way to do it—make sure the presentation truly focuses on items of interest to the client. That sounds basic, and it is , but it also requires sounding out a good sample of investors. Don't rely on what just a handful have to say.

Also, keep in mind that these are sophisticated investors. The speakers you choose should be money managers who have proven themselves over time and who are good on their feet.

CLIENT NEWSLETTERS

Newsletters are excellent vehicles for cross-selling funds and apprising clients of your latest investment approaches. Newsletters that are focused, substantive, visually appealing, and well-written can make a positive addition to your marketing effort. And they can be a great vehicle for that money manager on your staff whose opinions are sought and valued by investors.

A newsletter also gives your company regular visibility and exposure; just as one issue has been circulated and read and filed, chances are the next will reach your clients' desks.

Different newsletters targeting different segments of the institutional market can be very helpful if you can afford it. They can be monthly or quarterly, but they maintain and enhance your company's visibility within specific market segments.

SPEAKING OPPORTUNITIES

Another good way to reach your audience is through spokesmen. Some companies dispatch speakers to several engagements each month. Targeted audiences include professional groups comprising decision makers within current and potential client organizations. Examples include the American

Bankers Association (ABA) and conferences sponsored by publications such as *Institutional Investor* magazine.

Speeches should be informational, not sales-oriented. Attendees are there to gain useful information and will see through and resent a sales pitch. Look at the sales opportunity as *indirect.* The best approach is to address the subject with a sense of authority. Speaking engagements are a way to "strut your stuff" and show your company's expertise. Remember, client firms are looking for vendors who can play a consultative role. Speeches provide a means to demonstrate that ability.

Finally, if there are not enough invitations coming in, do not be shy about soliciting speaking engagements. Many organizations have a speakers committee, but developing the names of potential luncheon speakers or program participants is often the job of one or two staff people. Find out their names by calling the organization and sending them resumes of your company's experts in the field (or fields) covered by that organization's conferences. Include your executives, areas of expertise and list any previous speaking opportunities or published books or articles.

DIRECT MAIL

Direct-mail programs have their place as well. However, they can be an overused portion of the overall marketing strategy and budget for mutual funds. Generally, the institutional market is not as receptive to direct mail as the retail market. Institutional investors want a representative who is willing to meet face-to-face, spend time assessing their needs, and tailor a product to meet those needs. That approach is directly opposite to a mass mailing.

However, direct mailings can be effective tools in telling a specific segment of your institutional client base about major developments that will likely have an impact on them. Such mailings can be especially helpful to mutual fund companies that do not have strong newsletter programs.

CONCLUSION

Not every approach discussed in this chapter will work for every mutual fund company. Certainly, they must be considered against budgetary restraints. But the fact remains that the more *types* of marketing approaches a company is able to use, the more effective its overall marketing/sales efforts will be within the institutional market.

APPENDIX I: LARGEST U.S. BANK HOLDING COMPANIES

Bank	Location	Assets 12/31/86 (in Millions)
1. Citicorp	New York	196124
2. BankAmerica	San Francisco	104189
3.Chase Manhattan	New York	94766
4. Morgan (J.P.)	New York	76039
5. Manufacturers Hanover	New York	74397
6. Security Pacific	Los Angeles	62606
7. Chemical New York	New York	60564
8. Bankers Trust New York	New York	56420
9. First Interstate Bancorp	Los Angeles	55422
10. Wells Fargo	San Francisco	44577
11. First Chicago	Chicago	39148
12. Mellon Bank	Pittsburgh	34499
13. Bank of Boston	Boston	34045
14. Continental Illinois	Chicago	32809
15. First Bank System	Minneapolis	28012
16. NCNB	Charlotte, NC	27472
17. First Union	Charlotte, NC	26820
18. Suntrust Banks	Atlanta	26165
19. Marine Midland Banks	Buffalo	24790
20. Irving Bank	New York	24233

Appendix I: Largest U.S. Bank Holding Companies (Continued)

Bank	*Location*	*Assets 12/31/86 (in Millions)*
21. Bank of New England	Boston	22473
22. PNC Financial	Pittsburgh	22199
23. MCORP	Dallas	21887
24. Norwest	Minneapolis	21539
25. NBD Bancorp	Detroit	21176
26. Republicbank	Dallas	20944
27. Bank of New York	New York	20709
28. Barnett Banks of Florida	Jacksonville	20229
29. Texas Commerce Bancshares	Houston	19192
30. Citizens & Southern	Atlanta	18757
31. First Wachovia	Winston-Salem	18690
32. Interfirst	Dallas	17986
33. Republic New York	New York	17465
34. First Fidelity Bancorp.	Newark, NJ	15170
35. Sovran Financial	Norfolk, VA	14952
36. Corestates Financial	Philadelphia	14595
37. National City	Cleveland	14107
38. Hartford National	Hartford	13879
39. First City Bancorp. of Texas	Houston	13681
40. Banc One	Columbus, OH	12662
41. Southeast Banking	Miami	12469
42. Midlantic	Edison, NJ	11874
43. Fleet Financial Group	Provindence	11690
44. Fidelcor	Philadelphia	11392
45. Norstar Bancorp	Albany, NY	11132

Appendix I: Largest U.S. Bank Holding Companies (Concluded)

Bank	*Location*	*Assets 12/31/86 (in Millions)*
46. National Westminster Bank USA	New York	11080
47. Ameritrust	Cleveland	11068
48. Valley National	Phoenix	10716
49. Shawmut	Boston	10697
50. Harris Bankcorp	Chicago	10278

APPENDIX II: WORLD'S LARGEST BANKS

Rank 12/86			Deposits 12/31/86 (U.S. Dollars)
1	**Dai-Ichi Kangyo Bank Ltd., Tokyo (e)**	Japan	186,029,628,653s
2	**Fuji Bank, Ltd., Tokyo (e)**	Japan	166,547,333,964s
3	**Sumitomo Bank Ltd., Osaka(e)**	Japan	164,507,271,797s
4	**Mitsubishi Bank Ltd., Tokyo(e)**	Japan	158,671,131,135s
5	**Sanwa Bank Ltd., Osaka (e)**	Japan	151,871,893,602s
6	**Norinchukin Bank, Tokyo(e)**	Japan	144,233,722,754
7	**Industrial Bank of Japan, Ltd., Tokyo(e)**	Japan	137,424,332,628s
8	**Credit Agricole Mutuel, Paris**	France	133,396,066,200
9	**Banque Nationale de Paris**	France	121,830,138,297s
10	**Deutsche Bank, Frankfurt**	Germany	121,574,053,210s
11	**Credit Lyonnais, Paris**	France	115,235,251,599s
12	**Tokai Bank Ltd., Nagoya(e)**	Japan	113,260,733,674s
13	**Mitsubishi Trust & Banking Corp., Tokyo(e)**	Japan	110,529,232,627u
14	**Sumitomo Trust & Banking Co., Ltd., Osaka(e)**	Japan	110,136,767,202u
15	**National Westminster Bank Plc, London**	United Kingdom	107,831,802,000s
16	**Mitsui Bank, Ltd., Tokyo (e)**	Japan	104,352,303,044
17	**Citibank NA, New York**	United States	102,933,000,000
18	**Societe Generale, Paris**	France	99,084,964,111s
19	**Mitsui Trust & Banking Co., Ltd., Tokyo(e)**	Japan	98,919,395,905u
20	**Long-Term Credit Bank of Japan Ltd., Tokyo (e)**	Japan	98,645,684,071u
21	**Barclays Plc, London**	United Kingdom	96,793,866,000s
22	**Dresdner Bank, Frankfurt**	Germany	95,656,271,900s
23	**Taiyo Kobe Bank, Ltd., Kobe(e)**	Japan	91,240,394,399u
24	**Daiwa Bank, Ltd., Osaka(e)**	Japan	88,296,103,555u
25	**Bank of Tokyo, Ltd.(e)**	Japan	86,863,648,487s
26	**Yasuda Trust & Banking Co. Ltd., Tokyo (e)**	Japan	85,901,361,491
27	**Union Bank of Switzerland, Zurich**	Switzerland	81,743,463,927u
28	**Hongkong and Shanghai Banking Corp., Hong Kong**	Hong Kong	77,975,856,000s
29	**Bank of America NT&SA, San Francisco**	United States	76,084,000,000
30	**Swiss Bank Corp., Basle**	Switzerland	74,603,109,260u
31	**Commerzbank, Frankfurt**	Germany	72,143,790,542s
32	**Toyo Trust & Banking Co. Ltd., Tokyo (e)**	Japan	71,515,662,009
33	**Westdeutsche Landesbank Girozentrale, Duesseldorf**	Germany	71,512,709,800s
34	**Nippon Credit Bank, Ltd., Tokyo(e)**	Japan	68,801,207,211u

35	**Bayerische Vereinsbank, Munich**	Germany	68,383,919,785s
36	**Midland Bank Plc, London**	United Kingdom	68,293,524,000s
37	**Banca Nazionale del Lavoro, Rome**	Italy	64,609,892,244s
38	**Shoko Chukin Bank, Tokyo (e)**	Japan	64,259,656,298
39	**Lloyds Bank Plc, London**	United Kingdom	63,171,732,000s
40	**Chase Manhattan Bank NA, New York**	United States	60,899,893,000
41	**Royal Bank of Canada, Montreal**	Canada	60,645,504,466s
42	**Bayerische Hypotheken-und Wechsel-Bank, Munich**	Germany	59,504,546,763s
43	**Kyowa Bank, Ltd., Tokyo(e)**	Japan	57,828,988,316s
44	**Credit Suisse, Zurich**	Switzerland	57,277,935,000u
45	**Algemene Bank Nederland, Amsterdam**	Netherlands	54,833,290,200s
46	**Bayerische Landesbank Girozentrale, Munich**	Germany	54,559,121,921s
47	**Bank of Montreal**	Canada	53,896,029,841s
48	**Amsterdam-Rotterdam Bank, Amsterdam**	Netherlands	52,916,557,200s
49	**Saitama Bank Ltd., Urawa (e)**	Japan	51,716,634,926s
50	**Rabobank Nederland, Utrecht**	Netherlands	51,558,650,122s
51	**Zenshinren Bank, Tokyo (e)**	Japan	50,138,162,635
52	**Banca Commerciale Italiana, Milan**	Italy	48,758,706,900s
53	**Canadian Imperial Bank of Commerce, Toronto**	Canada	48,598,024,718s
54	**Generale de Banque, Brussels**	Belgium	47,733,849,600s
55	**Manufacturers Hanover Trust Co., New York**	United States	46,117,000,000
56	**Norddeutsche Landesbank Girozentrale, Hannover**	Germany	46,060,755,534s
57	**Istituto Bancario San Paolo di Torino, Turin**	Italy	45,570,109,761s
58	**Banco di Roma, Rome**	Italy	45,089,069,400s
59	**Morgan Guaranty Trust Co., New York**	United States	44,935,863,000
60	**Monte dei Paschi di Siena**	Italy	44,697,269,783s
61	**Chuo Trust & Banking Co., Ltd., Tokyo(e)**	Japan	43,566,253,775u
62	**Bank of Yokohama, Ltd. (e)**	Japan	42,889,379,687s
63	**Credito Italiano, Milan**	Italy	41,743,201,411s
64	**Rafidain Bank, Baghdad**	Iraq	41,142,034,096
65	**Cassa di Risparmio delle Provincie Lombarde, Milan**	Italy	40,766,186,376s
66	**Standard Chartered Bank, London**	United Kingdom	40,479,644,400s
67	**Chemical Bank, New York**	United States	39,163,000,000
68	**Bank of Nova Scotia, Toronto**	Canada	38,402,067,075s
69	**Banco di Napoli, Naples**	Italy	38,397,409,679u
70	**Banque Paribas, Paris (q)**	France	35,539,246,410s
71	**Kredietbank International Group, Brussels(c)**	Belgium	34,734,056,700s
72	**Security Pacific National Bank, Los Angeles**	United States	34,574,626,000

73	Bankers Trust Co., New York	United States	34,162,759,000
74	Deutsche Genossenschaftsbank, Frankfurt	Germany	33,923,983,324s
75	Wells Fargo Bank NA, San Francisco	United States	33,286,916,000
76	Banque Bruxelles Lambert, Brussels (e)	Belgium	31,634,086,614s
77	Groupe Des Banques Populaires, Paris	France	31,066,200,000s
78	Toronto Dominion Bank	Canada	30,729,419,438s
79	Hessische Landesbank-Girozentrale, Frankfurt	Germany	30,360,538,442s
80	Hokkaido Takushoku Bank, Ltd., Sapporo (e)	Japan	29,925,938,842u
81	Bank fuer Gemeinwirtschaft, Frankfurt	Germany	29,155,926,353s
82	Banque Indosuez, Paris	France	28,124,466,210s
83	Nederlandsche Middenstandsbank, Amsterdam	Netherlands	27,947,485,800s
84	Banco do Brasil, Brasilia	Brazil	27,471,479,199s
85	Bank Melli Iran, Tehran(g)	Iran	27,366,900,000
86	State Bank of India, Bombay	India	26,301,069,600s
87	Caisse Generale d'Epargne et de Retraite, Brussels	Belgium	26,279,840,800u
88	Banco Central, Madrid	Spain	25,407,503,240s
89	Credit Commercial de France, Paris	France	25,347,875,318s
90	Hokuriku Bank Ltd., Toyama (e)	Japan	25,063,182,188
91	Westpac Banking Corp., Sydney(e)	Australia	24,946,078,987s
92	First National Bank, Chicago	United States	24,909,690,000
93	Chiba Bank, Ltd. (e)	Japan	24,846,666,966
94	Joyo Bank, Ltd., Mito(e)	Japan	24,376,317,482
95	Shizuoka Bank Ltd. (e)	Japan	24,250,553,613
96	Australia & New Zealand Banking Group, Ltd., Melbourne (e)	Australia	23,969,248,906s
97	Ashikaga Bank, Ltd., Utsunomiya(e)	Japan	22,800,423,833
98	International Westminster Bank Plc, London	United Kingdom	22,481,940,000t
99	Creditanstalt-Bankverein, Vienna	Austria	21,854,135,710
100	PKbanken, Stockholm	Sweden	21,250,434,800s

(a)— Consolidated data, if available, are used for all banks that own over 50% of other banks. The consolidation includes only those affiliates in which ownership exceeds 50%. Unless otherwise noted after the name of the bank, all figures are for fiscal year after 9/30/86. (c)— Latest figures are for a different date than previous year. (d)— Or date one year prior to latest figures unless otherwise noted after name of bank. (e)— Data are for 9/30/86. (f)— Data are for 6/30/86. (g)— Latest data are prior to 6/30/86. (h)— A subsidiary of Compagnie Financiere de Credit Industriel et Commercial. (n)— New York cable rate for same date as bank's figures. (p)— See currency table for key to currency abbreviations. (q)— A subsidiary Compagnie Financiere de Paribas, Paris, a financial holding company. (s)— Consolidated data. (t)— Figures are included in the consolidated figures of parent bank. For that reason, the data for the bank are not included in the aggregate data totals for the Top 500 Banks. (u)— Data are not consolidated for affiliates more than 50% owned. (v)— Based on revised (w)— Member of the Al UBAF Banking Group, Neuilly, France, under whose name the seven UBAF banks operate in the international financial markets. (x)— A subsidiary of BCCI Holdings (Luxembourg) SA, a holding company with consolidated deposits of $15.6 billion and consolidated assets of $17.5 billion. (†)— Rank based on revised deposit total for 1985. (‡)— The 1985 data were not available last year. Rank bank would have had, if it had been included in the listing. N.A.— Not available.

APPENDIX III: LARGEST U.S. THRIFT INSTITUTIONS

Rank 6/87		Deposits June 30, 1987	Deposits June 30, 1986
1	Home Savings of America, FA, Irwindale, Calif.	21,315,735,000	20,632,904,000
2	Great Western Bank, FSB, Beverly Hills	18,336,206,000	17,116,165,000
3	American Savings & Loan Assn., Stockton, Calif.	17,373,865,000	16,617,214,000
4	California Fed. Savings & Loan Assn., Los Angeles	14,961,631,000	14,217,789,000
5	Meritor Savings Bank, Philadelphia	12,799,221,000	12,754,770,000
6	Glendale Federal Savings & Loan Assn., Calif.	12,789,621,000	11,660,817,000
7	Goldome, Buffalo, N.Y. (c,d)	10,831,727,000	11,170,249,000†
8	First Nationwide Bank, FSB, San Francisco	10,462,329,000	9,651,948,000
9	Great American First Savings Bank, San Diego, Calif.	9,106,812,000	8,410,010,000
10	Home Federal Savings & Loan Assn. of San Diego, Calif.	9,103,000,000	7,706,519,000
11	World Savings, FS&LA, Oakland, Calif.	7,900,507,000	7,790,359,000
12	Empire of America, FSB, Buffalo, N.Y. (d,e)	7,681,812,000	7,392,558,000†
13	Coast Savings & Loan Assn., Los Angeles	7,624,621,000	4,891,469,000
14	CrossLand Savings FSB, Brooklyn, New York	7,308,896,000	7,074,210,000
15	City Federal Savings Bank, Bedminster, N.J.	6,976,567,000	7,199,062,000
16	Dime Savings Bank of New York FSB, Garden City	6,880,401,000	6,708,617,000
17	Anchor Savings Bank FSB, Northport, N.Y.	6,372,570,000	6,376,930,000
18	Columbia Savings & Loan Assn., Beverly Hills	5,927,074,000	4,685,369,000
19	Gibraltar Savings, Beverly Hills	5,874,331,000	6,280,690,000
20	Imperial Savings Assn., San Diego, Calif.	5,555,182,000	5,891,565,000
21	Bowery Savings Bank, New York	5,109,922,000	5,090,167,000
22	First Federal of Michigan, Detroit	4,967,725,381	4,906,236,000
23	Citicorp Savings, FS&LA, San Francisco	4,863,528,000	3,177,685,000
24	Talman Home Federal Savings & Loan Assn., Chicago	4,624,384,000	4,833,627,000
25	People's Bank, Bridgeport, Conn.	4,584,490,000	4,019,429,000
26	Standard Federal Bank, Troy, Mich.	4,413,355,534	4,239,350,603
27	CenTrust Savings Bank, Miami	4,263,682,000	3,161,966,000
28	Long Island Savings Bank FSB, Syosset, N.Y.	4,204,528,000	4,120,098,000
29	Western Savings & Loan Assn., Phoenix, Ariz.	4,061,804,000	3,635,065,282
30	MeraBank, FSB, Phoenix, Ariz.	4,043,594,000	3,554,895,000
31	Carteret Savings Bank, FA, Morristown, N.J.	4,006,672,000	4,164,208,000
32	Atlantic Financial Federal, Bala Cynwyd, Pa.	3,987,251,000	3,961,786,000
33	Gibraltar Savings Assn., Houston	3,914,649,570	3,387,805,339
34	Dollar-Dry Dock Savings Bank, Bronx, New York	3,912,060,000	4,364,323,000

35	Northeast Savings, FA, Hartford, Conn.	3,902,359,000	3,311,825,000
36	Citicorp Savings of Illinois, FS&LA, Chicago	3,758,895,000	3,746,984,000
37	Howard Savings Bank, Newark, N.J.	3,749,833,000	3,372,697,000
38	Washington Mutual Savings Bank, Seattle	3,652,844,000	3,248,856,000
39	TCF Banking & Savings, FA, Minneapolis	3,644,545,000	3,131,113,000
40	Sears Savings Bank, Glendale, Calif.	3,617,400,000	5,115,309,000
41	Florida Federal Savings & Loan Assn., St. Petersburg	3,514,347,000	3,432,332,836
42	United Savings Assn., Houston	3,423,324,000	3,224,412,000
43	TransOhio Savings Bank, Cleveland	3,392,943,000	2,568,221,000
44	Emigrant Savings Bank, New York	3,172,033,964	3,180,297,695
45	Commercial Federal Savings & Loan Assn., Omaha, Neb.	3,155,660,000	1,703,118,000
46	First Federal Savings & Loan Assn., Rochester, N.Y.	3,127,292,000	3,268,025,000
47	Perpetual Savings Bank, FSB, McLean, Va.	3,012,455,000	3,000,000,000
48	University Savings Assn., Houston	3,003,648,000	2,714,818,000
49	Community Federal Savings & Loan Assn., St. Louis, Mo.	2,931,021,000	3,205,626,000
50	Lincoln Savings & Loan Assn., Irvine, Calif.	2,916,000,000	2,662,792,000
51	Green Point Savings Bank, Brooklyn, New York	2,915,024,344	2,659,072,044
52	Bright Banc Savings Assn., Dallas	2,912,700,000	3,278,467,000
53	American Savings Bank FSB, New York	2,897,608,000	2,965,611,000
54	Benjamin Franklin Federal S & L Assn., Portland, Ore.	2,871,312,000	2,782,064,895
55	AmeriFirst Federal Savings & Loan Assn., Miami	2,853,865,000	2,879,662,000
56	Sunbelt Savings Assn., Dallas	2,836,081,236	2,730,459,911
57	Manhattan Savings Bank, New York	2,703,686,000	2,680,631,038
58	First Texas Savings Assn., Dallas	2,666,608,967	2,732,885,143
59	Chevy Chase Savings Bank, FSB, Md.	2,633,529,611	2,305,083,798
60	Old Stone Bank FSB, Providence, R.I.	2,562,553,000	2,116,717,000
61	Apple Bank For Savings, New York	2,523,900,000	1,667,882,000
62	Georgia Federal Bank, FSB, Atlanta	2,500,000,000	2,197,367,000
63	Hudson City Savings Bank, Paramus, N.J.	2,488,900,678	2,396,217,946
64	Farm & Home Savings Assn., Nevada, Mo.	2,469,442,000	2,573,383,000
65	Far West Savings & Loan Assn., Newport Beach, Calif.	2,405,400,000	1,934,135,000
66	Homestead Savings, FS&LA, San Francisco	2,403,104,000	2,320,796,000
67	Far West Federal Bank, Portland, Ore.	2,384,379,000	1,453,497,399
68	Society for Savings, Hartford, Conn.	2,366,742,000	2,047,593,000
69	Fidelity Federal S & L Assn., Glendale, Calif.	2,358,231,000	2,260,463,000
70	Downey Savings & Loan Assn., Costa Mesa, Calif.	2,344,591,663	2,028,041,000
71	Bank Western FSB, Denver	2,343,907,000	2,409,020,000
72	Seamen's Bank for Savings FSB, New York	2,297,857,000	2,441,637,000

73	**Williamsburgh Savings Bank, Brooklyn, New York**	2,253,649,926	2,249,031,128
74	**Midwest Federal Savings & Loan Assn., Minneapolis**	2,232,671,000	2,058,752,000
75	**First Minnesota Savings Bank FSB, St. Paul**	2,228,188,000	2,378,427,000
76	**First Federal Savings & Loan Assn., Pittsburgh**	2,215,000,000	2,101,577,000
77	**Valley Federal S & L Assn., Van Nuys, Calif.**	2,206,328,000	2,044,327,000
78	**San Jacinto Savings Assn., Houston**	2,204,141,550	2,166,289,281
79	**Franklin Savings Assn., Ottawa, Kan.**	2,196,907,000	1,410,383,000
80	**Capitol Federal Savings & Loan Assn., Topeka, Kan.**	2,176,345,000	2,084,032,742
81	**American Savings & Loan Assn. of Florida, Miami**	2,150,172,000	2,088,252,000
82	**Rochester Community Savings Bank, N.Y.**	2,143,124,000	2,142,860,000
83	**Lincoln Savings Bank FSB, New York**	2,130,996,000	2,104,144,000
84	**St. Paul Federal Bank for Savings, Chicago**	2,099,254,083	2,001,609,747
85	**Santa Barbara Savings & Loan Assn., Calif.**	2,087,722,000	2,062,712,493
86	**Pacific First Federal Savings Bank, Tacoma, Wash.**	2,058,090,000	1,900,352,000
87	**Guarantee Savings, FS&LA, Fresno, Calif.**	2,020,950,000	2,124,700,000
88	**Citizens Federal Savings & Loan Assn., Miami**	2,000,892,341	1,328,519,340
89	**Hill Financial Savings Assn., Red Hill, Pa.**	1,984,747,232	1,760,527,723
90	**Citizens Federal Savings & Loan Assn., Dayton, Ohio**	1,974,861,461	1,914,392,000
91	**Coral Gables Federal Savings & Loan Assn., Fla.**	1,970,746,917	2,043,299,873
92	**Horizon Financial, FA, Southampton, Pa.**	1,963,253,000	1,687,162,000
93	**Astoria Federal Savings & Loan Assn., Queens, New York**	1,954,856,569	1,836,094,402
94	**Dollar Bank FSB, Pittsburgh**	1,925,517,000	1,934,586,000
95	**Lamar Savings Assn., Austin, Tex.**	1,915,000,000	1,874,968,726
96	**Greater New York Savings Bank, New York**	1,910,246,000	2,036,437,000
97	**East River Savings Bank, New York**	1,888,871,704	1,968,317,521
98	**Guaranty Federal Savings & Loan Assn., Galveston, Tex.**	1,861,673,377	1,629,787,000
99	**Pima Savings & Loan Assn., Tucson, Ariz.**	1,833,151,000	1,583,506,000
100	**Mercury Savings, FS&LA; Huntington Beach, Calif.**	1,808,192,000	1,754,586,000

This **preliminary** listing of the top 100 savings banks and S&Ls is based solely on data from an **American Banker** questionnaire. **Total deposits and savings accounts** include: non-interest earning demand and NOW accounts; accounts earning in excess of regular rate in certificates with denominations of $100,000 or more and in other accounts; and accounts earning at or below regular rate in interest-earning NOW accounts, in passbook accounts, and all other accounts, except escrowed accounts. **Regulatory Net Worth** includes permanent, reserve, or guarantee stock; paid-in surplus; qualifying mutual capital certificates; income capital/net worth certificates; qualifying subordinated debentures; appraised equity capital; reserves; undivided profits; and net undistributed income. **(a)— Charter Types:** 1-Mutual Savings Bank; 2-Stock Savings Bank; (3)-Mutual Savings & Loan Association; (4)- Stock Savings & Loan Association. **(b)— Insurance Types:** 1-FDIC-Insured; 2-FSLIC-Insured; 3-State Insured. **(c)**— Formerly Goldome FSB. Changed title in 8/87 when it converted from a federally-chartered mutual savings bank to a state-chartered stock savings bank. **(d)**— All data shown are on a consolidated GAAP ("general accepted accounting principles") basis. **(e)**— Converted from a mutual to stock savings bank in Nov. 1986. **(†)**— Restated. Originally reported unconsolidated data. **(‡)**— Rank unaffected by restatement. **(★)**— Rank institution would have had, if the restated data had been used.

APPENDIX IV: WORLD'S LEADING NON-BANK FINANCIAL COMPANIES

(in market capitalization, June 30, 1987)

Firm	*Country*	*Industry*	*Market Capitalization (Millions)*
1. Nomura Securities	Japan	Securities	$54,300.0
2. Mitsubishi Trust	Japan	Financial Svcs.	28,310.6
3. Sumitomo Trust	Japan	Financial Svcs.	27,889.7
4. Daiwa Securities	Japan	Securities	23,152.4
5. Mitsubishi Estate	Japan	Real Estate	23,019.0
6. Nikko Securities	Japan	Securities	21,115.5
7. Tokio Marine & Fire	Japan	Insurance	19,915.7
8. Yamaichi Securities	Japan	Securities	17,737.2
9. Assicurazione Generali	Italy	Insurance	17,493.4
10. Mitsui Trust	Japan	Financial Svcs.	17,422.0
11. American Express Co.	U.S.	Financial Svcs.	15,363.0
12. Allianz Aktie	West Germany	Insurance	13,195.5
13. Yasuda Trust	Japan	Financial Svcs.	12,654.3
14. American International Gp.	U.S.	Insurance	11,566.7
15. Mitsui Real Estate	Japan	Real Estate	10,152.1
16. Aetna Life & Casualty	U.S.	Insurance	6,681.7
17. Prudential Corp.	U.S.	Insurance	6,382.7
18. Munchener Ruck	West Germany	Insurance	6,315.8
19. Yasuda Fire & Marine	Japan	Insurance	6,255.0
20. General Re Corp.	U.S.	Insurance	5,578.2
21. Zurich Vers.	Switzerland	Insurance	5,333.0
22. Riunione Adriatica di Sicurta	Italy	Insurance	5,265.9
23. Taisho Fire & Marine	Japan	Insurance	5,207.7
24. American General Corp.	U.S.	Insurance	5,158.1
25. Cigna Corp.	U.S.	Insurance	4,982.7

Source: Morgan Stanley International Perspective.

APPENDIX V: LEADING UNDERWRITERS OF SECURITIES ISSUANCES IN U.S. MARKETS (July 1, 1986–June 30, 1987)

Rank	*Firm*	*$ Amount in Millions*	*Number of Issues*
1	Salomon Brothers	46,145.5	295
2	First Boston	44,262.3	240
3	Merrill Lynch Capital Markets	35,446.8	266
4	Morgan Stanley	32,171.4	220
5	Goldman, Sachs	31,836.1	239
6	Drexel Burnham Lambert	24,127.7	234
7	Shearson Lehman Brothers	20,942.0	198
8	Kidder, Peabody	13,225.0	131
9	Bear, Stearns	5,958.3	78
10	Prudential-Bache Securities	4,510.0	60
11	Smith Barney, Harris Upham	4,341.9	68
12	PaineWebber	3,945.5	69
13	Dillon, Read	3,470.4	33
14	Alex. Brown & Sons	3,251.6	53
15	Dean Witter Reynolds	2,971.7	41
Industry Totals		297,312.6	3022

Source: IDD Information Services.

APPENDIX VI: LEADING UNDERWRITERS OF COMMON STOCK (July 1, 1986–June 30, 1987)

Rank	*Firm*	*$ Amount in Millions*	*Number Issues Managed*
1	Goldman, Sachs	6,035.6	46
2	Merrill Lynch Capital Markets	5,241.0	78
3	Shearson Lehman Brothers	4,025.8	53
4	Drexel Burnham Lambert	3,316.4	58
5	First Boston	3,098.9	26
6	Alex. Brown & Sons	2,741.6	46
7	Wheat, First Securities	2,333.4	6
8	Morgan Stanley	2,190.3	39
9	Kidder, Peabody	1,995.1	45
10	Salomon Brothers	1,734.0	25
11	PaineWebber	1,195.0	35
12	Allen	1,122.7	7
13	Smith Barney, Harris Upham	784.6	24
14	Dean Witter Reynolds	715.8	19
15	E. F. Hutton	675.3	18
Industry Totals		44,702.2	1,110

Source: IDD Information Services.

APPENDIX VII: LEADING UNDERWRITERS OF STRAIGHT PREFERRED DEBT (July 1, 1986–June 30, 1987)

Rank	*Firm*	*$ Amount in Millions*	*Number Issues Managed*
1	Salomon Brothers	1,570.0	25
2	Goldman, Sachs	1,192.0	19
3	Merrill Lynch Capital Markets	1,153.0	19
4	First Boston	1,076.5	13
5	Shearson Lehman Brothers	1,028.0	10
6	Morgan Stanley	851.2	11
7	Drexel Burnham Lambert	737.0	13
8	Oppenheimer	445.0	5
9	Bear, Stearns	350.0	5
10	Kidder, Peabody	214.0	4
11	PaineWebber	110.4	4
12	Prudential-Bache Securities	75.0	1
13	E. F. Hutton	60.6	2
14	Rauscher Pierce Refsnes	40.0	1
15	Interstate Securities	10.0	1
Industry Totals		8,920.4	135

Source: IDD Information Services.

APPENDIX VIII: LEADING UNDERWRITERS OF STRAIGHT DEBT (July 1, 1986–June 30, 1987)

Rank	*Manager*	*$ Amount in Millions*	*Number Issues Managed*
1	Salomon Brothers	42,171.5	238
2	First Boston	38,938.1	191
3	Merrill Lynch Capital Markets	28,311.5	158
4	Morgan Stanley	27,225.4	152
5	Goldman, Sachs	23,061.0	157
6	Drexel Burnham Lambert	16,592.1	115
7	Shearson Lehman Brothers	14,825.4	120
8	Kidder, Peabody	9,626.4	68
9	Bear, Stearns	4,532.2	43
10	Prudential-Bache Securities	3,842.7	35
11	Dillon, Read	3,053.1	23
12	PaineWebber	2,368.4	25
13	Smith Barney, Harris Upham	2,207.4	33
14	Dean Witter Reynolds	1,921.9	16
15	Citicorp	1,232.4	14
Industry Totals		226,490.7	1,521

Source: IDD Information Services.

APPENDIX IX: LEADING UNDERWRITERS OF CONVERTIBLE DEBT (July 1, 1986–June 30, 1987)

Rank	*Manager*	*$ Amount in Millions*	*Number Issues Managed*
1	Drexel Burnham Lambert	2,179.3	37
2	Smith Barney, Harris Upham	1,200.0	9
3	Morgan Stanley	1,179.5	14
4	Goldman, Sachs	1,060.0	12
5	First Boston	720.0	5
6	Salomon Brothers	620.0	6
7	Kidder, Peabody	472.0	8
8	Lazard Freres	465.0	6
9	Alex. Brown & Sons	465.0	6
10	Shearson Lehman Brothers	430.0	6
11	Bear, Stearns	355.0	8
12	Merrill Lynch Capital Markets	300.0	6
13	Donaldson, Lufkin & Jenrette	204.1	6
14	Dean Witter Reynolds	145.0	4
15	Allen	115.0	2
Industry Totals		11,031.11	184

Source: IDD Information Services.

APPENDIX X: LEADING UNDERWRITERS OF CONVERTIBLE PREFERRED DEBT (July 1, 1986–June 30, 1987)

Rank	*Firm*	*$ Amount in Millions*	*Number Issues Managed*
1	Drexel Burnham Lambert	1,303.0	11
2	Kidder, Peabody	917.5	6
3	Morgan Stanley	725.0	4
4	Shearson Lehman Brothers	606.8	8
5	Goldman, Sachs	487.5	5
6	Merrill Lynch Capital Markets	441.2	5
7	First Boston	428.7	5
8	Bear, Stearns	307.5	4
9	Donaldson, Lufkin & Jenrette	200.0	2
10	PaineWebber	196.7	4
11	Dean Witter Reynolds	189.0	2
12	Smith Barney, Harris Upham	150.0	2
13	Salomon Brothers	50.0	1
14	Alex. Brown & Sons	45.0	1
15	L.F. Rothschild	21.2	1
Industry Totals		6,142.2	71

Source: IDD Information Services.

APPENDIX XI: LARGEST LIFE INSURANCE COMPANIES

1986 Ranking	*Firm*	*Total Life Insurance in Force (in Billions)*
1	Prudential of America	602.4
2	Metropolitan Life	519.4
3	Equitable Life Assurance	291.2
4	Aetna Life, CT	213.1
5	New York Life	186.8
6	John Hancock Mutual Life	166.5
7	TransAmerica Occidental	164.5
8	Lincoln National Life	157.0
9	Massachusetts Ind. & Life	156.1
10	Travelers Insurance	151.3
11	Sun Life of Canada	144.1
12	Northwestern Mutual Life	137.1
13	Connecticut General Life	120.8
14	Great-West Life Assurance	112.6
15	Manufacturers Life	107.7
16	State Farm Life	106.0
17	Crown Life	89.3
18	General Reassurance Corp.	85.1
19	General American Life	84.6
20	Confederation Life	81.8

Appendix XI: Largest Life Insurance Companies (Continued)

1986 Ranking	*Firm*	*Total Life Insurance In Force (in Billions)*
21	Massachusetts Mutual Life	76.6
22	Principal Mutual Life	72.2
23	Canada Life Assurance	70.2
24	Minnesota Mutual Life	70.1
25	Continental Assurance	69.1
26	Allstate Life	67.7
27	Guardian Life of America	65.8
28	Phoenix Mutual Life	65.5
29	London Life	63.5
30	Cuna Mutual Ins. Society	63.1
31	North Amer. Reassurance	59.5
32	New England Mutual Life	59.4
33	Provident L & A	59.2
34	Northwestern National Life	58.6
35	Mutual Life of New York	57.5
36	Equitable Variable Life	56.8
37	Mutual Benefit Life NJ	55.6
38	Mutual Life of Canada	52.3
39	Hartford L & A	52.1
40	Connecticut Mutual Life	47.7
41	United of Omaha Life	47.5
42	Southwestern Life	46.4
43	Executive Life, CA	45.5
44	New York Life Ins & Annuity	39.1
45	North Amer Life Assurance	38.5

Appendix XI: Largest Life Insurance Companies (Concluded)

1986 Ranking	*Frim*	*Total Life Insurance in Force (in Billions)*
46	Life of Virginia	36.1
47	Amer Life Ins, DE	36.1
48	Jackson National MI	36.0
49	State Mutual Life Assur	35.6
50	Metropolitan Ins & Annuity	34.2

Source: National Underwriter.

APPENDIX XII: LIFE INSURANCE SALES BY TYPES OF POLICIES

	Percent of Policies			Percent of Volume		
	Adult male	*Adult female*	*Juvenile*	*Adult male*	*Adult female*	*Juvenile*
Whole life—continuous pay	42%	47%	41%	26%	30%	42%
Whole life—continuous pay, term rider	1	1	+	1	1	+
Whole life—limited pay	9	14	36	2	4	21
Modified life	7	6	8	7	6	7
Level term and modified term	6	4	3	14	11	2
Decreasing term	3	2	—	4	4	—
Policies with family plan	11	13	—	14	18	—
Enhancement	1	1	+	1	1	1
Universal life	12	5	4	23	16	19
Variable life	5	2	2	7	5	5
Other combined coverages	3	5	6	1	4	3
	100%	100%	100%	100%	100%	100%

	Average Size Policy			Percent of Premium		
	Adult male	Adult female	Juvenile	Adult male	Adult female	Juvenile
Whole life—continuous pay	$18,820	$10,800	$12,450	42%	45%	39%
Whole life—continuous pay, term rider	32,170	23,700	**	1	1	+
Whole life—limited pay	6,430	5,600	7,080	4	11	30
Modified life	28,810	18,130	12,040	8	8	7
Level term and modified term	71,690	44,730	10,000	5	3	1
Decreasing term	42,440	38,830	—	3	1	—
Policies with family plan	39,790	23,160	—	9	12	—
Enhancement	21,890	22,110	**	1	1	+
Universal life	61,780	51,670	53,640	18	11	13
Variable life	47,620	35,850	28,960	7	4	4
Other combined coverages	17,780	14,630	5,590	2	3	6
	$31,010	$17,090	$12,210	100%	100%	100%

	Premium per Policy			*Premium per $1,000*		
	Adult male	*Adult female*	*Juvenile*	*Adult male*	*Adult female*	*Juvenile*
Whole life—continuous pay	$419	$235	$106	$22.30	$21.70	$ 8.50
Whole life—continuous pay, term rider	413	250	**	12.80	10.50	**
Whole life—limited pay	199	188	96	31.00	33.50	13.60
Modified life	459	303	97	15.90	16.70	8.10
Level term and modified term	337	186	43	4.70	14.20	4.30
Decreasing term	350	228	—	8.30	5.90	—
Policies with family plan	375	233	—	9.40	10.10	—
Enhancement	500	331	**	22.80	15.00	**
Universal life	650	503	324	10.50	9.70	6.00
Variable life	657	460	210	13.80	12.80	7.30
Other combined coverages	251	176	109	14.10	12.00	19.60
	$423	$248	$112	$13.60	$14.50	$9.10

+Less than ½ of 1 percent
—No cases
**Fewer than 10 cases
Source: Life Insurance Marketing and Research Association, Inc.

APPENDIX XIII: LIFE INSURANCE SALES BY POLICY SIZE

	Percent of Policies			Percent of Volume		
	Adult male	Adult female	Juvenile	Adult male	Adult female	Juvenile
$100,001-$500,000*	3%	+	+	16%	4%	2%
$100,000	4	1%	1%	12	8	5
$50,001-$99,999	9	3	+	19	12	2
$50,000	11	6	4	17	16	18
$25,001-$49,999	11	7	5	12	14	12
$25,000	12	10	7	10	15	13
$15,001-$24,999	4	4	2	3	5	3
$15,000	4	5	4	2	4	5
$10,001-$14,999	2	3	1	1	2	1
$10,000	13	17	27	4	10	23
$5,001-$9,999	3	5	3	1	2	2
$5,000	12	19	27	2	6	11
Under $5,000	12	20	19	1	2	3
	100%	100%	100%	100%	100%	100%

	Average Size Policy			Percent of Premium		
	Adult male	Adult female	Juvenile	Adult male	Adult female	Juvenile
$100,001-$500,000*	$173,670	$(150,200)	**	11%	2%	1%
$100,000	100,000	100,000	$(100,000)	10	4	3
$50,001-$99,999	67,900	65,180	**	14	8	2
$50,000	50,000	50,000	50,000	15	11	13
$25,001-$49,999	34,060	33,630	30,000	14	10	10
$25,000	25,000	25,000	25,000	12	13	11
$15,001-$24,999	19,580	19,800	20,530	3	4	2
$15,000	15,000	15,000	15,000	3	5	4
$10,001-$14,999	12,330	12,200	(11,800)	1	2	1
$10,000	10,000	10,000	10,000	7	13	25
$5,001-$9,999	7,040	7,100	7,190	1	3	2
$5,000	5,000	5,000	5,000	5	13	16
Under $5,000	2,070	1,980	2,210	4	12	10
	$31,010	$17,090	$12,210	100%	100%	100%

	Premium per Policy			Premium per $1,000		
	Adult male	Adult female	Juvenile	Adult male	Adult female	Juvenile
$100,001-$500,000*	$1,609	$(1,031)	**	$ 9.30	$(6.90)	**
$100,000	1,044	665	$(466)	10.40	6.70	$(4.70)
$50,001-$99,999	697	632	**	10.30	9.70	**
$50,000	580	481	328	11.60	9.60	6.60
$25,001-$49,999	496	366	228	14.50	10.90	7.60
$25,000	408	311	191	16.30	12.40	7.60
$15,001-$24,999	322	244	167	16.40	12.30	8.10
$15,000	291	228	112	19.40	15.20	7.50
$10,001-$14,999	279	206	(110)	22.60	16.90	(9.40)
$10,000	237	199	102	23.70	19.90	10.20
$5,001-$9,999	213	158	80	30.20	22.30	11.10
$5,000	183	167	67	36.60	33.40	13.40
Under $5,000	147	149	58	71.30	75.30	26.10
	$423	$248	$112	$13.60	$14.50	$9.10

*Policies over $500,000 were normalized to that amount
+Less than ½ of 1 percent
( )Based on 10 to 25 cases
**Fewer than 10 cases

APPENDIX XIV: LIFE INSURANCE SALES BY CLIENTS' OCCUPATIONS

	Percent of Policies		*Percent of Volume*	
	Adult male	*Adult female*	*Adult male*	*Adult female*
Professional, semi-professional, sales rep	12%	9%	17%	14%
Executive, manager	11	3	18	6
Farm executive	1	+	2	+
Clerical, sales clerk	6	21	6	26
Crafts worker, operative	43	11	38	11
Service worker, unskilled worker, military	19	18	15	16
Student (age 15 and over)	8	10	4	6
Homemaker	—	28	—	21
	100%	100%	100%	100%

	Average Size Policy		Percent of Premium	
	Adult male	Adult female	Adult male	Adult female
Professional, semi-professional, sales rep	$48,470	$29,760	17%	13%
Executive, manager	55,180	35,710	18	6
Farm executive	52,510	**	3	+
Clerical, sales clerk	31,940	22,660	5	22
Crafts worker, operative	29,950	17,960	39	11
Service worker, unskilled worker, military	26,790	16,990	15	16
Student (age 15 and over)	14,950	12,080	3	5
Homemaker	—	13,480	—	27
	$33,400	$18,490	100%	100%

	Premium per Policy		Premium per $1,000	
	Adult male	*Adult female*	*Adult male*	*Adult female*
Professional, semi-professional, sales rep	$599	$357	$12.40	$12.00
Executive, manager	727	522	13.20	14.60
Farm executive	796	**	15.20	**
Clerical, sales clerk	370	260	11.60	11.50
Crafts worker, operative	395	250	13.20	13.90
Service worker, unskilled worker, military	343	226	12.80	13.30
Student (age 15 and over)	153	132	10.30	10.90
Homemaker	—	237	—	17.60
	$428	$250	$12.80	$13.50

**Fewer than 10 cases
—No cases
+Less than ½ of 1 percent
Source: Life Insurance Marketing and Research Association, Inc.

APPENDIX XV: MUTUAL FUND SALES BY INVESTMENT OBJECTIVE

(January to December 1986—In $ millions)

	Total	Aggressive Growth	Growth	Growth and Income	Precious Metals	International	Balanced
1986							
JAN	15,087.3	874.8	884.8	1,529.6	57.8	307.5	268.1
FEB	15,433.4	891.5	926.1	1,617.8	47.3	502.3	269.0
MAR	19,110.7	1,085.3	1,268.5	1,879.0	46.6	851.9	439.3
APR	22,624.7	1,486.2	1,542.7	2,693.9	36.9	1,082.7	613.1
MAY	16,615.2	873.3	943.1	1,648.8	21.6	681.2	288.5
JUN	15,518.5	882.6	911.0	1,743.1	18.2	482.2	257.1
JUL	18,273.0	819.1	1,117.2	1,569.3	18.7	646.0	209.7
AUG	18,335.6	723.3	1,039.1	1,848.6	40.2	915.6	186.3
SEP	16,555.4	493.1	872.4	1,753.1	113.7	587.7	184.1
OCT	18,789.6	537.9	932.2	2,073.4	59.2	488.1	173.5
NOV	17,925.6	642.0	904.8	1,994.3	144.6	441.3	186.5
DEC	21,578.9	616.5	1,186.7	3,161.2	51.9	657.7	265.8
TOTAL	215,847.9	9,925.7	12,528.6	23,512.1	656.6	7,644.1	3,341.0

	Income	*Option Income*	*Government*	*GNMA*	*Corporate Bond*	*Long-Term Municipal*	*State Municipal*
1986							
JAN	744.2	187.4	3,856.2	2,071.3	1,333.4	1,861.6	1,110.7
FEB	789.3	204.8	3,881.4	2,134.1	1,265.0	1,786.4	1,118.6
MAR	958.0	211.6	4,689.6	2,859.2	1,544.9	2,027.5	1,249.2
APR	1,255.4	340.0	5,280.3	2,644.2	2,137.3	2,129.0	1,383.1
MAY	1,071.6	349.1	3,985.7	2,119.6	1,694.4	1,753.4	1,185.0
JUN	912.3	314.4	3,342.1	2,284.9	1,715.2	1,615.8	1,039.6
JUL	889.3	289.4	3,874.1	3,727.0	1,930.0	1,856.6	1,326.5
AUG	964.2	273.6	4,351.1	2,693.9	1,843.6	2,164.4	1,291.7
SEP	1,006.7	237.4	4,366.4	1,806.2	1,841.5	2,045.8	1,247.1
OCT	1,272.2	221.8	5,059.3	2,198.8	2,012.9	2,336.5	1,423.6
NOV	1,338.6	255.3	4,738.3	1,904.8	1,838.1	2,212.9	1,324.0
DEC	1,049.1	219.5	5,576.2	2,329.9	2,074.2	2,870.0	1,520.3
TOTAL	12,251.0	3,104.4	53,000.6	28,773.8	21,230.6	24,660.0	15,219.4

Source: Investment Company Institute.

APPENDIX XVI: LEADING MANAGERS OF TAX-EXEMPT FUNDS

Firm	$ Million Under Management
1. Prudential Asset Mgmt.	54,106
2. Wells Fargo Investment	53,237
3. J.P. Morgan	48,173
4. Bankers Trust-Investment	46,900
5. Metropolitan Life	39,705
6. Aetna Life	38,287
7. State Street Bank	23,572
8. Alliance Capital Mgmt.	23,362
9. Travelers Cos.	22,067
10. CIGNA Asset Advisers	20,795
11. Jennison Capital Associates	20,000
12. Citicorp Investment	18,608
13. MHIC	17,713
14. Loomis, Sayles	16,028
15. Chase Investors	15,500
16. Mellon Capital Mgmt.	15,000
17. John Hancock Financial	14,825
18. Mellon Bond Associates	14,579
19. Capital Guardian Trust	14,408
20. Pacific Investment	12,277
21. The Principal	12,260
22. State Street Research	11,827
23. Miller, Anderson and Sherrerd	11,500
24. Lehman Mgmt.	11,469
25. Fiduciary Trust	11,445
26. Scudder Stevens & Clark	11,300
27. Delaware Investment	11,103
28. New York Life	10,648
29. Boston Co.	10,355
30. Trust Co. of the West	10,173
31. American Nat'l Bank, Chicago	10,100
32. INVESCO Capital Mgmt.	9,991

Firm	$ Million Under Management
33. Oppenheimer Capital	9,865
34. Fayez Sarofim	9,222
35. Fischer, Francis, Trees & Watts	9,100
36. Wellington Mgmt.	9,076
37. T. Rowe Price	9,051
38. First Chicago Investment	9,013
39. Morgan Stanley Asset Mgmt.	8,752
40. Harris Trust & Savings Bank	8,463
41. Criterion Group	8,198
42. Mass Mutual Life	8,100
43. RCM Capital Mgmt.	8,025
44. Equitable Capital Mgmt.	7,847
45. Batterymarch Financial	7,771
46. Northern Trust	7,438
47. Sanford C. Bernstein	7,300
48. Fidelity Mgmt.	7,000
49. Lazard Freres	6,910
50. MONY	6,703
51. Brown Brothers Harriman	6,572
52. BEA Associates	6,193
53. Lincoln Capital Mgmt.	5,996
54. AmeriTrust	5,965
55. Equitable Real Estate	5,805
56. Capital Supervisors	5,786
57. RepublicBank Dallas	5,719
58. Mutual Benefit Life	5,673
59. Neuberger and Berman	5,538
60. The New England	5,385
61. Favia Hill & Associates	5,313
62. Stein Roe & Farnham	5,300
63. Putnam Cos.	5,296
64. Fidelity Mgmt. Trust	5,244
65. Jamison, Eaton & Wood	5,503
66. Common Fund	4,950
67. National Investment	4,828
68. Boatmen's Nat'l Bank	4,790
69. Barrow, Hanley, Mewhinney	4,777
70. Copley Real Estate Advisors	4,700
71. Transamerica Investment	4,677
72. ASB Capital Mgmt.	4,654
73. Security Pacific	4,611

Firm	$ Million Under Management
74. Lincoln Nat'l Pension	4,600
75. Frank Russell Mgmt.*	4,484
76. Trusco Capital Mgmt.	4,400
77. Centerre Trust	4,365
78. Columbia Mgmt.	4,347
79. MacKay-Shields Financial	4,300
80. Forstmann-Leff Associates	4,179
81. First Wachovia	4,073
82. Duff & Phelps	4,032
83. Investment Advisers	4,000
84. Irving Trust	4,000
85. McMorgan	4,000
86. Nat'l Bank of Detroit	4,000
87. Provident Nat'l Assurance	3,949
88. Pacific Financial Cos.	3,829
89. Pittsburgh Nat'l Bank	3,725
90. Dodge & Cox	3,690
91. Kemper Financial Services	3,591
92. Bank of New York	3,500
93. NCNB	3,479
94. Kennedy Associates	3,465
95. Provident Capital Mgmt.	3,456
96. First Asset Mgmt.	3,452
97. UNUM Life	3,440
98. Dewey Square Investors	3,400
99. Glenmede Trust	3,400
100. Trinity Investment	3,393

*Manager of managers
Source: Pension & Investment Age.

APPENDIX XVII: LEADING INVESTMENT ADVISORS FOR TAX-EXEMPT FUNDS

Firm	$ Million Under Management
1. Metropolitan Life	81,581
2. Aetna Life	60,226
3. Fidelity Mgmt.	58,000
4. Prudential Asset Mgmt.	54,106
5. Wells Fargo Investment	53,571
6. Travelers Cos.	51,899
7. J.P. Morgan	49,703
8. Bankers Trust-Investment	48,200
9. CIGNA Asset Advisers	44,100
10. Kemper Financial Services	39,346
11. John Hancock Financial	36,884
12. Scudder, Stevens & Clark	36,079
13. Putnam Cos.	32,451
14. Alliance Capital Mgmt.	31,139
15. Equitable Real Estate	29,355
16. Equitable Capital Mgmt.	29,069
17. New York Life	29,035
18. Wellington Mgmt.	28,976
19. Citicorp Investment	26,600
20. State Street Bank	26,473
21. Townsend Asset Mgmt.	25,043
22. Vanguard Group	25,000
23. Northern Trust	20,726
24. MHIC	20,655
25. T. Rowe Price	20,200
26. Loomis, Sayles	20,168
27. Jennison Capital Associates	20,000
28. Smith Breeden	20,000
29. MONY	18,100
30. Mass Mutual Life	18,000
31. Mitchell Hutchins	17,932
32. Wilmington Trust	17,849

Firm	$ Million Under Management
33. Chase Investors	17,300
34. American Capital Mgmt.	17,047
35. The Principal	16,994
36. Boston Co.	16,609
37. Lehman Mgmt.	16,077
38. Capital Research & Mgmt.	15,614
39. JMB Institutional Realty	15,300
40. Mellon Capital Mgmt.	15,000
41. Mellon Bond Associates	14,855
42. Massachusetts Financial	14,669
43. Capital Guardian Trust	14,483
44. Fiduciary Trust	14,013
45. U.S. Trust Co., N.Y.	13,561
46. The New England	13,504
47. Harris Trust & Savings Bank	13,117
48. State Street Research	12,991
49. Criterion Group	12,704
50. Daiwa International Capital	12,500
51. Bernstein-Macaulay	12,375
52. Pacific Investment Mgmt.	12,349
53. Bank of New York	12,287
54. County Investment Mgmt.	12,081
55. Brown Brothers Harriman	11,657
56. Neuberger and Berman	11,547
57. Miller, Anderson and Sherrerd	11,500
58. Delaware Investment Advisers	11,400
59. AmeriTrust	11,177
60. American National, Chicago	11,025
61. Stein Roe & Franham	10,800
62. Trust Co. of the West	10,735
63. BA Investment Mgmt.	10,690
64. Fayez Sarofim	10,688
65. Transamerica Investment	10,406
66. Morgan Stanley Asset Mgmt.	10,281
67. Oppenheimer Capital	10,241
68. INVESCO Capital Mgmt.	10,091
69. Henderson International	10,000
70. Fischer, Francis, Trees & Watts	9,900
71. Centerre Trust	9,632
72. Templeton International	9,600
73. Batterymarch Financial	9,234

Firm	$ Million Under Management
74. Connecticut Mutual Life	9,142
75. First Chicago Investment Advisors	9,013
76. National Bank of Detroit	9,000
77. RCM Capital Mgmt.	8,991
78. Irving Trust	8,600
79. Lord, Abbett	8,596
80. RepublicBank Dallas	8,544
81. Sanford C. Bernstein	8,500
82. AIM Mgmt.	8,268
83. First Wachovia	8,000
84. Lazard Freres	7,996
85. Manufacturers National Bank	7,881
86. Boatmen's National Bank	7,464
87. NCNB	7,248
88. Texas Commerce Bank	7,198
89. J&W Scligman	7,102
90. AIG Global	7,000
91. UNUM Life	6,951
92. National City Bank	6,900
93. Bank One, Indianapolis	6,871
94. Standish, Ayer & Wood	6,859
95. Copley Real Estate Advisors	6,800
96. Shearson Asset Mgmt.	6,737
97. BEA Associates	6,485
98. Nationwide Insurance	6,443
99. Fidelity Bank	6,232
100. Continental Assurance	6,154
Total	**1,811,475**

Source: Pension & Investment Age.

APPENDIX XVIII: 25 LARGEST REAL ESTATE MANAGERS RANKED BY EQUITY REAL ESTATE ASSETS

Managers	*$ millions*
Equitable Real Estate Investment Management	5,252
Prudential Asset Management Group	5,149
Copley Real Estate Advisors	4,700
Heitman Advisory	3,025
RREEF Funds	3,017
Aldrich, Eastman & Waltch	1,900
Corporate Property Investors	1,900
LaSalle Advisors	1,710
JMB Institutional Realty	1,600
Aetna Life Insurance	1,554
Boston Co.	1,515
Eastdil Realty	1,366
J.P. Morgan Investment Management	1,278
Fidelity Bank	1,250
Richard Ellis	1,150
Trust Co. of the West	1,098
CIGNA Asset Advisers	1,083
First Chicago Investment Advisors	901
Jones Lang Wootton	900
Security Capital Real Estate	898
F.I.A. Associates	845
John Hancock Financial Services	782
Coldwell Banker	775
First Wachovia	750
Lehndorff & Babson	670
Total	**44,068**

Source: Pension & Investment Age.

APPENDIX XIX: DERIVATIVE FINANCIAL PRODUCTS ON MAJOR U.S. EXCHANGES

American Stock Exchange
114 Equity Options
Computer Technology Index Options
Oil Index Options
Institutional Index Options
Major Market Index Options

Chicago Board of Trade
T-Bond Futures
T-Bond Options
10-Year T-Note Futures
10-Year T-Note Option
Major Market Index Futures
Municipal Bond Index Futures

Chicago Board Options Exchange
151 Equity Options
S&P 100 Options
S&P 500 Options
British Pound Options
Canadian Dollar Options
Deutschemark Options
Japanese Yen Options
Swiss Franc Options
T-Bond Options
5-Year T-Note Options

Appendix XIX: Derivative Financial Products On Major U.S. Exchanges (Continued)

Chicago Mercantile Exchange
British Pound Futures
Canadian Dollar Futures
Deutschemark Futures
Japanese Yen Futures
Swiss Franc Futures
British Pound Options
Canadian Dollar Options
Deutschemark Options
Japanese Yen Options
Swiss Franc Options
S&P 500 Index Futures
S&P 500 Option
Eurodollar Futures
Eurodollar Options
T-Bill Futures

Comex
Gold Futures
Silver Futures
Gold Options
Silver Options

Finex
U.S. Dollar Index Futures
U.S. Dollar Index Options
European Currency Unit Futures
Five Year U.S. Treasury Note Futures

Kansas City Board of Trade
Value Line Average Index Futures

Appendix XX: Derivative Financial Products On Major U.S. Exchanges (Concluded)

New York Futures Exchange
NYSE Composite Index Futures
NYSE Composite Index Options
CRB Index Futures

New York Stock Exchange
12 Equity Options
Composite Index Options
Beta Index Options

Pacific Stock Exchange
72 Equity Options
Tcchnology Index Options
Financial News Composite Index Options
Financial News Composite Index Futures

Philadelphia Stock Exchange
82 Equity Options
Australian Dollar Options
British Pound Options
Canadian Dollar Options
Deutschemark Options
Japanese Yen Options
Swiss Franc Options
Value Line Avg. Index Options

APPENDIX XX: BUSINESS GROWTH: NEW BUSINESS STARTS BY REGIONS AND STATES

(1985 versus 1986)

	1985		1986		% Change	
	Firms	*Employees*	*Firms*	*Employees*	*Firms*	*Employees*
New England	**11,609**	**58,921**	**14,006**	**60,171**	**20.6%**	**2.1%**
Maine	814	3,908	1,011	4,534	24.2%	16.0%
New Hampshire	1,074	5,405	1,415	5,238	31.8%	−3.1%
Vermont	511	2,682	685	2,468	34.1%	−8.0%
Massachusetts	5,222	28,187	6,239	27,306	19.5%	−3.1%
Connecticut	3,223	14,297	3,822	16,663	18.6%	16.5%
Rhode Island	765	4,442	834	3,962	9.0%	−10.8%
Middle Atlantic	**36,922**	**182,133**	**41,759**	**176,106**	**13.1%**	**−3.3%**
New York	19,190	91,053	21,609	87,035	12.6%	−4.4%
New Jersey	8,596	41,273	10,341	44,410	20.3%	7.6%
Pennsylvania	9,136	49,807	9,809	44,661	7.4%	−10.3%
East North Central	**35,923**	**189,976**	**35,339**	**161,329**	**−1.6%**	**−15.1%**
Ohio	8,262	45,647	8,869	42,231	7.3%	−7.5%
Indiana	3,968	26,061	4,023	20,224	1.4%	−22.4%
Illinois	11,958	59,154	10,504	46,094	−12.2%	−22.4%
Michigan	8,144	39,531	8,495	34,892	4.3%	−11.7%
Wisconsin	3,591	19,583	3,448	17,888	−4.0%	−8.7%

	1985		1986		% Change	
	Firms	*Employees*	*Firms*	*Employees*	*Firms*	*Employees*
West North Central	**14,488**	**84,585**	**13,730**	**75,734**	**−5.2%**	**−10.5%**
Minnesota	3,521	18,930	3,535	19,241	0.4%	1.6%
Iowa	1,864	10,350	1,618	9,127	−13.2%	−11.8%
Missouri	4,424	27,381	4,316	24,400	−2.4%	−10.9%
North Dakota	453	2,342	448	2,356	−1.1%	0.6%
South Dakota	474	2,801	461	2,287	−2.7%	−18.4%
Nebraska	1,237	7,423	1,161	6,399	−6.1%	−13.8%
Kansas	2,515	15,358	2,191	11,924	−12.9%	−22.4%
South Atlantic	**46,637**	**253,331**	**47,160**	**238,057**	**1.1%**	**−6.0%**
Maryland	4,766	22,578	5,132	24,272	7.7%	7.5%
Delaware	648	2,799	631	3,322	−2.6%	18.7%
District of Columbia	880	6,298	848	4,240	−3.6%	−32.7%
Virginia	5,783	31,258	6,030	30,217	4.3%	−3.3%
West Virginia	1,200	7,124	1,418	8,140	−1.0%	−14.6%
North Carolina	5,278	31,313	5,225	26,731	18.2%	−14.3%
South Carolina	2,801	18,334	2,864	16,838	2.2%	−8.2%
Georgia	6,790	44,222	7,303	39,703	7.6%	−10.2%
Florida	18,491	89,405	17,709	84,594	−4.2%	−5.4%

	1985		1986		% Change	
	Firms	*Employees*	*Firms*	*Employees*	*Firms*	*Employees*
East South Central	**12,257**	**73,233**	**12,694**	**70,585**	**3.6%**	**−3.6%**
Kentucky	2,934	17,500	3,269	17,210	11.4%	−1.7%
Tennessee	4,502	27,073	4,312	26,228	−4.2%	−3.1%
Alabama	3,221	18,647	3,236	16,893	0.5%	−9.4%
Mississippi	1,600	10,013	1,877	10,254	17.3%	2.4%
West South Central	**35,915**	**204,584**	**30,916**	**161,441**	**−13.9%**	**−21.1%**
Arkansas	1,965	11,402	1,908	11,468	−2.9%	0.6%
Oklahoma	3,574	21,979	2,954	16,111	−15.0%	−26.7%
Louisiana	4,402	24,271	4,141	21,088	−5.9%	−13.1%
Texas	26,073	146,932	21,913	112,774	−16.0%	−23.2%

	1985		*1986*		*% Change*	
	Firms	*Employees*	*Firms*	*Employees*	*Firms*	*Employees*
Mountain	**16,967**	**92,187**	**16,159**	**79,796**	**−4.8%**	**−13.4%**
Montana	920	4,049	812	3,048	−11.7%	−24.7%
Idaho	1,071	6,266	1,107	4,226	−5.0%	−32.6%
Wyoming	521	2,404	525	1,593	0.8%	−33.7%
Colorado	5,265	28,828	5,292	24,940	0.5%	−13.5%
New Mexico	1,454	7,267	1,407	7,302	−3.2%	0.5%
Arizona	4,736	26,022	4,283	23,231	−9.6%	−10.7%
Utah	1,796	10,354	1,731	8,626	−3.6%	−16.7%
Nevada	1,204	6,997	1,092	6,830	−9.3%	−2.4%
Pacific	**39,052**	**221,065**	**39,834**	**196,784**	**2.0%**	**−11.0%**
Alaska	1,018	4,062	705	2,763	−30.7%	−32.0%
Hawaii	1,019	6,457	1,065	6,662	4.5%	3.2%
Washington	5,311	27,351	5,238	22,636	−1.4%	−17.2%
Oregon	2,767	15,466	2,975	13,687	7.5%	−11.5%
California	28,937	167,729	29,851	151,036	3.2%	−10.0%
Total States and Regions	**249,770**	**1,360,015**	**251,597**	**1,220,003**	**0.7%**	**−10.3%**

Source: The Dun & Bradstreet Corporation, *Business Starts Record,* 1986.

APPENDIX XXI: NEW BUSINESS STARTS IN FINANCIAL SERVICES BY REGIONS AND STATES

(1985 versus 1986)

Finance, Insurance & Real Estate						
Banking	524	12,099	471	11,956	−10.1%	−1.2%
Credit agencies, except banks	1,411	11,523	1,555	12,449	10.2%	8.0%
Security, commodity brokers & services	1,103	7,702	1,167	8,028	5.8%	4.2%
Insurance carriers	373	4,185	339	4,025	−9.1%	−3.8%
Insurance agents, brokers & services	1,304	7,267	1,317	7,309	1.0%	0.6%
Real estate	10,050	47,905	11,108	44,109	10.5%	−7.9%
Combined real estate, insurance, etc.	24	126	26	177	8.3%	40.5%
Holding & other investment offices	921	8,264	1,050	9,428	14.0%	14.1%
Total Finance, Insurance & Real Estate	**15,710**	**99,071**	**17,033**	**97,481**	**8.4%**	**−1.6%**

Source: The Dun & Bradstreet Corporation, *Business Starts Record,* 1986.

APPENDIX XXII: 1986 U.S. PER CAPITA INCOME BY STATE

	Income	*Rank*	*Chg.*
U.S.	$14,641		+5.3
Ala.	11,336	42	+5.4
Alaska	17,796	3	−3.5
Ariz.	13,474	27	+5.1
Ark.	11,073	47	+4.9
Calif.	16,904	6	+5.4
Colo.	15,234	12	+3.8
Conn.	19,600	1	+7.5
Del.	15,010	13	+4.9
D.C.	19,397		+5.6
Fla.	14,646	19	+5.4
Ga.	13,446	28	+6.4
Hawaii	14,886	16	+5.7
Idaho	11,223	45	+3.4
Ill.	15,586	9	+5.4
Ind.	13,136	32	+5.7
Iowa	13,348	29	+6.7
Kan.	14,650	18	+5.3
Ky.	11,238	44	+4.5
La.	11,193	46	−0.7
Maine	12,790	33	+7.9
Md.	16,864	7	+5.5
Mass.	17,722	4	+8.1
Mich.	14,775	17	+5.7
Minn.	14,994	15	+6.0
Miss.	9,716	50	+4.7
Mo.	13,789	24	+5.1
Mont.	11,803	40	+7.0
Neb.	13,742	25	+5.4

	Income	*Rank*	*Chg.*
Nev.	15,437	10	+4.9
N.H.	15,911	8	+7.1
N.J.	18,626	2	+7.1
N.M.	11,422	41	+1.9
N.Y.	17,111	5	+7.3
N.C.	12,438	36	+6.4
N.D.	12,472	35	+4.5
Ohio	13,933	22	+4.9
Okla.	12,283	37	+0.9
Ore.	13,328	31	+5.1
Pa.	14,249	21	+5.2
R.I.	14,579	20	+6.6
S.C.	11,299	43	+5.1
S.D.	11,814	39	+7.1
Tenn.	12,002	38	+6.4
Texas	13,478	26	−0.1
Utah	10,981	48	+3.0
Vt.	13,348	30	+7.5
Va.	15,408	11	+6.4
Wash.	15,009	14	+6.2
W.Va.	10,576	49	+4.9
Wis.	13,909	23	+5.8
Wyo.	12,781	34	−1.2

Source: Associated Press

APPENDIX XXIII: PROFESSIONAL ORGANIZATIONS

The following professional organizations conduct programs on financial marketing and related topics:

American Bankers Association
1120 Connecticut Avenue, NW
Washington, D.C. 20036
(202) 467-4000

American Marketing Association
250 South Wacker Drive
Suite 200
Chicago, Illinois 60606
(312) 648-0536

Bank Administration Institute
60 Gould Center
2550 Golf Road
Rolling Meadows, Illinois 60008
(312) 228-6200

Bank Marketing Association
309 West Washington Street
Chicago, Illinois 60606
(312) 782-1442

Financial Institutions Marketing Association
111 East Wacker Drive
Chicago, Illinois 60601
(312) 938-2570

Futures Industry Association
1825 Eye Street, NW
Suite 1040
Washington, D.C. 20006
(202) 466-5460

International Association of Business Communicators
870 Market Street
Suite 940
San Francisco, California 94102
(415) 433-3400

National Investor Relations Institute
1730 M Street, NW
Washington, D.C. 20036
(202) 861-0630

Public Relations Society of America
845 Third Avenue
New York, New York 10022
(212) 826-1750

Securities Industry Association
120 Broadway
New York, New York 10271
(212) 608-1500

United States League of Savings Institutions
111 East Wacker Drive
Chicago, Illinois 60601
(312) 644-3100

Index

Chapter One

Stephen A. Kerns

Stephen A. Kerns is Vice President of the Weiser Group, a consulting firm that provides marketing advice to a wide range of banks, brokerage houses, insurance companies and other financial service organizations. Mr. Kerns has had extensive experience in developing and implementing financial marketing strategies in his present position with the Weiser Group, as well as in his earlier position with the Chicago Board of Options Exchange.

MARKETING FINANCIAL SERVICES IN A DEREGULATED ENVIRONMENT

Stephen A. Kerns
Vice President
Weiser Group

In the not too distant past, there were a relatively small number of people marketing financial products and services. The marketing emphasis for most financial services providers did not sufficiently exist to create a separate financial services discipline within the marketing field.

That has certainly changed. Some of the most sophisticated marketers in America today work for or on behalf of financial services companies. Many marketing consulting firms and advertising and public relations agencies specialize in financial services marketing. Nearly all the major, national advertising and public relations shops have financial services departments, or at least a stable of financial specialists on staff.

This is all part of the growth of financial services generally. It is an industry growing in the number of products and services brought to market, the number of competitors within individual product areas, and the number of competitors within geographic markets.

These, in turn, are the fruits of deregulation.

There has been so much talk about "The Age of Deregulation" and debate whether it is good or bad, that some key facts occasionally get lost: Deregulation is here, it's continuing and it shows no sign of stopping.

It is an evolutionary process. And, like any form of evolution, it is difficult to determine at what stage in the process we currently find ourselves. How much longer will Glass-Steagall stay in effect? Will savings and loans begin selling insurance? What new derivative markets will the futures and options industries create? How close are we to trading stocks through that long-anticipated "black box" computer system?

For financial services marketers, these questions take on a strategic focus: Who is my competition, and who will my competition be next year? What image does my organization need to project, and to whom? Which market segments are interested in our products and services? How do we determine market interest in each of the growing number of products we offer? How do we assess the value our customers will place on these products?

And what changes need to be made now so we can continue to compete in a changing marketing environment?

It is unwise to look at other industries for strategic answers, because marketing programs supporting financial services—whether provided by a major investment banking firm or a neighborhood S&L—are inherently unlike any other marketing efforts for any other goods or services.

It is not just that there are no tires to kick or doors to slam. The relationship of a financial services customer to his or her financial services provider is different from any other business relationship. After all, the underlying marketing claim of all financial services is that they will directly help a customer's financial health.

MARKETING TO KEEP UP WITH DEREGULATION

For a financial services marketer, deregulation has caused basic changes in strategic thinking. However, these tend to fall under three basic marketing concerns: competition, product attributes and customer service.

A New Competitive Outlook

Financial institutions face new and more complex types of competition. It is not enough merely to recognize that the big boys are coming into your turf, for example, and that they are likely to outspend your advertising budget. Marketers need to assess, on a product-by-product basis, what the *real* impact of this new competition is. Can your new competitor get by with a lower margin, and thereby undercut your existing pricing structure? How does its delivery system compare with yours? Who composes its salesforce? And how many of your customers already have some relationship with this new competitor?